Yearbook of Phraseology 1
2010

Yearbook of Phraseology 1
2010

Editor

Koenraad Kuiper

De Gruyter Mouton

ISBN 978-3-11-022261-6
e-ISBN 978-3-11-022262-3
ISSN 1868-632X
ISSN online 1868-6338

Bibliographic information published by the Deutsche Nationalbibliothek

The Deutsche Nationalbibliothek lists this publication in the Deutsche Nationalbibliografie;
detailed bibliographic data are available in the Internet at http://dnb.d-nb.de.

© 2010 Walter de Gruyter GmbH & Co. KG, Berlin/New York

Printing: AZ Druck und Datentechnik GmbH, Kempten
∞ Printed on acid-free paper

Printed in Germany

www.degruyter.com

Managing Editor

Koenraad Kuiper
Department of Linguistics
University of Canterbury
Private Bag 4800
Christchurch 8020
New Zealand
E-mail:
kon.kuiper@canterbury.ac.nz

Editors

Harald Burger
Universität Zürich, Switzerland

Jean-Pierre Colson
Université Catholique de Louvain, Belgium

Jarmo Korhonen
University of Helsinki, Finland

Annette Sabban
Universität Hildesheim, Germany

Review Editor

Andreas Langlotz, Université de Lausanne, Switzerland

Editorial Board

František Čermak
Univerzita Karlova v Praze,
Prague, Czech Republic

Dmitrij Dobrovol'skij
Universität Wien, Austria

Christiane Fellbaum
Princeton University, USA

Natalia Filatkina
Universität Trier, Germany

Csaba Földes
Panonische Universität,
Vesprem, Hungary

Sylviane Granger
Université Catholique de Louvain,
Belgium

Annelies Häcki Buhofer
Universität Basel, Switzerland

Erla Hallsteinsdóttir
Syddansk Universitet, Denmark

Salah Mejri
Paris VIII, France

Wolfgang Mieder
University of Vermont, USA

Antonio Pamies-Betrán
Universidad de Granada, Spain

Andrew Pawley
Australian National University, Australia

Elizabeth Piirainen
Steinfurt, Germany

Kathrin Steyer
Institut für deutsche Sprache,
Mannheim, Germany

Diana van Lancker-Sidtis
New York University, USA

Alison Wray
Cardiff University, UK

Contents

Koenraad Kuiper
   Editorial   ix

Articles

Sabine Fiedler
   Phraseology in a time of crisis: The language of bank
   advertisements before and during the financial crisis of
   2008–2010   1

Anita Naciscione
   Visual representation of phraseological image   19

Natalia Filatkina and Monika Hanauska
   Wissensstrukturierung und Wissensvermittlung durch
   Routineformeln: Am Beispiel ausgewählter althochdeutscher Texte   45

Dmitrij Dobrovol'skij and Elisabeth Piirainen
   Idioms: Motivation and etymology   73

Günter Schmale
   Ist ein idiomatischer Ausdruck immer expressiv? Korpusbasierte
   und fragebogengestützte Beobachtungen zu einer verbreiteten
   Prämisse   97

Erla Hallsteinsdóttir and Ken Farø
   Interlinguale Phraseologie   125

Anna Idström
    Inari Saami idioms of time   159

Comment

František Čermák
    Fifteen commandments of a phraseologist   179

Book reviews

Christiane Fellbaum (ed.): *Idioms and collocations: Corpus-based linguistic and lexicographic studies.* (Elena Dnestrovskaya)   183

Wolfgang Mieder: *"Yes we can": Barack Obama's proverbial rhetoric.* (Sabine Fiedler)   190

Thomas Kotschi, Ulrich Detges and Colette Cortès: *Wörterbuch französischer Nominalprädikate: Funktionsverbgefüge und feste Syntagmen der Form <être + Präposition + Nomen>.* (Annette Sabban)   194

Stefaniya Ptashnyk: *Phraseologische Modifikationen und ihre Funktionen im Text: Eine Studie am Beispiel der deutschsprachigen Presse.* (Martina Häcker)   198

Alison Wray: *Formulaic language: Pushing the boundaries.* (Sixta Quassdorf)   203

Editorial

Welcome to the *Yearbook of Phraseology*

KOENRAAD KUIPER

Welcome to the *Yearbook of Phraseology*, or, as the indigenous people of the islands of New Zealand would say formulaically, 'Haere mai, Haere mae, Haere mai'.

Why should we welcome this *Yearbook*? Why indeed should it see the light of day at all? The world is full of academic periodicals dealing with exotica of thousands of kinds. High aims were set for the Yearbook when it was proposed to the publishers. We said, "The YoP will be the pre-eminent periodical publication in phraseology with a high reputation among scholars in the field. It will publish only articles which make a significant contribution to the field. It will facilitate dialogue between Continental and English-speaking scholars in the field of phraseology and build a comprehensive understanding of the many facets of phraseology and thus establish the field on the global scale." On the one hand, these are high-sounding words and easily said. But on the other hand, there is no periodical publishing on all areas of phraseology exclusively. In fact, the field of phraseology is remarkably little known outside of northern Europe. While it exists at the crossroads of a number of disciplines it is certainly as central to linguistics as morphology and lexical semantics which deal with the properties of one word lexical items.

How does the *Yearbook* conceive of phraseology. In the proposal to the publisher we said, "Phraseology is the study of the phrasal lexicon of both native speakers and languages, and the study of the usage of phrasal lexemes. Phrasal lexemes are distinguished from other lexemes by having syntactic structure rather than word structure. As lexemes, they can be studied for both their formal properties and their usage properties.

The study of the phrasal lexicon of speakers is manifested in studies of the psycholinguistics of such items including their acquisition, production and perception. Where study is related to the phrasal lexicon of a language it supports areas such as the lexicography of idioms and restricted collocations, proverb studies and corpus linguistic investigations. The usage of phrasal lexemes leads, for example, to studies in formulaic varieties of speech and stylistics."

So the *Yearbook* has set out on an ambitious journey. In doing so it has needed friends. The sole scholarly society dealing with phraseology, the European Society of Phraseology has been its sponsor and without the active support of the management committee and advisory board as well as the membership of the Society this volume would not be in front of you. The publishers, Mouton de Gruyter, were prepared to accept the Society's proposal and have been most supportive. Members of the Editorial Board have been prepared to review and have done so promptly and carefully. In this first issue it is important to thank all these people.

However, the production of a *Yearbook of phraseology* is only a half way point. If the work represented in the *Yearbook* now and in the future is to make a significant contribution to the discipline of phraseology and its related disciplines it must also be read and disseminated. How successful that second phase will be is up to the scholarly community of those with an interest in phraseology.

Phraseology in a time of crisis: The language of bank advertisements before and during the financial crisis of 2008–2010

SABINE FIEDLER[1]

Abstract

This paper compares the phraseology of bank advertisements before and during the financial crisis of 2008–2010. A statistical analysis of the content of bank ads in newspapers from 2000 and 2009 shows how the banks' use of phraseology mirrors changes in people's attitudes in a time of economic turbulence. It seems that banks and their subsidiaries are reviewing their strategies and adapting their advertising campaigns to meet the requirements of the current climate. Rather than positioning themselves as sources of easy money, banks are reverting to images of honesty and sobriety. At a time when people's houses are being repossessed, slogans such as "If your bank can't keep up, leave them behind" (Abbey International) are being replaced with no-nonsense slogans such as "Your savings bank. Come rain or shine" (HSBC).

Keywords: phraseological unit; advertising; banks; financial service institutions.

1. Introduction

Many economists consider the financial crisis 2008–2010 to be the worst since the Great Depression of the 1930s. It contributed to the failure of key businesses and declines in consumer wealth worldwide. The trigger of the crisis was the bursting of the US housing bubble. The long-term trend of rising house prices had encouraged people to use their homes as cash machines. Using them as security, they had borrowed money to buy other things. Furthermore, people with low – or even no – income, who would normally not qualify for mortgages, had been encouraged to borrow money to achieve their dream of home ownership. Banks were lending recklessly and tempted people with very low mortgage rates for the first two or three years. This so-called sub-prime lending amounted to organised fraud. Bankers (and other agents along the "value chain") had no concept of social responsibility and did not care for the financial viability of the person responsible for paying off the loan. They had strong incentives to make aggressive loans and to create risky new products. Bonus culture encouraged short-termism and risk taking. When prices began declining in 2006 and mortgage rates rose, sub-prime mortgage holders were deluged with debts. They left their speculatively purchased homes as their mortgage balance sheet exceeded the value of their home. When Lehman Brothers declared bankruptcy in 2008 and other large financial institutions admitted that they were about to collapse, governments in several countries prepared rescue packages and banks were "bailed out" with taxpayers' money.

Although it was often argued that the regulatory system was at least as much to blame, because it failed to preserve the integrity of financial service firms or to protect the consumer (O'Driscoll 2009), the majority of people believed that the banks bore the bulk of the responsibility for the crisis, as surveys show (cf. MacWhirter 2008; Brandweek 2010). Wall Street banks had accumulated record profits before the crash creating opaque financial instruments that allowed them to dump their risk onto the wider economy. Bankers were mainly associated with questionable financial products, predatory lending practices, mortgage frauds and unbridled greed. The financial crisis led to a crisis of confidence in banks.

This paper compares the phraseology of bank advertisements before and during the financial crisis. The point of departure for dealing with this topic was my personal impression that in my collection of ads employing phraseological units (PUs) in the field of financial service advertisements the tone had suddenly changed in 2008/2009. Rather than positioning themselves as sources of easy money, banks were promoting an image of honesty and sobriety. I decided to test this hypothesis by undertaking a systematic analysis of British and American print advertisements.

2. Advertising

2.1. *Functions and influence*

Advertising is usually considered a genre, a type of cultural and social communication (MacRury 2009: 23). It is "a paid, non-personal communication about an organization and its products or services that is transmitted to a target audience through mass media, such as television, radio, newspapers, magazines, direct mail, outdoor displays, or mass-transit vehicles" (Lee and Johnson 2005: 3). The functions of advertising include information (about the features of the product, service or idea and its location of sale), persuasion (of consumers to buy a specific brand or to adopt a certain attitude towards a product or a company) and reminding (customers of a product so that they keep buying it instead of the competitor's brand) (Lee and Johnson 2005: 11).

Surveys demonstrate that advertisements do influence people's attitudes (cf. Bertrand et al. 2010; Mylonakis 2008). For example, the Nielsen IAG Financial Brand Confidence Study, which was conducted in March 2009 as a national online survey of 5,500 US respondents, shows that banks that advertise have greater consumer confidence.[2] People were asked about the factors that would increase confidence in the safety and soundness of their financial institution and they cited:

- Seeing regular advertising for that institution (25%)
- Receiving regular mail or email offers from that institution (25%)
- Regularly seeing internet offers/advertising from that institution (21%)
- Reading positive stories in the press about that institution (44%).

When asked about their own banks, insurance companies and investment firms, 55% of respondents who said they had seen more advertising for their financial institution reported having "complete confidence" in the financial health and soundness of their financial company and only 18% said they had "little or no confidence" in their company. However, among those who said they had seen less advertising, only 18% had "complete confidence" in their financial company and 45% said they had "little or no confidence" in their company. Richard Khaleel, an executive of Nielsen IAG's Financial Practice, concludes that during economic crises "out of sight" may not only mean "out of mind", but even "out of business".[3]

2.2. *Advertising as presentation of self*

Goffman shows how human behaviour in public situations is socially constructed (cf., for example, Goffman 1959, 1963, 1971). He portrays all the actions and activities that we do throughout the day as strategic encounters in which people attempt to sell a particular self-image. Goffman (1959) uses the imagery of the theatre. Social interaction is a drama. People use a process that he calls "the presentation of self" to give a certain impression in the minds of others. People perform the role(s) that are expected of them in a particular social situation and choose their stage, props, costumes in front of a specific audience. In order to keep their coherence and win credibility the actors are consistent in appearance (i.e. the items that reveal the performer's status) and manner (i.e. the role the performer expects to play). Their aim is to be believed. Credibility is manifested in verbal and non-verbal signifiers. We have a repertoire and vocabulary of manageable fronts which we adjust to different settings. The social fronts are institutionalised – others base expectations on us in our roles as, for example, a university teacher, car dealer, bank manager, etc.

As Goffman explains, the self moves between the front stage of publicity and back stage of privacy. In the back stage the front stage performances are prepared, which is why this space is more authentic and less social. Nevertheless, even in these private moments and spaces of social life some traces of ritual remain. Goffman describes different processes that are involved with the constitution of the self. The techniques of "impression management" include the concealment of errors, concealment of the process of the performance (only the final product is shown) and concealment of dirty work. These techniques are means of self-control to handle and avoid embarrassment.

Goffman's approach can also be applied to macro-sociological entities, such as organisations in which certain values define role-based interaction and drive organisational performance. We expect them, as well as the individual actor, to be ideally virtuous. The performers may consciously guide the audience for their own ends and usually foster impressions that reflect well upon themselves. They try to present a positive picture of themselves if possible or to rescue what they can in situations when the self is profoundly threatened.

Advertising can be seen as presentation of self in Goffman's sense. It is volitional and considered. Companies spend a great deal of money promoting an attractive "corporate self" in order to encourage people to trust and respond positively towards the company.

3. Phraseology

Phraseological units are lexicalized multiword items. Because of their connotative features they may fulfil various pragmatic functions in discourse. It is due to these features, along with their ready recognizability and the seemingly endless opportunities for creative application, that phraseological units are so often employed as part of the persuasive tactics of advertising. Their functions and use in advertisements have been described in a large number of studies about different languages (cf., for example, Bürli-Storz 1980; Mieder 2005; Vesalainen 2001; Balsliemke 2001; Sabban 1998; Burger 2003).

It is generally agreed that phraseology is culturally marked (Sabban 2007). Proverbs, catch-phrases, formulae and other types of PUs have always been a reflection of their time and place; they mirror people's ideas, experience and values as well as important social events. This is true for the time-honoured proverbs of the past. A classical example are the many proverbs on the position of women that exist in many languages and cultures (e.g. *A woman's place is in the home; Lange Haare, kurzer Verstand; A mulher e a mula, o pau as cura*). They are part of our collective memory, but in European cultures they are mainly used in an ironic or humorous sense today because their contents reflect beliefs and attitudes of the past that contradict our modern reality. The burning issues, cultural products and outstanding personalities of the modern era will, similarly, leave their phraseological tracks in our languages. *Tear down this wall, Life is like a box of chocolates*, and *Yes, we can* are only three examples of many that might be mentioned in this context.[4]

The war on Iraq, to mention an event in our present era, brought the following expressions into being or, at least, made them popular:

shock and awe
the axis of evil
friendly fire (which was already used in the Gulf War of 1991)
freedom fries[5]
the mother of all battles
weapons of mass destruction.

The fact that they are used figuratively in various domains now and that they are employed and modified in advertising can be seen as evidence of their currency.

(1) *Weapon of mass seduction* (car advertisement *Volvo*) (*The Courier-Mail* 14 March 2008)

(2) *The Mother of all Broadband* (*Virgin Media*) (*Daily Mirror* 3 Dec 2008)

Kuiper (2009: 157–176) has shown that social perturbations can manifest themselves in phraseological changes within a speech community. He found that during the Cultural Revolution in China the formulaic inventory underwent a number of significant changes. Taking these results into consideration, in the following section, I will examine the use of phraseology in bank advertisements before and during the financial crisis. The analysis will focus on the kinds of pragmatic messages that PUs convey to readers.

6   Sabine Fiedler

4. Phraseological units in financial service ads

4.1. General remarks

Phraseology in bank advertisements is of general interest to phraseology research from at least two perspectives.[6] Firstly, as in advertising in general, PUs (i.e. proverbs, sayings, catch-phrases, quotations and other types of prefabricated speech) work as eye catchers. They attract the reader's attention as they strike them as something familiar and because of their images and spoken character (cf. Fiedler 2007). They are often employed in creative ways to enhance expressiveness or to evoke comical effects.

(3)   *Money doesn't grow on trees. But it does in our branches* (*Savings & Loans*) (Adelaide, March 2008)

(4)   *Avoid paying inheritance tax. Where there's a Will, there's a way.* (*Irongate*) (*The Daily Telegraph* 7 Oct 2000)

Especially popular in bank ads is the proverb *Don't put all your eggs in one basket*. The well-known sentence that – in its financial interpretation – admonishes us not to risk all our money in one investment instead of spreading it out among several because we may ruin ourselves if we do is mainly found in the form of a provocative negation:

(5)   *All your eggs in one basket can now be a good thing* ... (*The cooperative bank*) (*The Guardian Weekly* 6 Aug 2009)

(6)   *Don't Crack Over Your Money. Now you really CAN put all your eggs in one basket.* (*Greater Rome Bank*) (*Rome News Tribune* 20 July 2008)

Ambiguity is produced deliberately when elements of collocations that have the status of terms in banking (*cut the closing costs, fix a mortgage*) are taken literally.

(7)   *We'll cut the closing costs. You cut the* (pictures of grass, flowers, and a hedge) (New York, August 2007)

(8)   *Wish you could fix your current great mortgage rate?* (*HSBC*) (*The Daily Telegraph* 25 June 2009; the picture shows a house that is literally secured like a tent by means of pegs).

Secondly, banks and insurance companies often make use of catchy slogans in their advertising campaigns, such as *The Citi Never Sleeps* (Citibank).[7] These can gain currency and become winged words (catch phrases) and in this way a part of the phrasicon themselves.[8]

4.2. The use of phraseological units before the crisis

The messages expressed in bank ads before the crisis were mainly "Don't be satisfied with ordinary profits", "You are special", "You can easily gain more", "Don't be patient. Become active". Compare the following examples:

(9) *Easy money (Abbey National) (The Daily Telegraph* 11 Nov 2000)

(10) *Active Assets? Or Property Couch Potatoes? (Active Asset Account) (The Daily Telegraph* 4 Nov 2000)

(11) *Defy convention (Cahoot) (The Daily Telegraph* 16 Nov 2000)

(12) *Stop at the top. For high tax-free income every month look no further than the No.1 sector performer [...] (Perpetual) (The Daily Telegraph* 2 Dec 2000)

(13) *Make it happen. Standard solutions are not the best. (The Royal Bank of Scotland) (The Daily Telegraph* 1 Nov 2000)

We learn from bank advertisements before the crisis that they are not for people with narrow arguments (14), that a bank can make you happy and more hopeful (15). Banking is associated with gambling, as phrases such as *lucky winner* (*National Savings; The Daily Telegraph* 17 Nov 2000) imply. Other ads have people say *When it comes to my savings, size does matter* (*Intelligent Finance, The Daily Telegraph* 4 Nov 2000)

(14) (Charles Schulz has Snoopy say in a speech bubble:) *You can't discuss something with someone whose arguments are too narrow (Alliance Leicester) (The Daily Telegraph* 2 Dec 2000; Snoopy refers to Woodstock's narrow speech bubble with chicken scratch marks. The ad goes on: *We have a good deal to talk about*)

(15) *Uplifting thoughts #32 Henderson Global Players wins 1999 Best Overseas Fund Manager (The Daily Telegraph* 6 Nov 2000)

4.3. The use of phraseological units during the crisis

The negative influence of financial service ads on people prior to the crisis has frequently been a focus of criticism. In an article in the *New York Times* on 15 August 2008, "Home Equity Frenzy Was a Bank Ad Come True", Louise Story takes the catchy advertising slogan "Live Richly", which was created in 1999 for *Citicorp*, as a starting point for her argument that advertising "urged people to lighten up about money". As Elizabeth Warren, a professor at Harvard Law School who has studied consumer debt and bankruptcy, says, "financial companies used advertising to foster the idea that it is good, even smart, to borrow money". Advertisements changed the language of home loans and with it Americans' attitudes towards debt.[9] It became socially acceptable for everyone to accumulate debt. The article was followed by more than 50 comments, in which people mainly agreed with the author. Among other things, they wrote that it is also due to advertising campaigns that "keeping up with the Joneses", "live for today, the hell with tomorrow", the "Me, Now" mentality as well as "Buy now, pay later" have become leifmotifs of the present generation.

As described in section 1, having now become a focus of adverse attention, banks face an image crisis. They have to convey positive and reassuring messages in order to re-establish trust, restore the relationships with their customers and to fight their discredited self. Increased advertising is one way to be heard. My examination of the English-speaking press reveals that the majority of banks and their agencies try to combat their crisis of confidence through advertising. They adapt the contents of their messages to the current mood. They are, however, responding in different ways. The strategic foci of bank advertisements created in response to the crisis can be classified into the following types:

(A)   Focus on values such as security, solidity and reliability

Bankers aim to reassure customers that their institutions are well capitalized so that existing as well as future customers' money is safe. They focus their long-standing tradition.

(16)   *We offer strength and stability. (PNC)* (*The Washington Post Sunday* 16 Aug 2009)

(17)   *Safe, sound and growing (Rabobank)* (*The Tribune* 9 Sept 2009)

(18)   *Markets change. Our search for value hasn't. (Franklin Templeton Investments)* (*Time Magazine* 23/2009)

In 2008, for example, the investment firm T. Rowe Price ran an ad campaign with the headline "Confidence". A T. Rowe Price spokesman, Steve Norwitz, explained: "(...) we wanted to reassure investors that T. Rowe Price, with its long history, has been through this kind of market turmoil before; and we have the experience and expertise to be able to take advantage of opportunities and manage portfolios effectively in the midst of chaos. (...) and we are playing off that brand positioning with this ad."

(B) Focus on close contact with customers ("We put you first")
Today banks emphasize their links to the local community. They show real bankers with real names addressing their customers.

(19) *Louis Dhanaraj, Banking Center Manager: We don't want customers to lose their houses.* (*Bank of America*) (*Money & Main Street* 8/2009)

Some banks and financial institutions published open letters or manifestos to reassure customers in times of uncertainty (e.g. *A letter to customers of the Royal Bank of Scotland Group* published in *The Independent* on 1 Aug 2009 and *The Declaration of Financial Independence* signed by *INGDirect* published on the Internet in November 2009). This strategy includes the aspect of transparency and clarity. Customers have to understand the products a bank offers.

(20) *(...) we created our Clarity Commitment – a simple, one-page loan summary written in plain language* (*Bank of America*) (*Money & Main Street* 8/2009)

(C) Focus on present needs
Several banks and financial institutions use the crisis to stress that they have understood what is necessary in the present situation. This mainly refers to cash flow.

(21) *We're giving state capitols what they need most – capital* (*J.P. Morgan Chase & Co.*) (*USA Today* 1 Sept 2009)

Ads are designed to evoke positive feelings by showing people who received loans to open up businesses.

(22) *"City National helped me build my dream"* (*Pink Magazine*, Los Angeles Sept 2009)

(D) Focus on ecological campaigns

Several banks are trying to be seen as "going green". For example, *HSBC* introduced the initiative "Green Sale". They offer a range of financial products and promise to donate some of the money to environmental charities and funds. In Germany, *Deutsche Bank* is in the process of modernizing its headquarters in Frankfurt/Main. The offices will be renamed "Greentowers" because the bank plans to create an ecologically sustainable building as an active contribution to climate protection. The insurance company *Générali* offers car insurance at reduced rates for clean vehicles, and the *Royal Bank of Scotland* provides loans for firms that create a healthy economy, e.g. recycling plants. On *CNN*, in a *Crédit Agricole* commercial, we hear Sean Connery say: *Back to common sense. It's time for green banking* (5 Feb 2010).

My comparative study is based on bank advertisements in *The Daily Telegraph* that were published from October through December 2000 and those that appeared from May through October 2009. The corpus includes 300 ads for each group. The analysis revealed that the ads of 2009 expressed values such as "security/solidity", "tradition" and "customer-orientation" to a higher degree than those published before the crisis (cf. Figure 1). This result was basically confirmed by the data obtained from a comparison between financial service ads found in *Time Magazine* in 2000/2001 and 2008/2009 (cf. Figure 2), although the absolute number of ads run by financial companies in this magazine is relatively low (23 for the period 2000/01 and 18 for 2008/09).

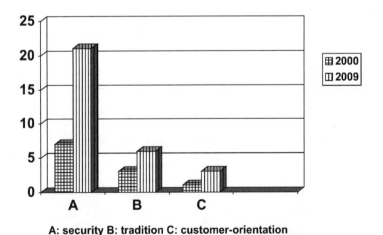

A: security B: tradition C: customer-orientation

Figure 1. Contents of bank ads in *The Daily Telegraph*

Phraseology in a time of crisis 11

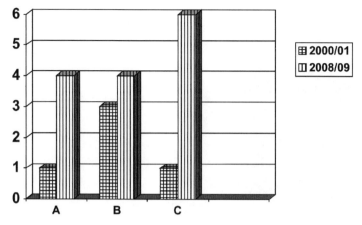

A: security B: tradition C: customer-orientation

Figure 2. Contents of bank ads in *Time Magazine*

Let us now have a closer look at how these differences are reflected in the use of phraseology. The PUs used in my corpus of financial service ads confirm the trends described above. PUs expressing sobriety and safety are found more often in ads published now. Banks have become *comfort zones* (*Bradford & Bingley*; *The Daily Telegraph* 29 June 2009), and *peace of mind* seems to be the dominant phrase (see Figure 3):

(23) *Peace of mind with the flexibility to change your mind* (*Bank of America*) (*Time Magazine* 9/2009)

Other advertisements now include proverbs and phrases that make us aware that there are good and bad times in life.

(24) *A wise plan... rain or shine* (*Principal*) (*Time Magazine* 14, 2009)

(25) *Life happens. Be ready* (*Principal*) (*Time Magazine* 27, 2008)

Proverbial phrases that are related to gambling and irresponsible recklessness are negated:

(26) *Insuring deposits up to '100,000' without anyone losing a 'cent'* (FDIC, *Time Magazine* 1, 2008; showing a 100,000-dollar bill and a Lincoln one-cent coin)

Think of life insurance from New York Life as a gift of financial protection. Since 1845, we've provided peace of mind through the toughest times. And we have the highest ratings for financial strength.* You see, as a mutual company, owned by our policyholders, we share your goal of providing for your family's long-term security. Give them the most selfless gift of all, a more secure future.

THE COMPANY YOU KEEP®
www.newyorklife.com

*Standard & Poor's (AAA), A. M. Best (A++), Moody's (Aaa) and Fitch (AAA) for financial strength. Source: Individual Third Party Ratings Reports (as of 3/18/09).
© 2009 New York Life Insurance Company, 51 Madison Avenue, New York, NY 10010

Figure 3. *(Time Magazine 23/2009)*

(27) *heads you win ... tails you win (first direct)* (*The Daily Telegraph* 20 May 2009; the three dots each time are followed by a picture of a one-cent coin)

An expression that has become popular in the crisis and the Presidential election campaign 2008 is *Main Street* (Mieder 2009). It refers metonymically to the interests of everyday working-class people and small business owners and is often contrasted with Wall Street. An information brochure for bank customers received the title *Money & Main St.* Its subtitle reads: *How economic headlines are affecting everyday Americans*. The insurance company *New York Life* uses the phrase to stress their commitment to their customers:

(28) *We're Main Street Not Wall Street New York Life* (*Time Magazine* 16/2008)

The following tables list PUs found in financial service ads in *The Daily Telegraph* and *Time Magazine* before and during the crisis:

2000/2001

uplifting thoughts
lucky winner
size does(n't) matter
easy money
narrow argument
couch potato
banking on the hoof
small, medium or large?
scale new heights
stop at the top
defy convention
make it happen
Is water wet?

2008/2009

peace of mind
(we help people to) save and meet their financial goals
(come) rain or shine
comfort zone
let the storm pass by
make peace with (your mind/your money)
Main Street (not Wall Street)
(a bank you can) bank on
we make money with you, not off you
safe haven
with both feet firmly on the ground
(your financial world is) out of control. You need someone to depend on
go through tough times
plain English
we call a spade a spade

The phrasicon of the English language contains very large resources so that users can choose and have enough units at their disposal to present themselves as they wish. In addition, there are expressions which were coined or popularized in the financial crisis 2008–2010. In English, these are phrases and slogans such as *bad bank, foul debts, Chapter 11, scrappage scheme, Cash for Clunkers, Turn Rust into Lust.* They have also entered other languages, either as loan translations or in English. A German TV quiz show recently included the following question:

> *Die aktuelle Finanzkrise wurde ausgelöst von:*
>
> *A: passiven Depots* *B: phlegmatischen Fonds*
> *C: lethargischen Zinsen* *D: faulen Krediten*[10]

Time will tell if expressions like these will stay in the language or soon fade out.

The tables support the results shown in Figures 1 and 2. The differences between "good times marketing" and "crisis marketing" can also be seen in the use of phraseology. The situation should, however, not be depicted in black and white. For example, phrases such as *I will take my clients seriously* (*J.P. Morgan* in the *Time Magazine* on 14 Feb 2000) and *With age comes wisdom. With advice comes wealth* (*Rabo Robeca Bank* in the *Time Magazine* on 1 May 2001) are also found in the 2000/2001 corpus, and the modified proverb *Now you can put all your eggs in one basket* (see Section 4.1.) was published in ads of several institutions in 2008 and 2009. In the *Daily Telegraph* on 8 May 2009 it appeared only few pages after a report on the consequences of the financial crisis.

The advertisement is a semiotically complex genre. Its effects rely on the connection between image and language. As we have seen in some of the examples above, the function of visual elements can go beyond mere illustration. In (26) and (27), images constitute the text. They are part of the message and must be "translated" into verbal elements. Play on words can be found in (7) and (8), where parts of the collocations are represented by pictures to activate their literal meanings. These few examples suffice to illustrate how the interaction between visual and verbal elements can be exploited to gain attention and involvement of the audience (cf. Naciscione 2001; Stöckl 2004). This, however, would be a subject for another article. With regard to the topic of this paper, icons and vignettes are worth mentioning, as their use is different in advertisements before and during the crises. In the past we could find images such as mountain tops and broken chains, symbolizing high rates and freedom or independence. The new icons are the safe (representing security), the lighthouse (giving orientation) and the life belt (promising rescue). Symbols like these are part of the social setting projecting the front in Goffman's sense.

5. Conclusion

A comparative analysis of advertisements run by banks and financial institutions in 2000/2001 and 2008/2009 shows changes in the content of slogans and other phraseological units. Proverbs and phrases expressing risk, adventure and non-conformity were dominant in ads prior to the crisis. Crisis-sensitive advertisements in 2008/2009 place the customer at the centre. Old-fashioned banking virtues of stability, confidence in financial services, convenience as well as solidity and tradition of institutions are emphasised as the cornerstones of a new value system; innovative strategies, such as "green banking" are devised to show that banks are ready for the future.

Given the findings of this study, we predict that once the financial crisis is over, banks will once again change the content of their advertisements to exploit the mood of the times. There are already some signs of this, now, one and a half years after Lehman's collapse. Many banks have recovered more quickly than expected and risk-taking and aggressive securities trading are mounting a comeback. As Richard Bove, an analyst at Rochdale Securities wrote, "People come to Wall Street to make money" (*The Los Angeles Times. Business* September 14, 2009).

University of Leipzig

Notes

Correspondence address: sfiedler@rz.uni-leipzig.de

1. I would like to thank Kon Kuiper for very helpful comments on an earlier draft of this article. It would not exist without his support.
2. Cf. http://en-us.nielsen.com/main/news/news_releases/2009/march/advertising_builds (accessed 25 May 2010).
3. The connection between exposure to advertisements and attitude has been shown by tests in social psychology (cf. Perloff 2003: 59–61).
4. *Mr. Gorbachev, tear down this wall!* was the famous challenge from US President Ronald Reagan to the Soviet leader to destroy the Berlin Wall in his speech on 12 June 1987. *My momma always said: Life is like a box of chocolates. You never know what you're gonna get.* is a memorable line from the film *Forrest Gump* (1994). *Yes we can!* was the slogan used by Barack Obama in the 2008 presidential campaign.
5. Word of the year 2003. Dent (2005: 157) describes it as "an alternative term for 'French fries', chosen by some Americans as a critique of the French protest against the invasion of Iraq".
6. A third aspect worth being considered might be the existence of a number of slogans that were created by financial experts and that are associated with the banking sector, such as stock market rules (e.g. *Never catch a falling knife; Sell in May and go away. But remember to be back in September*).

7. Cf., for example, the following taglines: *The world's local bank* (HSBC), *The company you keep* (*New York Life*), *The way up* (*City National Bank*), *Value from Ideas* (*Santander*), *Precise in a world that isn't* (*SPDR*), *Count on more* (*UMB*), *Don't take chances. Take charge* (*American Express*).
8. I could give an in-joke from my own family as an example. When the bank *BfG* received a new identity as the financial service provider *SEB (Skandinaviska Enskilda Banken)* in 2001, this process was supported by a large-scale advertising campaign on TV featuring Peter Ustinov. The well-known actor stressed the bank's new image saying in English, "More than a bank". Up to the present day, when our family is in the garden and one of us is about to sit on our bench there is a good chance of hearing this phrase. (The funny thing about it is the fact that 'bank' is a mistranslation of the German word 'Bank' here, a frequent blunder of German learners of English.)
9. "Second mortgages", which had an unappealing ring, were called "home equity (loans)", which has a connotation of ownership and fairness.
10. "Quiz mit Jörg Pilawa" on 16 Sept 2009. It can be compared with "Who wants to be a millionaire?" Translation: The present financial crisis was caused by A: passive deposits, B: phlegmatic funds; C: lethargic interests, D: foul debts (The German word *faul* can also mean *lazy*).

References

Balsliemke, Petra. 2001. *"Da sieht die Welt schon anders aus." Phraseologismen in der Anzeigenwerbung: Modifikation und Funktion in Text-Bild-Beziehungen.* Baltmannsweiler: Schneider.

Bertrand, Marianne, Dean Karlan, Sendhil Mullainathan, Eldar Sharif & Jonathan Zinman. 2010. What's advertising content worth? Evidence from a consumer credit marketing field experiment. *Quarterly Journal of Economics* 125(1). 263–306.

Brandweek. 2010. Distrusting the bankers. *Brandweek* 51(4). 25 Jan 2010.

Burger, Harald. 2003. Das idiomatische "Bild" und seine Modifikationen durch materielle Bilder – theoretische und empirische Aspekte. In Carmen Mellado Blanco (ed.), *Beiträge zur Phraseologie aus textueller Sicht*, 98–113. Hamburg: Kovač.

Bürli-Storz, Claudia. 1980. *Deliberate ambiguity in advertising.* Bern: Francke.

Dent, Susie. 2005. *Fanboys and overdogs: The language report.* Oxford: Oxford University Press.

Fiedler, Sabine. 2007. *English phraseology: A coursebook.* Frankfurt/M.: Peter Lang.

Goffman, Erving. 1959. *The presentation of self in everyday life.* New York: Doubleday & Company.

Goffman, Erving. 1963. *Behavior in public places: Notes on the social organization of gatherings.* New York: Free Press/MacMillan.

Goffmann, Erving. 1971. *Relations in public: Microstudies of the public order.* New York: Basic Books.

Kuiper, Koenraad. 2009. *Formulaic genres.* London: Palgrave Macmillan.

Lee, Monie & Johnson, Carla. 2005. *Principles of advertising: A global perspective*, 2nd edn. New York: Haworth Press.
MacRury, Iain. 2009. *Advertising*. London: Routledge.
MacWhirter, Ian. 2008. Everything you want to know about the bank crisis. *New Statesman* 5 May 2008. 22–24.
Mieder, Wolfgang. 2005. "A proverb is worth a thousand words": Folk wisdom in modern mass media. *Proverbium* 22. 167–244.
Mieder, Wolfgang. 2009. *Yes we can: Barack Obama's proverbial rhetoric*. New York: Peter Lang.
Mylonakis, John. 2008. The influence of banking advertising on bank customers: An examination of Greek bank customers' choices. *Banks and Bank Systems* 3(4). 44–49.
Naciscione, Anita. 2001. *Phraseological units in discourse: Towards applied stylistics*. Riga: Latvian Academy of Culture.
O'Driscoll, Gerald P. Jr. 2009. The financial crisis: Origins and consequences. *The Intercollegiate Review* Fall 2009. 4–12.
Perloff, Richard M. 2003. *The dynamics of persuasion: Communication and attitudes in the 21st Century*. 2nd edn. Hillsdale, NJ: Lawrence Erlbaum.
Sabban, Annette. 1998. *Okkasionelle Variationen sprachlicher Schematismen: Eine Analyse französischer und deutscher Werbetexte*. Tübingen: Narr.
Sabban, Annette. 2008. Critical observations on the culture-boundness of phraseology. In Sylviana Granger & Fanny Meunier (eds.), *Phraseology: An interdisciplinary perspective*, 229–242. Amsterdam: Benjamins.
Stöckl, Hartmut. 2004. *Die Sprache im Bild – Das Bild in der Sprache*. Berlin: de Gruyter.
Vesalainen, Marjo. 2001. *Prospektwerbung: Vergleichende rhetorische und sprachwissenschaftliche Untersuchungen an deutschen und finnischen Werbematerialien*. Frankfurt/M.: Lang.

Visual representation of phraseological image[1]

ANITA NACISCIONE

Abstract

Visual representation of a phraseological image is of stylistic and cognitive interest because it brings out the creative aspects of the verbal and the visual in multimodal discourse. A cognitive approach to the instantial stylistic use of phraseological units[2] (PUs) focuses on how they are perceived, understood, and interpreted. In a visual representation, the process of creating a mental image relies on close ties between the visual and the verbal, and knowledge of the political, socio-cultural, and semiotic implications. Visual representation performs a semantic and stylistic function; it enhances and interprets the image of a metaphorical PU and creates new meaning. It stretches the imagination and sustains figurative thought. Thus, phraseological metaphor exists not only in thought and language; it also exists in visual representation and its perception.

Keywords: phraseological metaphor; cognitive stylistic approach; visual representation; multimodal discourse; visual allusion.

1. Introduction

Visualisation is involved in metaphor recognition. Aristotle noted that metaphor can bring an image before our very eyes (1991: 247). In other words, metaphor makes an image mentally visible. In cognitive psychology the image is generally viewed as a mental representation, as "a picture in the head". Perception of an image, whether lexical or phraseological, is a cognitive process that creates a mental picture in the imagination, a kind of visualisation in the mind's eye, which may be subjective. For instance, we would each visualise the base metaphor[3] of the PU *to skate on thin ice*[4] in our own way. However, an illustration presents a personal angle of vision (see Figure 1).

20 Anita Naciscione

Figure 1. *To skate on thin ice*

Visual representation of an image serves to create a new guided mode of perception which we are led to accept since seeing is persuasive. A cognitive approach to language use concentrates on meaning and its development (Geeraerts 2006). In this paper I am concerned with visual aspects of metaphorical thought representation and with the creative use of phraseological metaphor in verbal and visual discourse.[5] The paper explores the benefits of a cognitive approach to visual representation of instantial stylistic use[6] and focuses on perception and comprehension of the verbal and the visual.

This paper draws on the basic findings of cognitive science, which has established metaphor as a figure of both thought and language. The use of figurative language has been recognised as part of human cognition both in literary texts and everyday speech (Lakoff and Johnson 2003 [1980]; Gibbs 1999 [1994], 1995, 2005; Steen 1994, 2009 [2007]; Katz 1998 et al.). The cognitive approach has served as a basis for the development of cognitive stylistics (Lakoff and Turner 1989; Gibbs 1995, 1999, 2002, 2008; Semino and Culpeper 2002; Steen 2002a, 2002b; Stockwell 2002; Gavins and Steen 2003 et al.).

Metaphors occur not only in thought and language, but also in pictures (Forceville 1991, 1994, 1996, 2008). In visual representation, metaphor forms part of the conceptual metaphor UNDERSTANDING IS SEEING, "what enables you to see is metaphorically what enables you to understand" (Lakoff and

Turner 1989: 94). Cognitive science seeks to understand "the internal mental representations responsible for higher-order mental functions", among them vision and language (Harrington 2002: 125). Cognitive psychologists argue against the traditional split between vision and thinking, emphasising that the sense of sight is the most efficient organ of human cognition (Arnheim 1997 [1969]: 14).

2. Visual representation of instantial stylistic use

Stylistic changes of PUs in pictures is an issue that has long fascinated researchers (for example, Mieder 1989, 1993; Forceville 1991, 1994, 1996, 2008; Naciscione 2001a, 2005; Lundmark 2003, 2005; Stöckl 2004; Fiedler 2007; Burger 2007, 2008; Kuiper 2009).

Visual instantiation of phraseological meaning is not merely a feature of traditional illustrations. In instantial stylistic use, the visual representation of phraseological units performs a different semantic and stylistic function from core use;[7] it enhances and interprets the image, bringing the literal meaning to the fore. Illustrations open up the possibility of making human thought visible and creating a visual effect; they provide food for thought or, as Arnheim puts it, they form visual thinking (1997 [1969]). The picture from Thurber's book *The beast in me and other animals* (1973 [1928]: 269) is an apt drawing about the nature of human beings. Stylistically, it is a visual pun (see Figure 2).

The caption, coupled with the visual impact, brings out the literal meaning of the constituents of the PU *to throw one's weight about/around*,[8] which is metaphorical in its base form. Metaphorical meaning is grounded in bodily

"*I'm getting tired of you throwing your weight around.*"

Figure 2. *Throwing your weight around*

experiences.[9] Together with the visual impact of physical perception, the textual message creates a more powerful stylistic effect. In visual representation, the cognitive link between thought, language, and sight provides a significant insight as we turn from abstract phraseological meaning to the sense of sight. The shift from figurative to literal or from literal to figurative results in a pun. This pattern demonstrates the function of the sense of sight[10] in mental and visual perception.

In literary discourse, the visual may be involved in meaning change and development, contributing to figurative networks in discourse. The new visualisation becomes part of the mental world.[11] In *Alice's Adventures in Wonderland*, Lewis Carroll and his illustrator Tenniel repeat the PU *to grin like a Cheshire cat* both verbally and visually. The image of the Cheshire Cat appears in three pictures over a stretch of three chapters, sustaining figurative thought. In the first picture, Alice is looking up at the Cat, who is sitting in a tree grinning from ear to ear.

Figure 3. *A grin without the Cat*

The second picture features the famous grin of the Cat (see Figure 3), which lingers after the Cat has vanished. The third picture presents the Cat's head (see Figure 4) above the Queen, who is ready to cut off everybody's head, including the Cat's.

Her order cannot be carried out as the executioner does not know how to cut off a head without a body from which to cut it.

This presentation of an image is a breach of the traditional way of using illustrations in children's books, resulting in "uncommon nonsense" (Carroll

Figure 4. *The Cat's head*

1928: 142) typical of the genre of English Children's Nonsense Literature. Visual representation of instantial use is one of the ways of depicting a world of logical improbability.

The famous grin, metonymically standing for the Cheshire cat, is a verbal and visual extension of a phraseological image (Carroll 1928: 80–116), creating a sustained visual pun.[12] In discourse, a phraseological pun may permeate a stretch of text, creating a visual narrative and contributing to its coherence and cohesion,[13] as is the case in this text. A dynamic, reiterated visualisation of a phraseological image is a technique of image development in text; it reveals the potential of visual and verbal sustainability of the PU.

Change and development of phraseological meaning is not merely a feature of illustrations in a literary discourse, as we have seen from Thurber and from Lewis Carroll's *Alice's Adventures in Wonderland*. Instantial stylistic use is a mode of figuration that also forms part of various types of newspaper and internet texts, which combine verbal and visual representation in creative thinking. The media exploit semantic, stylistic, semiotic, and psychological elements to achieve an economic, political, or social effect. This especially applies to advertising texts, which frequently resort to stylistic use in visual representation due to its persuasive power.

Many researchers focus on the interface between language and image in printed media, that is, the relationship between linguistic images and material pictures, such as photographs, paintings, cartoons, etc. (for instance, Mieder 1989; Forceville 1994; Stöckl 2004; Goodman 2006; Burger 2007, 2008). Stöckl's article is a study of the language-image link with respect to advertising and journalism. Stöckl comes to the conclusion that "there is a strong pictorial element in language and a linguistic element in images" (2004: 10). Printed material, advertisements included, usually combines and establishes interactions between verbal and pictorial information (Forceville and Urios-Aparisi 2009: 3).

Burger's research centres around the question whether and, if so, how the linguistic image is influenced by the material picture (*das idiomatische Bild* vs *das materielle Bild*, to use the German terms), especially in advertising (see Burger 2008: 121–135). This leads to another interesting issue: whether the message of the verbal representation of the phraseological image is influenced by the quality and type of visual representation. This aspect receives detailed attention in Burger's article (2008). Whether more or less effective modifications exist from the point of view of the recipient is of great importance for the applied field of advertising and marketing in establishing the best ways to reach the target audience, which is vital for production and distribution. Burger's investigation is based on empirical research. He offers an innovative approach to enable optimization of phraseological resources in the world of advertising. However, investigation of the recipient's viewpoint is not the aim of this current research (see Burger 2008).

Indeed, my aim is to focus on the benefits of a cognitive approach to such phenomena and to explore how the phraseological image is used to construct meaning in visual representation. Each new piece of scholarly research expands the horizon of investigation in multimodal discourse, bringing out the great variety of metaphorical and metonymic conceptualisation in advertising (Forceville 2008, 2009; Forceville and Urios-Aparisi 2009: 3–17).

Use of multimodal metaphor is a common feature of the stylistic use of PUs on the internet. The increasing need for new forms of expression has resulted in creative, sophisticated pathways for representing a message. The visual also offers endless opportunities, lending a new dimension by further developing and reinforcing the image which the figurative meaning has evoked. Let me take one PU and examine a number of its virtual representations. Over the last decade the internet has hosted many images featuring the PU *money laundering*. Though this term is informal as to its stylistic level, it is in standard use in criminal law; for example, the official name of the related US law is the *Money Laundering Statute*. Thus, it is a terminological PU or a terminological phraseologism according to Nikulina (2005).

Figure 5. *Laundered bills*

Although visual discourse is usually coupled with verbal text in close interaction, cases may arise where no verbal text exists. Here the visual narrative constitutes the whole discourse of the representation. The picture of laundered bills[14] (see Figure 5) contains no text or caption. This is a case of creative visualisation of an abstract concept constituted by metaphor.[15] The picture is used to give visual shape to the concept of money laundering, to illustrate a "theory constitutive metaphor", and to help explicate it (Gibbs 1999 [1994]: 169–179). The visual representation enhances comprehension, which involves parallel perception, the reader being simultaneously aware of the figurative thought in legal language and of the literal meaning.

The globalised practice of using both verbal and nonverbal techniques in the media and on the internet has resulted in multimodal discourse[16] which employs features from more than one semiotic mode of communication simultaneously (Goodman 1996: 69; Kress and Van Leeuwen 1996; Machin 2007; Forceville

2008: 463). This development is also seen in numerous sites dealing with money laundering and conferences dedicated to it (see Figures 6, 7, 8).

Figure 6. *Conference on money laundering*

"How elements in visual and verbal modes interact on the page is a central issue in multimodal texts" (Goodman 1996: 69). Use of symbols is one visualisation technique that helps to depict the abstract in terms of the concrete in multimodal manifestations. In Figure 6 the dollar sign $ produces a special visual effect that adds a new visual and semantic dimension to the phraseological image that would not be available in a standard text.

A further development of the image of money laundering has resulted in a logo (see Figures 6, 8) featuring a washtub with a currency sign in it. The graphic of the washtub provides a metonymic link to laundering; thus in this instantiation, metonymy is one of the aspects of meaning construction (Gibbs 2003: 27–40, 2007: 20–28; Panther 2005: 353; Barcelona 2007).

Metonymy brings out the role of visual representation in the extension of the image of a metaphorical PU; thus it is a case of metonymy and metaphor working

Figure 7. *Logo of money laundering*

concurrently. This is what I would call concurrent use of several stylistic patterns within the context of one PU, providing semantic and stylistic cohesion.[17] The logo of a washtub with a currency sign in it is frequently used for conferences and specialist websites devoted to money laundering. Numerous conferences have been held on money laundering in the EU; hence the euro € symbol. Graphic properties are generally used to represent the extra-linguistic world in an accurate manner. For identification of instantial graphic implications, it is important to know the socio-cultural background, in this case the use and symbolic meaning of the currency sign.

Visual representation frequently involves the use of semiotic elements due to their clear-cut graphic persuasive power. In Figure 8 the symbolic meaning is incorporated in a modified STOP sign, a command to terminate the activity.[18]

Figure 8. *Stop!*

The graphic also contains the dollar sign $, which is perceived as a symbol of money. Thus, the multimodal enactment of a phraseological image is another mode of presenting the message and visualising thought. Textual information is supported by pictorial perception. Semiotic elements help to retrieve and visualise the phraseological image. This determines the significance of multi-modality in meaning construal and interpretation of a pictorial metaphor (see Forceville 2008). The visual effect merges with the verbal in creating a visual pun; it is a way in which "words, typography and pictures are woven together to form multimodal texts" (Goodman and Graddol 1996: 1). The graphic representation is inextricably linked with the content of the article. The symbol $ performs a semantic function. The visual creation stretches the usual system of typography and affects the relation between the visual and the verbal.

Multimodal metaphor is frequently used in graphic design of book covers. For instance, the cover of Nick Kochan's book *The washing machine* (2005) (see Figure 9) featuring a washing machine at work, laundering bills, is sufficient to retrieve the base form of the PU *money laundering* from long-term memory.

The subtitle "How Money Laundering and Terrorist Financing Soils Us" reinforces and explains the idea. It is clear that a washing machine presupposes

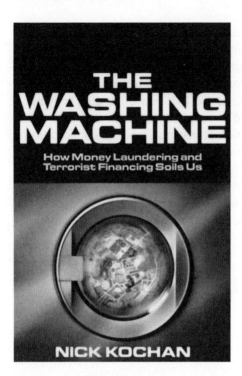

Figure 9. *The Washing Machine*

laundering. The bills that are being laundered imply that this is *dirty money*; you do not wash clean things. This is another PU with metaphorical links to the PU *money laundering* and an extension of the phraseological image *soils*. Thus, the cover of the book is what I would call a <u>visual allusion</u>[19] to the image of *money laundering*, accompanied by extended phraseological metaphor. Concurrently it also resorts to punning, as both the figurative and direct meanings are clear to vision and understanding. Moreover, instantial use of the PU in the title performs an umbrella function, encompassing the entire text of the book.

Another example; the stylistic pattern of visual pun is used in the book cover of *Reigning <u>cats and dogs</u>* by Katharine Macdonogh (1999), which offers visual representation of pampered royal pets in paintings and photographs since the Renaissance on both front and back covers, hinting implicitly at the existence of an impressive array of them in royal history. The cover employs the pattern of replacement of a constituent of the PU <u>*to rain cats and dogs/raining cats and dogs*</u>, resulting in a homophonic pun: a common technique in book cover design. Thus, skilful instantial visualisation of phraseological image is common in both literary and media discourses.

3. A discourse dimension

Visual representation of stylistic use has not exhausted its potential. The development of media and multimodal possibilities offers new and unexpected turns in visual discourse. An interesting aspect of visual representation is the visual development of figurative meaning, which makes identification and interpretation of stylistic use in multimodal texts more difficult. It is common for magazines to use a PU on their cover and pick it up again in the cover story, which provides further extension of the metaphorical thought, though it may be pages away. Only the interrelation between the two modes of expression provides a full understanding of the multimodal text. Interaction between the visual and its verbal counterpart has "a perceptual immediacy" that is lacking in language alone (Forceville 2008: 463).

Visual comprehension is facilitated by "metaphor networks" (Trim 2007). Understanding the functional load of both visual image and language helps to bridge the cognitive gap between the textual and the visual, as they cannot be viewed separately. For instance, *The Spectator* often uses a phraseological image in the design of its cover. The following visual representation goes back to 10 January 1998 (see Figure 10).

Modern psychological research on perception has revealed the worth of pictures in communicating thought, which is enshrined in the well-known proverb <u>a picture is worth a/ten thousand words</u> (Mieder 1992: 463) as part of current popular wisdom.[20] A pictorial representation helps us to draw inferences as the eye is involved in active exploration. It is a visual experience in an attempt to establish the base form, which in this case does not appear anywhere – either on the cover of the magazine or in the text of the article or its title.

Visual perception, backed by semantic and stylistic analysis, allows us to draw the conclusion that the visual representation in Figure 10 is a case of concurrent visual and verbal allusion to the metaphorical PU *to skate on thin ice*, which is based on common metaphorical mapping, that is, in its base form the PU is a conventional phraseological metaphor. The sub-image *spin*, which is graphically presented on the ice, is a term in figure skating, while at the same time it is an extension of the base metaphor of the PU, creating a visual pun. Importantly, sub-images form an essential part of the given extended metaphor while the tie between the sub-images is metonymic. Skating and spinning are linked metonymically, with both constituting a single extended metaphorical image. Concurrently, *spin* is also a direct allusion to another PU, <u>spin doctors</u>, PR professionals who specialise in spin tactics to manipulate public opinion and provide favourable biases. The meaning of the PU *to skate on thin ice* is enhanced by the ominous headline *Heading for trouble*.

Figure 10. The Spectator, *10 January 1998*

The cover story appears on Page 8. Its headline *Spinning out of Control* (see Figure 11) catches the eye and the mind. It forms part of the extended metaphor, which creates a new meaning and reflects sustained metaphorical thought.

With the images of Alastair Campbell and Peter Mandelson in the foreground, spinning out of control illustrates the idea of the PR profession on course to self-destruct. The metaphorical extension helps to bridge the distance and establish the semantic and stylistic link between cover page and cover story.

The idea of the text-forming potential of PUs is not new in phraseological research (Chernyshova 1974; Zhantlesova 1978; Dobrovol'skij 1980; Moshiashvili 1982; Naciscione 1997, 1998; Sabban 2006, 2007; Fiedler 2007; Trim 2007). The text-forming function of metaphorical networks is also manifest in the use of visual representation. As the phraseological image is extended over the whole article, it calls for a sustained mental vision in one's mind's eye. The sub-image, which forms part of the associative metaphorical network, reflects an extended metaphorical thought. Cohesion secures continuity of phraseological ties in discourse, including visual representation. The new visualisation

SPINNING OUT OF CONTROL

PR is the profession of the decade. But, says **Jenny McCartney**, *the industry may be on the point of self-destruction*

Figure 11. *Spinning out of control, p. 8*

becomes part of the mental world. Spiegel believes that visualisation is an essential structure of narrative as we think and feel through our eyes (1976: 18–25).

Creative expression of a new idea is achieved by an instantiation of extended metaphor, pun, and allusion in a process of meaning extension in one visual context. Thus, it is not only a matter of a metaphor network; I would call it a *figurative network* as it involves an area of figuration and a range of stylistic techniques. The visual implications of the pun help to shift from direct meaning to figurative meaning and back again. A sustained visual image becomes an essential part of the meaning of the PU in the given instantiation. The abstract idea has been translated into visual form to represent a hazardous situation. The textual and the visual representation of a thought process is influenced by political, social, and cultural contexts that lie behind the specific space and time the image is used.

The process of understanding and interpreting meaning requires "cognitive effort that takes place in real time, starting with the first moments when people move their eyes across the page" (Gibbs 1999: 15). In this case it refers to both the visual representation and the headline, which attract the reader's attention. "Interpretation involves both conscious and unconscious mental processes" (Gibbs 1999: 331). I follow Arnheim in believing that "visual perception is an active concern of the mind" (1997 [1969]: 37); hence, the importance of stylistic awareness and the training of a discerning eye. In discourse the language becomes alive, new meanings are created and sustained. It is essential to develop an understanding of the discoursal dimensions of phraseological metaphor, including those in visual discourse. Extended phraseological metaphor is enhanced and developed by a pictorial illustration of the instantial image to create a visual impact. This is a case of visual sustainability. It works, provided the basic principle remains: cohesion and coherence of the verbal and the visual. The example shows that extended phraseological metaphor is used to reflect extended figurative thought.

4. Implicit visual messages

Visual representation of a phraseological image may convey implicit messages that are not directly expressed in text. This is a creative instantiation of visual allusion in a serious financial text (Figure 12). The allusion is to the base form of the PU *to put all one's eggs in one basket*. Recognition and interpretation of a creative representation may be cognitively challenging, especially in cases of allusion. Importantly, with no textual presence of any of the base constituents, the visual impact becomes the key to comprehension.

Visual allusion is achieved as the PU is retrieved from long-term memory and we establish the base form. *Eggs* and *basket* are the implicit verbal elements of the PU, while at the same time they constitute the explicit visual presence of the phraseological image. Verbal absence turns into a presence due to visual representation. Emergence of the figurative meaning of the PU vis-à-vis visual representation of the literal meaning of *eggs* and *basket* results in a visual pun. The dual perception is enhanced as these constituents have been visually foregrounded[21] in the article. You cannot miss the eggs and the basket when casting an eye on the page. The implicit presence of the invisible base form is indispensable to secure comprehension. *Eggs* and *basket* have also been psychologically foregrounded, turning into figurative constituents of the PU due to the natural perceptual link between sight and thought.

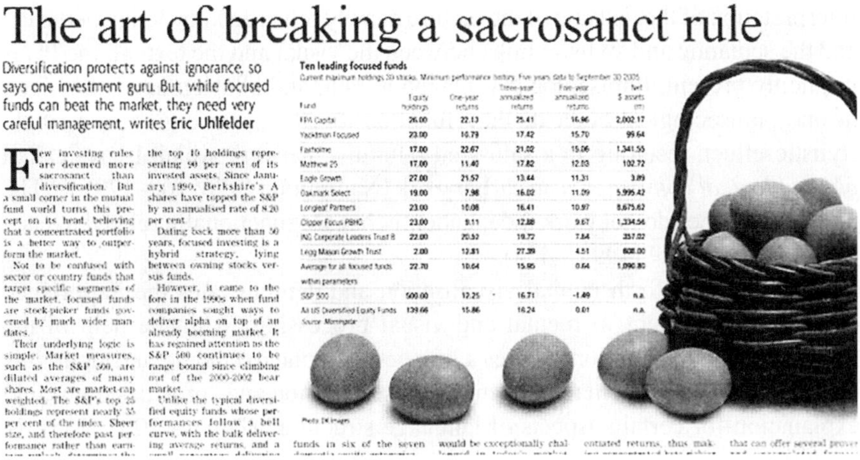

The art of breaking a sacrosanct rule

Diversification protects against ignorance, so says one investment guru. But, while focused funds can beat the market, they need very careful management, writes Eric Uhlfelder

Few investing rules are deemed more sacrosanct than diversification. But a small corner in the mutual fund world turns this precept on its head, believing that a concentrated portfolio is a better way to outperform the market.

Not to be confused with sector or country funds that target specific segments of the market, focused funds are stock-picker funds governed by much wider mandates.

Their underlying logic is simple. Market measures, such as the S&P 500, are diluted averages of many shares. Most are market-cap weighted. The S&P's top 25 holdings represent nearly 35 per cent of the index. Sheer size, and therefore past performance rather than earn-

the top 10 holdings representing 50 per cent of its invested assets. Since January 1990, Berkshire's A shares have topped the S&P by an annualised rate of 8.20 per cent.

Dating back more than 50 years, focused investing is a hybrid strategy, lying between owning stocks versus funds.

However, it came to the fore in the 1990s when fund companies sought ways to deliver alpha on top of an already booming market. It has regained attention as the S&P 500 continues to be range bound since climbing out of the 2000-2002 bear market.

Unlike the typical diversified equity funds whose performances follow a bell curve, with the bulk delivering average returns, and a

funds in six of the seven

would be exceptionally chal

entuated returns, thus mak

that can offer several prove

Figure 12. Financial Times, *fm*, 28 November 2005, p. 13

The headline *The art of breaking a sacrosanct rule* provides an important cue; it acts as a response-producing stimulus. *Breaking* plays a dual role: it is the explicit metaphorical *break* as part of *to break a rule* with insertion of the highly appropriate epithet *sacrosanct*, while at the same time it is also a subtle metaphorical sub-image in an allusion to the implicit PU. *Breaking* is the only textually visible link to the base form, providing associations of contiguity. As the article is devoted to the art of breaking the inviolable investment rule of diversification of equity funds versus focused funds, *breaking* is inevitably part of both *breaking a sacrosanct rule* and the danger of *putting all one's eggs in one basket*. The natural desire to understand leads to the link between the eggs and the basket, and breaking the sacrosanct rule of risk management. The visual representation becomes a genuine part of the concept of risk. The link between the visible and the invisible is a dimension that allows us to gain an insight and draw inferences. The visible spurs our imagination and helps us to conceive the phraseological image, which is sustained throughout the text. It lingers at the back of our mind as the article explores the alternative of focused funds versus the traditional piece of financial wisdom not to put all your eggs in one basket.

This instantiation reveals the interconnection of stylistic techniques in that it shows how a phraseological metaphor turns into a visual pun. "PUs can be visualised without mentioning a single constituent" (Fiedler 2007: 104), as in this case when the base form of the metaphorical PU *to put all one's eggs in one basket* appears neither in the text of the article nor in the headline, nor indeed is a caption present. However, we infer the absent presence of the PU.

Interpretation of the text and of the picture heavily relies on knowledge of the PU and the semantic and stylistic links between the visual and the textual; the PU is implicitly present. Phraseological metaphor, pun, and allusion are intertwined in one phraseological context; they function together, converging in a single stylistic effect, resulting in a saturated figurative network which I have called *phraseological convergence* in earlier work (Naciscione 1976: 168–179).[22] "The individual tropes do not work independently but are functionally related to each other" (Gibbs 1999 [1994]: 454).

The pun calls forth mental visualisation and demonstrates the importance of the sense of sight in mental and visual processing. With the help of the sense of vision, perception secures a link between understanding and sight. It is perception that derives mainly from the sense of vision and "provides motivated explanation for certain aspects of language structure" (Popova 2003: 135). In cognitive psychology, sight is viewed as a primary sense in cognition; people rely on sight more than on other senses. The experience of metaphor reveals the importance of mental sight in the perception of abstract notions, while physical sight implies a perceptual awareness which aids comprehension of figurative language. In this case it is the instantial use of a metaphorical PU, in which a visual pun is combined with extended metaphor, resulting in an allusion. Thus, visual representation is a technique for expressing an implicit message and sustaining figurative thought. Cases of multimodal use call for both imagination and a creative approach in their instantiation and for more advanced cognitive skills in inference and interpretation.

5. Visual literacy as a cognitive skill

Stylistic use in multimodal texts is more demanding in identification and interpretation. It is important to understand figurative language and see its connection with visual representation. Although cognitive linguistics has it that, "figurative language does not require special cognitive processes to be produced and understood" (Gibbs 1999 [1994]: 17), in visual representation the process of perception and comprehension is a pursuit of hidden connections and cohesion of the textual and the visual, which is equally important to cognitive stylistics and applied areas, for instance, advertising. Experience has it that understanding of cohesive ties is crucial for comprehension, while failure to recognise cohesion and insightful associative links is "the common cause of misreading" (McRae 1996: 35).

Cognitive psychologists see visual perception as a cognitive activity. "The human mind perceives, shapes and interprets its image of the outer world with all its conscious and unconscious powers" (Arnheim 1974 [1954]: 461) to establish the message and resolve the subtle complexity of the situation, using available linguistic and background knowledge. A semantic and stylistic tie is established with the base metaphor of the PU, although it does not appear in the text. Visual discourse is an interesting "perceptual experience" (Gibbs 1999 [1994]: 79) as we feel the invisible presence of the PU in the face of the visible absence of its base form.

To understand the case of visual allusion in Figure 13, we need encyclopaedic knowledge of the political discord in the EU over the Lisbon Treaty. The relevant historical fact is the second Irish Referendum (02.10.2009.) reversing the decision of the first (12.06.2008). This is represented visually by the stray Irish sheep returning to its flock (the flock is bodily present, that is, it is visually represented in the picture). The available textual information is scanty: the name "Ireland" on the straying black sheep and "EU Treaty" on the enclosure gate with twelve stars as a symbol of the EU.

Figure 13. *P. Pismestrovic*, Kleine Zeitung, *Austria, 20 June 2008*
  Cartoon by Pismestrovic, Kleine Zeitung, Austria© *CAI/NYT Syndication*

Visual perception supported by this information leads to identification of figurative meaning and the base form: *there is a black sheep in every flock* > *the black sheep of the family* > *a black sheep*. However, as Mieder points out, a decontextualised proverb is meaningless in itself; it is the metaphor of the proverb that enables us to employ it in so many different contexts, including advertisements and cartoons (1989: 20–21). The same applies to all PUs. Innovative stylistic alterations are common in the use of traditional proverbs and their variants, as is also seen from the extensive collection of Wolfgang Mieder's international archive of proverbs in Burlington, Vermont (Mieder and Litovkina 1999: 3). In order to disambiguate a particular stylistic instantiation, it is necessary both to have a good knowledge of the base form and the figurative means employed. Comprehension of the figurative links between the visual and the verbal is a cognitive act, as is creativity; hence the importance of visual literacy[23] as a cognitive skill. Visual literacy is fundamental to understanding the coherence and cohesion of the visual and the textual.

On the other hand, a new instantiation is enabled due to use of the PU as a language unit and a pattern of instantial stylistic use, such as pun, extended metaphor, metonymy, or allusion. To be creative implies going beyond standard form and meaning, and beyond conventional vision. When exploring creativity, Pope shows that creativity emerges every time some existing language material (words, images, sounds) is transformed into something judged to be fresh and valuable. Creativity does not come from nothing or from nowhere; it embraces "radical forms of re-creation and includes actively engaged kinds of re-vision, re-membering and re-familiarisation" (Pope 2005: xvii). Moreover, visual discourse calls for new ways of both creation and interpretation. "Multimodal texts demonstrate linguistic and artistic creativity, and creative multimodality reveals how language functions" (Goodman 2006: 244).

6. Conclusion

This paper takes a closer look at the creative aspects of verbal and visual representation of phraseological image in multimodal discourse from a cognitive perspective. The image-bearing constituents of phraseological units lend themselves well to creative textual and visual representation, including abstract qualities and implicit messages. The phraseological image is sustained as thought develops, contributing to the creation of a visual narrative. The visual reflects experience beyond the possibilities offered by a text. The cognitive approach elucidates the comprehension and interpretation of phraseological metaphor in verbal and visual discourse and brings out its role in the communication of figurative thought.

Mental visualisation of instantial stylistic use forms part of cognitive performance, enhanced by visual representation of the extended image. Visualisation is a reflection of figurative thought. I would argue that phraseological metaphor occurs not only in thought and language, it also occurs in visual representation and its perception. Visual representation of a phraseological image engages both the eye and the mind.

Comprehension and interpretation rely on cohesive ties between the visual and the verbal. Visual literacy is a cognitive skill which advances sociolinguistic competence; the ability to perceive, comprehend, and interpret the stylistic, social, and cultural message of a visualised phraseological image. Skills of visual literacy have become increasingly important as the nature of pictures has changed. Pictures do not merely illustrate the text or emerge as an afterthought; they frequently provide further development of thought. Training a discerning eye in stylistic awareness enhances our cognitive abilities for mental representation and processing.

In conclusion, visual representation is a non-verbal mode of expression that is perceived by sight. In visual discourse the phraseological image is evoked pictorially with or without a verbal text, and cohesion of phraseological meaning is retained. A number of stylistic patterns may be employed in one visual representation: metaphor, metonymy, pun, allusion and others, forming a subtle network of associations, and figurative and literal meanings. To date, visual representation of PUs is a less examined mode of their stylistic use. Exploration of phraseological metaphor in multimodal discourse opens up new pathways for further research and makes a good case for including studies in this field in general research on phraseology.

Latvian Academy of Culture

Notes

Correspondence address: naciscione@parks.lv

1. This article is published as part of Ch. 6 of my book: Naciscione, Anita. 2010. *Stylistic Use of Phraseologtcal Units in Discourse*. Amsterdam & Philadelphia: John Benjamins Publishing Company.
2. *The phraseological unit* is a stable, cohesive combination of words with a fully or partially figurative meaning. For the basic terms in phraseology, see Naciscione 2001b.
3. *The base metaphor* is a metaphor which forms part of the image of the PU in its base form. *The base form* is stored in the long-term memory of the language user as a

language unit. It is accessed when a discourse situation calls for it. It is the dictionary form and meaning, recorded as the head phrase.
4. I have indicated the forms of PUs for emphasis: instantial elements are in italic while base forms are in italic and underlined.
5. *Visual discourse* is a coherent visual representation of instantial use with the aim of creating a visual narrative. In visual discourse, the phraseological image is evoked pictorially with or without a verbal text, and cohesion of phraseological meaning is retained.
6. *Instantial stylistic use* is a particular instance of a unique stylistic application of a PU in discourse, resulting in significant changes in its form and meaning determined by the thought and the context.
7. *Core use* is use of the PU in its most common form and meaning. In core use the PU does not acquire any additional stylistic features in discourse and does not exceed the boundaries of one sentence.
8. *To throw one's weight around* is an American variant of the PU.
9. "Metaphorical thought is grounded in non-metaphorical aspects of recurring bodily experiences or experiential gestalts" (Gibbs 1999 [1994]: 16). For more on people's bodily experiences as part of the fundamental grounding for human cognition and language, see Gibbs 2005.
10. For the importance of a cognitive-linguistic view of the sense of sight in cognition of a literary text, see Popova 2003.
11. According to Spiegel, traditional visualisation in literature starts only in the fiction of the 19th century when the "visual perspective moves to the centre of a coherent and fully articulated literary form" (Spiegel 1976: 33).
12. For more examples of sustained visual puns in thought representation, see Naciscione 2005.
13. For an understanding of cohesion in phraseology, see Naciscione 2002.
14. This picture has been taken from the site of St. Kitts–Nevis. See *St. Kitts – Nevis financial service sector reviewed: Money laundering is a global problem* 2008.
15. For stylistic use of the PU *money laundering*, see Naciscione 2003, 2006.
16. *Multimodal discourse* is a discourse that applies stylistic techniques from more than one semiotic mode of expression. The verbal works together with the non-verbal in construction of new meaning in metaphorical and metonymic conceptualisations which are patterns of both thought and language.
17. For concurrent use of stylistic techniques in phraseological instantiations, see Naciscione (1976: 160–180, 2001b: 136–141). In phraseology, *concurrent use* is the simultaneous occurrence of several instantial changes reinforcing the message and creating a focal point within the framework of one PU. See also Gibbs (1999 [1994]: 449–454) for use of several tropes working together.
18. See *Satcor Report on International Conference "Stop Money Laundering"* 2002.
19. Cognitive research on multimodality has established a number of stylistic techniques in visual discourse: *visual metaphor*, *visual pun*, and *visual metonymy* and of late also *visual simile* or *pictorial simile* as Forceville calls it (2009: 466) as a separate stylistic means. I would argue for *visual allusion* as a distinctive pattern in its own

right. If a PU is involved, it is a case of *phraseological allusion*, which is a mental implicit verbal and/or visual reference to the image of a phraseological unit, which is represented in discourse by one or more explicit image-bearing constituents, and their instantial ties, hinting at the image (see Naciscione 2001b: 99–109).
20. For a discussion of the verbal and visual potential of this proverb, see Mieder (1993: 133–149).
21. For a detailed analysis of the theory of foregrounding and its stylistic and psychological aspects, see van Peer 1986. For features of prominence that differentiate the figure from the ground, making it more salient, see Stockwell (2002: 14–15).
22. The idea of convergence of several stylistic devices for emphasis was first expressed by Riffaterre (1959: 154–174).
23. By *visual literacy* I understand the ability to perceive, comprehend, and interpret visual representation of language. Kress and van Leeuwen (1996: 3) stress the importance of visual literacy as a matter of survival in visual communication.

References

Aristotle. 1991. *On rhetoric: A theory of civil discourse*. George A. Kennedy (trans.). Oxford: Oxford University Press.
Arnheim, Rudolf. 1974 [1954]. *Art and visual perception: A psychology of the creative eye*. Berkeley & Los Angeles: University of California Press.
Arnheim, Rudolf. 1997 [1969]. *Visual thinking*. Berkeley & Los Angeles: University of California Press.
Barcelona, Antonio. 2007. The role of metonymy in meaning construction at discourse level. In Günter Radden, Klaus-Michael Köpcke, Thomas Berg & Peter Siemund (eds.), *Aspects of meaning construction*, 51–75. Amsterdam & Philadelphia: John Benjamins.
Burger, Harald. 2007. Das idiomatische "Bild" – alte Fragen, neue Antworten? [Idiomatic "Image": Old questions, new answers?]. In Erika Krzisnik & Wolfgang Eismann (eds.), *Frazeologija v jezikoslovju in drugih vedah*, 121–135. Ljubljana: Filozofska fakulteta.
Burger, Harald. 2008. Das idiomatische "Bild" und seine Modifikationen durch materielle Bilder – theoretische und empirische Aspekte [Idiomatic "Image" and its modifications in pictures: Theoretical and empirical aspects]. In Carmen Mellado Blanco (ed.), *Beiträge zur Phraseologie aus textueller Sicht*, 89–113. Hamburg: Verlag Dr. Kovac.
Carroll, Lewis. 1928. *Alice's adventures in Wonderland*. London: Macmillan.
Chernyshova, Irina. I. 1974. Tekstoobrazuyushchiye potentsii frazeologicheskikh yedinits [Text-forming potential of phraseological units]. *Lingvistika teksta*, 159–166. Moscow: Moskovskiy pedagogicheskiy institut inostrannykh yazykov imeni M. Toreza.
Dobrovol'skij, Dmitrij. 1980. Zur Dialektik des Begriffs der textbildenden Potenzen von Phraseologismen. *Zeitschrift für Phonetik, Sprachwissenschaft und Kommunikationsforschung* 33. 690–700.

Fiedler, Sabine. 2007. *English phraseology: A coursebook*. Tübingen: Gunter Narr.
Forceville, Charles. 1991. Verbo–pictorial metaphor in advertisements. *Parlance* 3. 7–20.
Forceville, Charles. 1994. Pictorial metaphor in advertisements. *Metaphor and Symbolic Activity* 9(1). 1–29.
Forceville, Charles. 1996. *Pictorial metaphor in advertising*. London: Routledge.
Forceville, Charles. 2008. Metaphor in pictures and multimodal representations. In Raymond W. Gibbs (ed.), *Metaphor and thought*, 462–482. Cambridge: Cambridge University Press.
Forceville, Charles. 2009. Non-verbal and multimodal metaphor in a cognitivist framework: Agendas for research. In Charles J. Forceville & Eduardo Urios-Aparisi (eds.), *Multimodal metaphor*, 19–42. Berlin & New York: Mouton de Gruyter.
Forceville, Charles & Urios-Aparisi, Eduardo. 2009. Introduction. In Charles J. Forceville & Eduardo Urios-Aparisi (eds.), *Multimodal metaphor*, 3–17. Berlin & New York: Mouton de Gruyter.
Gavins, Joanna & Gerard Steen (eds.). 2003. *Cognitive poetics in practice*. London & New York: Routledge.
Geeraerts, Dirk. 2006. Introduction: A rough guide to cognitive linguistics. In Dirk Geeraerts (ed.), *Cognitive linguistics: Basic readings*, 1–28. Berlin & New York: Mouton de Gruyter.
Gibbs, Raymond W., Jr. 1999 [1994]. *The poetics of mind: Figurative thought, language and understanding*. Cambridge: Cambridge University Press.
Gibbs, Raymond W., Jr. 1995. Idiomaticity and human cognition. In Martin Everaert, Erik-Jan Van der Linden, André Schenk & Rob Schreuder (eds.), *Idioms: Structural and psychological perspectives*, 97–116. Hillsdale, NJ: Lawrence Erlbaum.
Gibbs, Raymond W., Jr. 1999. *Intentions in the experience of meaning*. Cambridge: Cambridge University Press.
Gibbs, Raymond W., Jr. 2002. Psycholinguistic comments on metaphor identification. *Language and Literature* 11(1). 78–84.
Gibbs, Raymond W., Jr. 2003. Prototypes in dynamic meaning construal. In Joanna Gavins & Gerard Steen (eds.), *Cognitive poetics in practice*, 27–40. London: Routledge.
Gibbs, Raymond W., Jr. 2005. *Embodiment and cognitive science*. Cambridge: Cambridge University Press.
Gibbs, Raymond W., Jr. 2007. Experimental tests of figurative meaning construction. In Günter Radden, Klaus-Michael Köpcke, Thomas Berg & Peter Siemund (eds.), *Aspects of meaning construction*, 19–32. Amsterdam & Philadelphia: John Benjamins.
Gibbs, Raymond W., Jr. (ed.). 2008. *The Cambridge handbook of metaphor and thought*. Cambridge: Cambridge University Press.
Goodman, Sharon. 1996. Visual English. In Sharon Goodman & David Graddol (eds.), *Redesigning English: New texts, new identities*, 38–72. London & New York: Routledge.
Goodman, Sharon. 2006. Word and image. In Sharon Goodman & Kay O'Haloran (eds.), *The art of English: Literary creativity*, 244–277. New York: Palgrave Macmillan.
Goodman, Sharon & Graddol David. 1996. Introduction. In Sharon Goodman & David Graddol (eds.), *Redesigning English: New texts, new identities*, 1–2. London & New York: Routledge.

Harrington, Michael. 2002. Cognitive perspectives on second language acquisition. In Robert Kaplan (ed.), *The Oxford handbook of applied linguistics*, 124–140. Oxford: Oxford University Press.
Katz, Albert N. 1998. Figurative language and figurative thought: A review. In Albert N. Katz, Cristina Cacciari, Raymond W. Gibbs & Mark Turner (eds.), *Figurative language and thought*, 3–43. Oxford: Oxford University Press.
Kochan, Nick. 2005. *The washing machine*. Mason, OH: Thomson South-Western.
Kress, Gunther & Theo Van Leeuwen. 1996. *Reading images: The grammar of visual design*. London: Routledge.
Kuiper, Koenraad. 2009. *Formulaic genres*. Basingstoke: Palgrave Macmillan.
Lakoff, George & Mark Johnson. 2003 [1980]. *Metaphors we live by*. Chicago: University of Chicago Press.
Lakoff, George & Mark Turner. 1989. *More than cool reason: A field guide to poetic metaphor*. Chicago: University of Chicago Press.
Lundmark, Carita. 2003. *Puns and blending: The case of print advertisements*. KU Leuven, ICLC8. http://wwwling.arts.kuleuven.ac.be/iclc/Papers/Lundmark.pdf (accessed 18 November 2009).
Lundmark, Carita. 2005. *Metaphor and creativity in British magazine advertising*. Luleå: Luleå University of Technology dissertation.
Macdonogh, Katharine. 1999. *Reigning cats and dogs*. New York: St. Martin's Press.
Machin, David. 2007. *Introduction to multimodal analysis*. London: Hodder Arnold.
McRae, John. 1996. Representational language learning: From language awareness to text awareness. In Ronald Carter & John McRae (eds.), *Language, literature and the learner: Creative classroom practice*, 16–40. London & New York: Longman.
Mieder, Wolfgang. 1989. *American proverbs: A study of texts and contexts*. Bern et al.: Peter Lang.
Mieder, Wolfgang. 1992. *A dictionary of American proverbs*. New York & Oxford: Oxford University Press.
Mieder, Wolfgang. 1993. *Proverbs are never out of season: Popular wisdom in the modern age*. New York & Oxford: Oxford University Press.
Mieder, Wolfgang & Anna T. Litovkina. 1999. *Twisted wisdom: Modern anti-proverbs*. Burlington: The University of Vermont.
Moshiashvili, Svetlana A. 1982. *Tekstoobrazuyushchiye funktsii frazeologicheskoi konfiguratsii v sverhfrazovom yedinstve* [Text-forming functions of phraseological configuration in a supra-phrasal unit]. Moscow: Moskovskiy pedagogicheskiy institut inostrannykh yazykov imeni M. Toreza dissertation.
Naciscione, Anita. 1976. *Okkazional'noye stilisticheskoye ispol'zovaniye frazeologitcheskikh edinits (na materiale proizvedeniy Chosera)* [Occasional stylistic changes of phraseological units: Based on the Complete Works of Chaucer]. Moscow: Moskovskiy pedagogicheskiy institut inostrannykh yazykov imeni M. Toreza dissertation.
Naciscione, Anita. 1997. Translation aspects of phraseological reiteration in discourse. In Andrejs Veisbergs (ed.), *Contrastive and applied linguistics* 607, 31–35. Riga: University of Latvia.
Naciscione, Anita. 1998. Phraseological puns in discourse. In Andrejs Veisbergs (ed.), *Contrastive and applied linguistics* VII, 70–84. Riga: University of Latvia.

Naciscione, Anita. 2001a. Frazeologisko vienību stilistiskais lietojums reklāmā [Stylistic use of phraseological units in advertising]. *Linguistica Lettica* 9. 169–177.
Naciscione, Anita. 2001b. *Phraseological units in discourse: Towards applied stylistics*. Riga: Latvian Academy of Culture.
Naciscione, Anita. 2002. Cohesion in phraseology. In *Proceedings of the tenth EURALEX international congress* II, 533–539. Copenhagen: Center for Sprogteknologi.
Naciscione, Anita. 2003. Translation of terminology: Why kill the metaphor? In Andrejs Veisbergs (ed.), *Proceedings of the third Riga symposium on pragmatic aspects of translation*, 102–115. Riga: University of Latvia & Aarhus School of Business.
Naciscione, Anita. 2005. Visual representation of phraseological metaphor in discourse: A cognitive approach. In Carmen R. Caldas-Coulthard & Michael Toolan (eds.), *The writer's craft, the culture's technology, PALA 2002*, 71–83. Amsterdam & New York: Rodopi.
Naciscione, Anita. 2006. Figurative language in translation: A cognitive approach to metaphorical terms. In Andrejs Veisbergs (ed.), *Pragmatic aspects of translation*, Proceedings of the fourth Riga international symposium, 102–118. Riga: University of Latvia.
Nikulina, Elena A. 2005. *Terminologizmy kak rezul'tat vzaimodeystviya i vzaimovliyaniya terminologii i frazeologii sovremennogo angliyskogo yazyka* [Terminologisms as a result of interaction and mutual influence between terminology and phraseology in Modern English]. Moscow: Moskovskiy Pedagogicheskiy gosudarstvenniy universitet habilitation dissertation.
Panther, Klaus-Uwe. 2005. The role of conceptual metonymy in meaning construction. In Francisco Ruiz de Mendoza Ibáñez & Sandra Peña Cervel (eds.), *Cognitive linguistics: Internal dynamics and interdisciplinary interaction*, 353–386. Berlin & New York: Mouton De Gruyter.
Peer, Willie van. 1986. *Stylistics and psychology: Investigations of foregrounding*. London: Croom Helm.
Pope, Rob. 2005. *Creativity: Theory, history, practice*. London & New York: Routledge.
Popova, Yanna. 2003. 'The fool sees with his nose': Metaphoric mappings in the sense of smell in Patrick Süskind's *Perfume*. *Language and Literature* 12(2). 135–151.
Riffaterre, Michael. 1959. Criteria for style analysis. *Word* 15(1). 154–174.
Sabban, Annette. 2006. Zur textbildenden Rolle von Phrasemen – mit einer Analyse von Musik-Moderationen und Kulturnachrichten im Hörfunk [On the role of phrasemes in text formation: Analysis of musical and cultural broadcasts]. In Ulrich Breuer & Irma Hyvärinen (eds.), *Wörter-Verbindungen. Festschrift für Jarmo Korhonen*, 275–290. Frankfurt am Main: Peter Lang.
Sabban, Annette. 2007. Textbildende Potenzen von Phrasemen [Text-building potential of phrasemes]. In Harald Burger, Dmitij Dobrovol'skij, Peter Kühn & Neal R. Norrick (eds.), *Phraseologie: Ein internationales Handbuch der zeitgenössischen Forschung*, 237–254. Berlin & New York: Walter de Gruyter.
Satcor Report on International Conference "Stop Money Laundering". 2002. http://www.antimoneylaundering.ukf.net/stopimages/stopsmall.jpg (accessed 19 September 2009).
Semino, Elena & Jonathan Culpeper (eds.). 2002. *Cognitive stylistics: Language and cognition in text analysis*. Amsterdam & Philadelphia: John Benjamins.

Spiegel, Alan. 1976. *Fiction and the camera eye: Visual consciousness in film and the modern novel.* Charlottesville: University Press of Virginia.
St. Kitts – Nevis financial service sector reviewed: Money laundering is a global problem. 2008. http://www.houstontriallawgooglyerblog.com/uploads/image/StanfordMoneyLaundering.jpg (accessed 19 September 2009).
Steen, Gerard. 1994. *Understanding metaphor in literature.* London & New York: Longman.
Steen, Gerard. 2002a. Identifying metaphor in language: A cognitive approach. *Style* 36(3). 386–407.
Steen, Gerard. 2002b. Towards a procedure for metaphor identification. *Language and Literature* 11(1). 17–33.
Steen, Gerard J. 2009 [2007]. *Finding metaphor in grammar and usage: A methodological analysis of theory and research.* Amsterdam & Philadelphia: John Benjamins.
Stöckl, Hartmut. 2004. In between modes: Language and image in printed media. In Eija Ventola, Cassily Charles & Martin Katlenbacher (eds.), *Perspectives on multimodality*, 9–30. Amsterdam & Philadelphia: John Benjamins.
Stockwell, Peter. 2002. *Cognitive poetics: An introduction.* London & New York: Routledge.
Thurber, James. 1973 [1928]. *The beast in me and other animals.* San Diego et al.: Harvest/HBJ.
Trim, Richard. 2007. *Metaphor networks: The comparative evolution of figurative language.* New York: Palgrave Macmillan.
Zhantlesova, Lidia P. 1978. Tekstoobrazuyushchaya rol' frazeologicheskikh yedinits v sverhfrazovom yedinstve [Text-forming role of phraseological units in supraphrasal context]. In *Sbornik nauchnykh trudov Moskovskogo pedagogicheskogo instituta inostrannykh yazykov imeni M. Toreza* 134, 228–244. Moscow: Moskovskiy pedagogicheskiy institut inostrannykh yazykov imeni M. Toreza.

Wissensstrukturierung und Wissensvermittlung durch Routineformeln: Am Beispiel ausgewählter althochdeutscher Texte

NATALIA FILATKINA and MONIKA HANAUSKA

Abstract

The following paper explores the role of routine formulae in the processes of knowledge structuring and transmission in the Early Middle Ages. The term "formulaic language" is understood as involving syntactically, semantically and pragmatically more or less fixed expressions or texts which are an important part of cultural practice and communication. Although recent phraseological research has demonstrated an important role for formulaic patterns in modern European languages, historical aspects of formulaic language have not received a great deal of attention, there existing only small number of studies dealing with this topic, mainly focused on one author or one type of text such as blessings or conversational guides.

By collecting and systematically exploiting a corpus of German historical texts from 750 to 1750, the research group "Historical Formulaic Language and Traditions of Communication" at the University of Trier, Germany is able to expand knowledge of the historical functions of formulaic language. The project has developed a methodology for investigation all types of historical formulaic patterns. Its database includes all Old High German texts with the exception of glosses.

The following paper concentrates on only one type of phrasal vocabulary – routine formulae and explores their use and pragmatic function in a number of vernacular Old High German texts. The study focuses on selected Old High German texts used for didactic purposes as well as biblical exegesis and biblical epics. Knowledge for this study is understood chiefly as a function of the scientific heritage of Antiquity and Christianity which was required to be made accessible to students in the medieval classroom. The paper presumes that formulaic language is a fundamental element of verbal communication in the Middle Ages and the Early Modern Period just as it is in contemporary communication. This assumption is supported by the fact that routine formulae do play a significant part in knowledge transmission in the Middle Ages and have many pragmatic functions in the source documents.

The selection of texts is based on the understanding that academic life in the Early Middle Ages was mainly dominated by monastic culture. In this environment, theological and philosophical knowledge was transmitted to students on the one hand and to educated scholars on the other, largely in Latin as a predominant academic language and as a connecting bridge for the scholars all over Western Europe. Vernacular languages such as Old High German did not play an important role in this context. Nevertheless, there are a small number of texts that show that Old High German was also a part of this scholarly tradition. In such texts as Williram's of Ebersberg paraphrase of the Song of the Songs, the biblical epic of Otfrid of Weißenburg or Notker's of St. Gall scholarly adaptation of classical authors and texts like Martianus Capella, Boethius or the Psalms, scholarly knowledge is transmitted to a monastic audience. In these texts, routine formulae play a significant role in knowledge transmission. The authors use formulaic patterns systematically to prepare their texts for their readers. Four main groups of routine formulae have been differentiated according to their chief pragmatic function.

The first group of routine formulae is used to direct the readers' attention to new or important contents. These expressions also introduce new content, and structure the text, e.g. <u>fernemet/firnim</u> ('notice, listen!'). In the second group the chief pragmatic function is to instruct the reader/listener by emphasizing important aspects of information, e.g. <u>ih sago dir</u> ('I may tell you'), <u>giuuisso uuizist thu thaz</u> ('you may know') or <u>ih uueiz uuola</u> ('I know well'). The routine formulae of the third group are mainly used to point to matters of interest, e.g. <u>hier ist ze uuizzene</u> ('here you have to know') or <u>hier ist ze merchene</u> ('here you have to notice'). The function of the fourth group is to explain previous passages which are difficult to understand or to translate into German, as e.g. <u>daz chît</u> ('this means') or <u>ih meino</u> ('I mean'). As routine formulae are often multifunctional, it is not always possible to strictly separate the first three groups from each other. There are many overlaps between these groups. It is therefore necessary to take the variety of pragmatic functions into account for an adequate description of these routine formulae.

The results of this study show an abundant usage of routine formulae, the diversity of their forms and functions as well as their importance to the structure of Old High German texts. That being so, new light has been thrown on the historical significance of formulaic language, and ways of investigating historical traditions of communication have been illustrated.

Keywords: routine formulae; Old High German; knowledge transfer; formulaic patterns; pragmatic function.

1. Einleitung

Der vorliegende Aufsatz widmet sich der Rolle der Routineformeln in historischen Texten der Wissensvermittlung und Wissensstrukturierung und bezieht diese Begriffe auf das gelehrte (u.a. biblische und theologische) Wissen der klösterlichen Schulausbildung im Frühen Mittelalter. Im Mittelpunkt stehen deshalb einige ausgewählte althochdeutsche[1] Texte, für die die Verwendung der wissensvermittelnden Routineformeln besonders charakteristisch ist. Die Auswahl der Texte beruht auf den Ergebnissen der systematischen Auswertung der gesamten althochdeutschen Überlieferung nach dem Auftreten formelhafter Wendungen durch die Nachwuchsforschergruppe „Historische Formelhafte Sprache und Traditionen des Formulierens (HiFoS)" an der Universität Trier.[2] Das Projekt widmet sich der epochenübergreifenden Dokumentation und Untersuchung der Gebrauchsdynamik und Variation der historischen formelhaften Wendungen in unterschiedlichen Textsorten aus der Zeitspanne zwischen ca. 750 bis ca. 1750. Es wird von der Überzeugung geleitet, dass Formelhaftigkeit ein Grundkonstituens der sprachlichen Repräsentation von Weltwissen ist. Im Mittelalter und in der Frühen Neuzeit war sie ein wesentliches Element der verbalen Kommunikation und kam vor allem mit Hilfe der syntaktisch, semantisch und pragmatisch mehr oder weniger fest werdenden bzw. gewordenen Wendungen oder Texte zustande. Diese stellten eine herausragende kulturelle Kommunikationspraktik mit besonderem Status dar und gestalteten die Traditionen des Formulierens. Sie basierten einerseits auf kulturell geprägten gesellschaftlichen Gebrauchskonventionen, waren aber andererseits historischen Veränderungsprozessen unterworfen.

Für die Gegenwart haben die Korpus- und Computerlinguistik bereits in den 90er Jahren des vergangenen Jahrhunderts empirisch anhand elektronischer Textkorpora nachgewiesen, in welch hohem Maße die meisten in Europa verbreiteten Sprachen formelhaft (syntaktisch und semantisch) geprägt sind.[3] Zu einer ähnlichen Schlussfolgerung kommen auch die Untersuchungen aus den Bereichen der Formulierungstheorie, Textsortenlinguistik und Ritualforschung. Der Hintergrundgedanke ist dabei, dass Wörter einer Sprache nicht isoliert voneinander funktionieren, sondern syntagmatisch und eben phraseologisch miteinander verbunden sind und nur in dieser Verbundenheit in verschiedenen Kommunikationssituationen Sinn ergeben. Viele der in der Kommunikation auszuführenden Sprachhandlungen sind konventionalisierte, ritualisierte Kommunikationsformen, die das Formulieren ökonomischer gestalten. Die Konventionalisierung, Routine in der Mündlichkeit (Coulmas 1981) wie in der Schriftlichkeit (Gülich 1997) oder – mit Feilke (1994: 366) – idiomatische Prägung entsteht zu einem wesentlichen Teil durch den Gebrauch von formelhaften Wendungen unterschiedlichster Typen. Linguistische und kulturhistorische

Analysen in der HiFoS-Nachwuchsforschergruppe lassen eine ähnliche Relevanz der Formelhaftigkeit für historische Formulierungstraditionen annehmen.

Im vorliegenden Aufsatz folgt der allgemeinen Zusammenfassung der wichtigsten Erkenntnisse im Bereich der gegenwartssprachlich bezogenen Routineformelforschung (Abschnitt 1) ein historischer Umriss (Abschnitt 2). Abschnitte 3 und 4 führen in die Methoden und Techniken der Wissensvermittlung im Frühen Mittelalter ein und bilden eine wichtige Verständnisgrundlage für die Darstellung der Funktionen von historischen Routineformeln in diesem Prozess (Abschnitt 5). Die Analyseergebnisse sind in Abschnitt 6 präsentiert.

2. Routineformeln in der gegenwartssprachlich bezogenen Phraseologieforschung

Routineformeln oder anders ausgedrückt kommunikative bzw. pragmatische Phraseologismen gehören seit Beginn der germanistischen Phraseologieforschung in den 60er Jahren des 20. Jahrhunderts zu ihrem Kernbestand. Darunter werden mehr oder weniger feste desemantisierte Wendungen verstanden, mit deren Hilfe immer wiederkehrende kommunikative Handlungen, die so genannten kommunikativen Routinen, bewältigt werden (Burger 2007: 57). Sie können dementsprechend als Entlastung oder Erleichterung bei Formulierungsschwierigkeiten eingesetzt werden.

Für die meisten in der Phraseologieforschung berücksichtigten Standardsprachen können die Routineformeln in vieler Hinsicht als gut erforscht gelten.[4] Besonders in solchen Kommunikationsbereichen wie informelle und formelle Kontakteröffnungen und -beendigungen wurde die konstitutive Rolle der Routineformeln bereits in mehreren Untersuchungen hervorgehoben: Für direkte und indirekte mündliche Gespräche sowie etwa schriftliche Brieftexte können in ihrer Grundstruktur mehr oder weniger stabile Schemata (formelhafte Texte) festgestellt werden, die mit Hilfe der Routineformeln organisiert sind, einzelne Kommunikationsschritte in diesen Situationen prägen und auf bestimmte soziale Ordnungen verweisen. Die Stabilität geht dabei mit Flexibilität einher: Den Kommunikationsbedingungen entsprechend kann die Struktur und folglich die Verwendung von Routineformeln eine unterschiedliche Entfaltung finden. Sowohl durch Flexibilität, aber auch gleichzeitig durch eine gewisse Stabilität können allgemeine kulturelle Zuweisungen erfolgen, z.B. zu bestimmten historischen Epochen, Institutionen, Altersgruppen, Bevölkerungsschichten, Sprachgemeinschaften usw. (Lüger 2007: 446). Der letzte Aspekt – die kulturelle Geprägtheit der Routineformeln und der interlinguale Vergleich ihrer Verwendung – hat oft den Gegenstand unterschiedlich umfangreicher kontrastiver Untersuchungen gebildet (Gülich und Henke 1979/1980; Coulmas 1981; Álvarez de la Granja 2008). Die Wichtigkeit der korrekten Verwendung von Routineformeln für die adäquate soziale Kompetenz in einer Fremdsprache wurde mehrmals seitens der didaktisch ausgerichteten Phraseologieforschung betont (Gülich und Henke 1979/1980; Kühn 1984; Lorenz-Bourjot und Lüger 2001: 85).

Die Forschung unterscheidet grundsätzlich zwischen situationsgebundenen und situationsunabhängigen Routineformeln (Burger et al. 1982: 105; Stein 1995). Für den Gebrauch dieser beiden Typen der Routineformeln als Handlungsmuster ist nicht so sehr das Wissen über ihre semantisch beschreibbare Bedeutung ausschlaggebend, sondern eher das Wissen über die pragmatischen Funktionen, die Routineformeln in der jeweiligen Kommunikationssituation übernehmen. Diese sind in der Regel sehr vielfältig und können bei ein und derselben Formel je nach der Situation und/oder Position im Text variieren. Aufgrund dieser Polyfunktionalität ist in Bezug auf eine Formel eher von einer dominanten Funktion auszugehen, die eng mit einem Spektrum an weiteren Funktionen verbunden ist.

Trotz dieser Schwierigkeit und mit Blick darauf wurden in der traditionellen Phraseologieforschung mehrere Versuche unternommen, Routineformeln nach ihren Funktionen zu klassifizieren. Eine dieser Klassifikationen (Coulmas 1981: 94) sei an dieser Stelle stellvertretend erwähnt. Obwohl sie in der rezenteren Forschung unterschiedlich und kontrovers diskutiert wurde, bildet sie die funktionale Vielfalt der Routineformeln umfassend ab, hat nicht das Ziel,

Tabelle 1. *Funktionen der Routineformeln nach Coulmas (1981: 94)*

soziale Funktionen	*diskursive Funktionen*
– Kontaktfunktion (Aufmerksamkeitserlangung und -steuerung, Höflichkeitssignale) – Stärkung der Verhaltenssicherheit (Zustimmungsformeln, Vorstellungs- und Entschuldigungsformeln) – Schibboleth-Funktion (gruppenspezifische Anredeformen, Ausdrücke sozialer Identität) – Konventionalitätsfunktion (z.B. Glückwünsche)	– Gesprächssteuerung (Eröffnungs- und Einleitungsformeln,Rederechtsverteidigungsformeln, Signale der Beitragsübergabe, Abschlussformeln) – Evaluation (psychoostensive Formeln, emotive und kognitive Einstellungskundgaben) – Metakommunikation (Verständnissicherung, Kommentar- und Korrekturformeln) – Entlastungsfunktion (Verzögerungsformeln als Anhangfragen, Pausenfüller, Hörersignale)

sie nach dem Prinzip der Monofunktionalität zu ordnen und eignet sich auch für historische Untersuchungen.

3. Routineformeln in der historisch ausgerichteten Phraseologieforschung

Wesentlich weniger Beachtung fanden bis jetzt historische Routineformeln. Für das 19. Jahrhundert hat Linke eine größere Studie (Linke 1996) vorgelegt und die Rolle der Phraseologie, darunter auch Routineformeln, in der bürgerlichen Konversationskultur herausgearbeitet: Im Kontext von Anstandsbesuchen, Tischgesprächen, gesellschaftlichen Anlässen wie Bällen, gemeinsamen Restaurantbesuchen usw. bildeten sich im 19. Jahrhundert phraseologische Wendungen heraus, die sich durch starke soziosemiotische Kraft auszeichnen (Burger 1998: 89–90). Ihre systematische Analyse anhand verschiedener (literarischer und nicht literarischer) Textsorten steht bis jetzt aus. Mit Blick auf das Bestreben, Deutsch rein zu reden und zu schreiben, sind den Routineformeln in den barocken Grammatiken, Kanzleibüchern, Stil- und Schreiblehren einzelne Kapitel gewidmet (Filatkina, im Druck).

Für das Frühmittelalter betont Burger (1977: 17–18) das häufige Vorkommen der Beteuerungsformeln, Ausrufeformeln, Grußformeln und Flüche mit starker Affinität zur gesprochenen Sprache. Eine umfangreiche Sammlung der Beteuerungsformeln primär aus einem Textdenkmal, Otfrids Evangelienbuch, legte Büge (1908) vor. Die geläufige Verwendung solcher Formeln wie *das sage ich dir für wahr, das glaubt mir, das mögt ihr gewiss wissen* führt Büge (1908: 2) der typischen Einstellung zur formelhaften Sprache am Anfang des 20. Jahrhunderts entsprechend auf volkstümliche Traditionen zurück und sieht darin vor allem „ein Kunstmittel zur lebhaften und kunstvollen Darstellung" (Büge 1908: 41). Die Routineformeln verteilen sich quantitativ unterschiedlich innerhalb einzelner Kapitel; ihr Einsatz überwiegend bei den Verben des Sagens und Wissens ist vor allem dadurch zu erklären, dass „der Dichter keinen bequemen Ausdruck wie *affirmare, confirmare, arquere*, oder wie im Neuhochdeutschen ‚versichern', ‚behaupten', ‚bestätigen'" (Büge 1908: 46) parat hatte und solche Verben umschreiben musste. In den mittelhochdeutschen Texten nehmen Beteuerungsformeln insbesondere in der Funktion der Wahrheitsbeteuerung stark zu.

An den Rändern eines lateinischen Manuskripts der Bibliothèque National in Paris und eines Manuskripts der Vatikanischen Bibliothek sind die so genannten *Altdeutschen* oder *Pariser Gespräche* überliefert (Sonderegger 1978: 284–285). Burger hat bereits (1983: 24–34) die Ergiebigkeit dieser Quellen für phraseologische Fragestellungen betont, allerdings unterlagen sie bis jetzt kaum einer systematischen Untersuchung. Dieser althochdeutsche (fränkische) Text mit lateinischer Übersetzung wurde von einem Franzosen aus dem Ende des 10. oder Anfang des 11. Jahrhunderts wohl für französische Reisende im deutschsprachigen Gebiet verfasst und besteht aus über 100 Sätzen, Dialogformen und Einzelwörtern. Der Text steht in der Überlieferungstradition der bereits im 3. Jahrhundert bekannten *Hermeneumata* – Gesprächsbücher der griechischen Konversation für lateinkundige Schüler (Haubrichs und Pfister 1990).

Die in den *Altdeutschen Gesprächen* überlieferten Sätze vermitteln sprachliches Wissen über die Alltagskommunikation in einer fremden Sprache: Sie stellen meistens imperativische Bitten oder Befehle (1), einige der ersten im Althochdeutschen überlieferten Beschimpfungen (2) sowie fränkische Interjektionen dar, zu denen interessanterweise meistens lateinische Übersetzungen X fehlen (3):

(1) *elpe . adiuua. Gimen min ros . i(d est). da | mihi^m. quum. Gimer min scelt . i(d est) scu | Gimer min spera. | Gimer min stap. i(d est) | fustum*
‚Hilfe! Gib mir mein Roß. Gib mir mein Schild. Gib mir meinen Speer. Gib mir meinen Stab.'

(2) *Vndes ars in tine naso . i(d est) canis culum in tuo naso*
‚Hundearsch in deine Nase'

(3) *Terue geu! Terue nain i . non*
‚Wahrlich ja! Wahrlich nein'

Ähnliches gilt ferner für die sog. Kasseler Glossen im Codex Casselanus theol. 4°24, der im 1. Viertel des 9. Jahrhunderts wohl in Regensburg niedergeschrieben wurde (Schröder 1981: 61–63). Sie weisen einen den *Altdeutschen Gesprächen* ähnlichen Aufbau auf: Auch hier finden sich neben den sachlich angeordneten Einzelwörtern Befehlswendungen und dialogische Routineformeln. Hier werden die mit dem Latein vertrauten (vermutlich italienischen?) Leser in bairischen Routineformeln und Wortformen unterwiesen, so dass sie sich mit Sprechern des Bairischen verständigen können.

(4) | | | |
|---|---|---|
| *Tundi meo capilli* | *skirminfahs* | ‚schere mein Haar' |
| *Radi me meo colli* | *skirminanhals* | ‚schere meinen Hals' |
| *Radi meo parba* | *skirminanpart* | ‚schere meinen Bart' |
| *Sic potest fieri* | *somacuuesan* | ‚vielleicht' |

Aus dieser Perspektive des mittelalterlichen Fremdsprachenunterrichts allgemein und des mittelalterlichen DaF-Unterrichts ganz konkret ist das Vorkommen von Beschimpfungen in den *Altdeutschen Gesprächen* und eine Stelle in den *Kasseler Glossen* zu verstehen:

(5) Stulti sunt Romani   Tole sint uualha   ‚Dumm sind die Romanen'
     Sapienti sunt Paioari   spahe sint peigira   ‚Klug sind die Baiern'

Penzl (1984: 392) macht darauf aufmerksam, dass es sich aus der Tradition der *Hermeneumata* ergibt, dass der Lehrer im Unterricht den Schüler über Persönliches ausfragte, ihn beschimpfte und lächerlich machte, um die Schüler zu größerem Fleiß und größerer Aufmerksamkeit zu ermuntern und von Ungezogenheit und Ungehorsam abzuhalten. Unter diesem Gesichtspunkt wären – so Penzl – auch die Routineformeln (5) zu beurteilen: Zur Tradition des Unterrichts gehört, dass der Lehrer seine Überlegenheit in Wissen und die Unwissenheit seines Schülers betont.

Aus heutiger Perspektive interessant ist nicht nur die sprachliche Eigenart des Formulierens im Althochdeutschen, die die *Kasseler Glossen* sowie die *Altdeutschen Gespräche* tradieren, sondern auch die Unterschiede der Gesprächskonventionen. Sie kommen am deutlichsten in der Struktur der Gespräche zum Ausdruck: Es finden sich viele Fragen an die Reisenden, die sehr eingehend und detailreich sind. Die Antworten sind dabei eher kurz, sie bestehen oft aus einem Wort oder fehlen ganz. Daraus ist möglicherweise zu schließen, dass es in althochdeutschen Zeiten wohl höflich war, an einen Fremden ganz persönliche Fragen zu richten. Der Fremde aber braucht durchaus nicht genaue Auskunft über seine Reise zu geben, wenn er das nicht wünscht.

Eine dezidierte Verwendung von Routineformeln ist ferner für mittelalterliche Segenssprüche konstitutiv. Trotz der Tatsache, dass Segenssprüche in der letzten Zeit immer öfter als Beispiele der historischen Fachsprache in den Fokus literaturwissenschaftlicher Untersuchungen geraten (Schulz 2000, 2003; Riecke 2004: 92–115), wurden sie bis jetzt kaum textlinguistisch und sprachhistorisch mit Blick auf ihre formelhafte Geprägtheit erforscht. An unterschiedlichen Stellen innerhalb eines Segensspruches kommen unterschiedliche Typen von formelhaften Wendungen, darunter auch Routineformeln, vor, und zwar in den (einleitenden) Historiolae, in den narrativen Passagen sowie in den handlungsorientierten Teilen. Sie fungieren als ein besonderes Mittel der Kommunikation mit dem Leser, als Mittel der Wahrheitsbeteuerung und Vermittlung des mittelalterlichen Wissens. Neben dieser Konstanz bei der Gestaltung der Textsorte an sich weisen Routineformeln in Segenssprüchen im Laufe der Geschichte Variationen auf, die sich sowohl auf der Mikroebene (hier verstanden als die

Morphosyntax und lexikalische Besetzung der phraseologischen Ausdrucksmittel), als auch auf der Makroebene der Texte (das heißt, ihre innere Organisation) feststellen lassen. Sie verändern sich in ihrer gestalterischen Rolle abhängig von den Veränderungen der Funktion der Textsorte „Segensspruch" insgesamt. Sie variieren ferner innerhalb der unterschiedlichen Typen der Segenssprüche.[5]

Einen besonderen Status der so genannten pragmatischen Kommentierungen in den mittelhochdeutschen Artusromanen hebt Eikelmann (1999: 304, 2002: 96) hervor. Dabei geht er auf formelhafte Wendungen wie *das ist ein altes sprichwort, das ist ein altgesprochenes wort, so sagt man* ein, die typologisch als Routineformeln zu klassifizieren sind. Sie signalisieren meistens die Gebräuchlichkeit von Sprichwörtern und tradieren das sprachlich-kulturelle Wissen, das ihre Verwendung voraussetzt. Eikelmann (2002: 96–97) stellt in ihrer Verwendung einen deutlichen Unterschied zur Gegenwart fest: Werden sie heute meist relativierend eingesetzt, hat sie das Mittelalter gezielt und vielgestaltig als Einleitungsformeln, Kommentare und Textparaphrasen genutzt, um Status und Funktion des Sprichworts zu betonen. Auf diese Weise vermitteln die Routineformeln das Wissen über Gebräuchlichkeit, Verbreitung und Wahrheitswert von Sprichwörtern und gewähren Einblicke in ihre kulturellen Verwendungstraditionen.

Friedrich (2006: 33–34, 2007: 1096–1097) zufolge sind für die mittelhochdeutschen. literarischen Texte ferner Bekräftigungs- und Beteuerungsformeln typisch, die Bezug auf Gott bzw. Personen oder Dinge nehmen, die dem Sprecher wichtig sind und auch allgemein als edel, wertvoll oder heilig gelten. Im deutlichen Unterschied zur heutigen Kommunikationspraxis steht die Verwendung von Begrüßungen, die in den mittelhochdeutschen Texten mit Ehrbezeugungen verbunden sind, z.B.: *gegruesset siestu, vroewe min, hail sistu, chuninc Marsilie!* usw. Einige Routineformeln weisen semantisch-pragmatische Unterschiede auf. So hat die Formel *durch got* in der Bedeutung ‚um Gottes Willen' nicht immer den gegenwärtigen Charakter einer Empörung: Die wörtliche Bedeutung ‚für Gott, Gottes eingedenk' verfügt teilweise auch noch über ihre ursprüngliche religiöse Dimension und erinnert den Angesprochenen an dessen Seelenheil, das er mit der rechten Handlungsweise bewahren soll, z.B.: *durch got nu senftet iwern haz* (Friedrich 2006: 34). Auch die Routineformel *gehabe dich wol* ist laut Friedrich (2006: 35–36) mittelhochdeutsch vorwiegend Trostformel ‚sei guten Mutes; keine Sorge; keine Angst'. Ihre häufige Verwendung beim Abschied sorgt dafür, dass sie auch (und auf dem Weg zum Neuhochdeutschen fast ausschließlich) als allgemein-wohlwollende Abschiedsformel verwendet wird.

Kaum erforscht bleibt die Rolle der Routineformeln in den historischen Prozessen der Strukturierung und Vermittlung des gelehrten Wissens. Sie soll deshalb im Mittelpunkt des vorliegenden Aufsatzes stehen.

4. Wissensvermittlung im Frühmittelalter

Als Orte der Gelehrsamkeit und der frühmittelalterlichen Wissenschaft sind in erster Linie die Klöster zu nennen.[6] Im Zentrum der wissenschaftlichen Auseinandersetzung stand die christliche Theologie. Schwerpunkt der klösterlichen Schulausbildung stellt daher die Vermittlung biblischer und theologischer Inhalte dar, allem voran die Auslegung biblischer Texte. Seit der Admonitio Generalis, die Karl der Große 789 erlassen hatte, um die professionelle Ausbildung des Klerus zu verbessern,[7] standen sowohl die Bibel selbst als auch Schriften der Kirchenväter sowie (spät)antiker Philosophen wie Boethius, Martianus Capella oder Terenz auf den Lehrplänen der Klosterschulen. Die antike Tradition der Sieben Freien Künste bildete seit der Admonitio Generalis wieder die Basis des lateinischsprachigen Unterrichts. In den Fächern des Triviums (Grammatik, Rhetorik und Dialektik) wurden die lateinischen Sprachkenntnisse vertieft und das Textverständnis gefördert. Im darauf aufbauenden Quadrivium, bestehend aus den naturwissenschaftlichen Fächern Arithmetik, Musik, Astronomie und Geometrie, wurden die Schüler auf das Studium der Theologie vorbereitet (Ochsenbein 1991: 137).

Allmählich wurde die Bedeutung des Trivium-Studiums weiter ausgebaut, diente es doch vornehmlich dem Verständnis und der christlichen Exegese der Bibel. Um einen festen Grundstock an Allgemeinwissen aufzubauen, beschäftigten sich die Schüler in den Trivium-Fächern in erster Linie mit christlichen philosophischen und theologischen Texten, die im Laufe der Zeit auch um Schriften antiker, nicht christlicher Autoren wie Ovid, Vergil oder Aristoteles erweitert wurden.[8]

Die schulische Wissensvermittlung erfolgte Baldzuhn (2002) zufolge bis ins Spätmittelalter mündlich. Schriftlichkeit und damit das stille Lesen statt des Hörens eines Lehrvortrags drang erst spät in den Unterricht ein. Die überlieferten Texte, die für den Schulkontext angefertigt wurden, stellen also Zeugnisse eines spezifischen Verhältnisses zwischen Mündlichkeit und Schriftlichkeit dar. Baldzuhn (2002: 167) bemerkt hierzu: „Gerade die gegen das Licht der mündlichen Lehrtradition betrachteten schriftlichen Quellen werden darin als Vermittlungsprodukt sichtbar, in dem oral und literal geprägte Kommunikationsstrategien ineinander greifen."

Neben der Wissensvermittlung im schulischen Kontext steht die Auseinandersetzung mit theologischen oder säkularen Themen wie beispielsweise der Bibelexegese, der theologischen Dogmatik, der christlichen Ethik, der Hagiographie oder der Historiographie, die in ihrer Intention an ein gebildetes klerikales Fachpublikum gerichtet waren.[9] Wissenschaftliche Werke des Frühmittelalters entstanden primär durch Kommentierung und/oder Kompilation, und stellten sich bewusst in den Dienst der christlichen Aneignung des Bildungsgutes (Goetz 2003: 256). Bildung und Wissenschaft hatten im Frühmittelalter also keinen Selbstzweck, sondern waren immer Instrumente der Vermittlung christlicher Inhalte. Es entstand dennoch – oder gerade deshalb – in allen Wissensgebieten eine reichhaltige lateinische Literatur, in der zwar vieles aus bereits vorhandenen Inhalten neu zusammengestellt und der Zeit angepasst wurde, gleichzeitig aber auch zahlreiche eigenständige Werke entstanden, die von der Bildungsgesellschaft des Frühmittelalters aufgenommen und in den wissenschaftlichen Diskurs überführt wurden.

Einen weiteren Bereich der Wissensvermittlung stellte die Unterweisung der Bevölkerung in Fragen des christlichen Glaubens dar: Das Ziel dieser Bestrebungen, die in erster Linie vom niederen Klerus getragen wurden, war es, essentielle Glaubensinhalte und Kenntnisse zumindest des Vaterunsers und des Glaubensbekenntnisses weiterzugeben (Haubrichs 1995: 58). Dabei richteten sich diese Bemühungen nicht nur an eine nicht-christliche Bevölkerung, wie sie bis ins 9./10. Jahrhundert noch in Teilen des Frankenreichs zu finden war (Kahl 2000: 669), sondern auch an eine bereits nominell dem Christentum angehörende Zielgruppe.

5. Wissensvermittelnde volkssprachige Texte im Frühmittelalter

Wie bereits erwähnt, fand die schulische Unterweisung des monastischen Klerus in den Klosterschulen statt. Für die Ausbildung nach dem Bildungsprogramm der Sieben Freien Künste wurde ein Kanon an grundlegenden Texten herangezogen, die einerseits auf spätantike und/oder frühchristliche Autoren wie Boethius, Martianus Capella, Cassiodor oder Prudentius (Glauche 1970: 76; Ochsenbein 1991: 138) zurückgingen und andererseits aus der Bibel stammten wie beispielsweise der Psalter, der eine zentrale Stellung nicht nur im monastischen Schulunterricht einnahm (Ochsenbein 1991: 140).

Diese Texte wurden in der Unterrichtssprache Latein gelesen und behandelt. Eines der Ziele, die die Ausbildung der jungen Mönche hatte, war die Vermittlung des Lateinischen als Sprache der Bibel und somit als Wissenschaftssprache schlechthin. Erst im beginnenden 11. Jahrhundert wurde ein Teil dieser Werke erstmals durch den St. Galler Schulmeister Notker den Deutschen in die Volkssprache übersetzt, um im Unterricht Verwendung zu finden. Doch Notker beließ es nicht bei einer reinen Übersetzung, sondern versuchte die komplexen Inhalte auch in der Volkssprache zu erklären. In einem Brief an den Bischof Heinrich von Sitten rechtfertigte Notker sein Vorgehen:

Scio tamen, quia primum abhorrebitis quasi ab insuetis, sed paulatim forte incipient se commendare vobis, et praevalebitis ad legendum et ad dinoscendum, quam cito capiuntur per patriam linguam, quae aut vix aut non integre capienda forent in lingua non propria.

‚Ich weiß dennoch, dass Ihr vielleicht zuerst erschrecken werdet, wie vor etwas Ungewohntem, aber allmählich werden sie vielleicht anfangen, sich euch zu empfehlen, und Ihr werdet beim Lesen und beim Erkennen durchdringen, wie schnell sie verstanden werden durch die Vatersprache, welche sie entweder mit Mühe oder nicht anständig beim Erfassen durchdringen können in der nicht eigenen Sprache.'

(Zitat und Übersetzung nach Hellgardt 1979: 13)

Notkers Intention war es also, den Zugang zu intellektuell anspruchsvollen Inhalten über die Muttersprache zu erleichtern. Das „Unerhörte" seines Vorgehens war es dabei, dass er nicht nur eine Übersetzung oder Glossierung anbot, sondern auch die Erklärung in der Volkssprache bereitstellte.[10] Notker übersetzte und kommentierte während seiner Zeit als Schulmeister unter anderem Texte, die im Dialektikunterricht herangezogen wurden, wie die aristotelischen Schriften *Categoriae, De interpretatione*, die in den Übersetzungen des Boethius vorlagen und weitere Schriften zur Logik wie *De syllogismis, De partibus logicae* und *De definitione*. Hinzu kommt die Übersetzung und Kommentierung eines Teils des allegorischen Werkes *De nuptiis Philologiae et Mercurii* des Martianus Capella. Diese Schriften wurden in Notkers Unterricht eingesetzt, worauf auch die entsprechende Aufbereitung der Texte hinweist: Einerseits wurde der lateinische Text so bearbeitet, dass die Schüler leichter einen Zugang zur syntaktischen Struktur fanden, andererseits wurde der Text mithilfe von formelhaften Wendungen, mithin Routineformeln, aber auch durch Sprichwörter angereichert, damit Wissensinhalte besser vermittelt werden konnten (Filatkina u.a. 2009).

Daneben wurden in den Klöstern auch Werke verfasst, die sich der Bibelexegese widmeten. Trotz der Dominanz des Lateinischen auf dem Gebiet der Bibelexegese entstanden seit der karolingischen Renaissance auch volkssprachige Texte, die nicht allein der Missionierung der Bevölkerung dienten, sondern auch für die Rezeption innerhalb des Klosters intendiert waren. So nimmt man an, dass beispielsweise das Evangelienbuch Otfrids von Weißenburg, das um 860/70 entstand, im Kloster sowohl der Privatlektüre der Mönche als auch der Tischlesung im Refektorium diente (Green 1987: 769). Die einzelnen Abschnitte dieses das Leben Jesu nacherzählenden Werkes werden immer wieder durch exegetische Exkurse unterbrochen, in denen die narrativen Inhalte erklärt und ausgelegt werden. Diese Exkurse dienen also der Vermittlung theologischer Lehren, durch die das Heilswirken Jesu deutlich gemacht wird. Es entsteht eine enge Verklammerung von Wiedergabe und Deutung des biblischen Textes, wie Hellgardt (1981: 146) feststellt.

Während sich mit dem Ende der karolingischen Herrschaft im 10. Jahrhundert eine Rückkehr zur Bildungssprache Latein abzeichnete,[11] setzte um 1000 mit der kommentierenden Übersetzung des Psalters durch Notker den Deutschen allmählich wieder eine volkssprachliche Schriftlichkeit ein, die freilich noch immer in engem Verhältnis zum Lateinischen stand. Mit der auf Augustinus, Cassiodor und Hieronymus fußenden Auslegung des Psalters als einem Grundtext der theologischen Bildung eines Klosterschülers versuchte Notker die vielschichtigen Inhalte der Bibelexegese für den schulischen Gebrauch aufzubereiten.

Die um 1060/65 entstandene Auslegung des Hohenliedes des Ebersberger Abtes Williram stellt eine weitere Form der exegetischen Bearbeitung eines biblischen Textes in der Volkssprache dar. Ähnlich wie Notker verwendete Williram eine deutsch-lateinische Mischsprache, die wichtige Inhalte zwar auf Deutsch darbietet, Fachtermini jedoch in der lateinischen *lingua sacra* belässt. Auch er stützte sich in seiner Auslegung des Hoheliedtextes auf anerkannte Kirchenlehrer wie Haimo von Auxerre und übertrug ihre Gedanken gekonnt in die Volkssprache. Der Rezipientenkreis der Hoheliedparaphrase ist jedoch – anders als bei Notker – nicht im schulischen Umfeld zu suchen, sondern vielmehr bei den lateinisch gebildeten Gelehrten der Zeit (Zerfaß 1995: 204). So stellte Williram neben seine deutsch-lateinische Prosaparaphrase eine kunstvolle lateinische Versparaphrase, die der intendierte Leser in Zusammenspiel mit dem Prosatext rezipieren sollte (Zerfaß 1995: 16). Gleichwohl sollte auch hier Wissen vermittelt werden: Wissen um die Auslegungspraxis des als rätselhaft empfundenen Hohenliedes, womit Williram einem Bedürfnis seiner Zeit nachkommt (Grabmeyer 1976: 397).

Interessant erscheint aus phraseologischer Sicht, dass die Wissensinhalte bei diesen doch sehr unterschiedlichen Texttypen vielfältig mit formelhaften Wendungen vermittelt werden. Im Folgenden soll anhand exemplarisch ausgewählter Texte, nämlich den Schultexten Notkers, den Exegesepassagen im Evangelienbuch Otfrids und der Hoheliedparaphrase Willirams untersucht werden, wie Routineformeln zur Textgliederung und Wissensvermittlung eingesetzt werden.

6. Strategien der Wissensstrukturierung und -vermittlung in althochdeutschen Texten unter Einsatz der Routineformeln

Die zum Teil hochkomplexen Inhalte der exegetischen oder schulischen Literatur, die in die Volkssprache transferiert wurden, mussten von den Bearbeitern so aufbereitet werden, dass sie von ihren intendierten Rezipienten verstanden werden konnten. Der Textautor bzw. -bearbeiter tritt also als Vermittler zwischen den Textinhalten und den Rezipienten. Auffällig hierbei ist die ausgiebige Verwendung von Routineformeln, die gerade diesem Zweck der Aufbereitung, der Textgliederung und der Wissensvermittlung dienen. Die hier vermittelten Inhalte stellen im Gegensatz zu den bereits besprochenen Beispielen kein Alltags-, sondern vielmehr eine Form von Spezialwissen dar, das an einen ganz speziellen Kreis von Empfängern, nämlich in der Regel an Klosterschüler und/ oder bereits gebildete Kleriker gerichtet ist.

Problematisch erweist sich die Frage nach der Rezeptionssituation der jeweiligen Texte, die einen Einfluss auf die Beurteilung der pragmatischen Dimension der eingesetzten Routineformeln hat: War der Text in erster Linie zum mündlichen Vortrag gedacht wie etwa für die Verwendung im Unterricht, wodurch die schriftlich belegten Routineformeln Sprechakte innerhalb einer medialen Mündlichkeit darstellten (vgl. Baldzuhn 2002: 164)? Oder war der Text zur stillen Lektüre intendiert, ohne die Möglichkeit eines mündlichen Vortrags zu berücksichtigen? Sichere Aussagen lassen sich hierzu nicht machen, beide Möglichkeiten müssen aber für jeden Text berücksichtigt werden, wie Green in Bezug auf das Evangelienbuch Otfrids feststellt (Green 1987: 769).

Deshalb erscheint ein textbezogener Ansatz, der die Routineformeln innerhalb ihres situativen Kontextes interpretiert, notwendig. Im Folgenden wird anhand ausgewählter Stellen bei Otfrid, Notker und Williram demonstriert, wie sie in ihren Texten Routineformeln einsetzen, um ihre Inhalte zu strukturieren und für den Rezipienten aufzubereiten. Wie oben bereits erwähnt, ist die Bestimmung einer dominanten pragmatischen Funktion in einigen Fällen nicht eindeutig, da Routineformeln polyfunktional sein können. Eine Beschreibung der Formeln erfordert daher immer auch die Einbeziehung ihres aus dem Kontext ableitbaren Funktionsspektrums (Filatkina 2007: 140). Im Sinne der in Abschnitt 1 zusammengefassten Überlegungen wird bei der folgenden Darstellung der verwendeten wissensstrukturierenden Routineformeln in Anlehnung an die Klassifikation Coulmas' eine dominante pragmatische Funktion angegeben, die jedoch erweitert wird durch ein Spektrum an zusätzlichen Funktionen, die die Formeln innerhalb des jeweiligen Kontextes zusätzlich erfüllen.[12]

6.1. *Aufmerksamkeitssteuernde Routineformeln*

Im Anschluss an die Erzählung von der Hochzeit in Kanaa, bei der Jesus Wasser zu Wein verwandelte, deutet Otfrid dieses Geschehen in einem Spiritualiter-Kapitel aus: Er beginnt seine Auslegung mit der Routineformel *fernemet sar in rihti*, mit der er einerseits die Aufmerksamkeit seiner Rezipienten für sich beansprucht, andererseits aber die erste wichtige Information einleitet, nämlich dass im theologischen Sinn Christus selbst für den Bräutigam steht:

(6) *Fernem(et) sar in rihti* . *thar (Christus) ther brutigomo si* | *ioh druta sine in lante* . *zi theru bruti ginante*
,Vernehmt sodann direkt, dort ist Christus der Bräutigam und seine Vertrauten im Land. zur Braut bestimmt.'
(Otfrid, Evangelienbuch 53v, II 9, 7; ID 9691)

Gerade weil diese Routineformel bei der Vermittlung der für das mittelalterliche Wissensbild wichtigen Kenntnisse und Überzeugen eingesetzt wird, wird sie oft mit den Wahrheitsbeteuerungen *in alauuari* oder *giuuisso* kombiniert:

(7) *Firnim in alauuari* . *thaz got ther fater uuari* | *ioh thaz kind eino* . *kristan bezeino*
,Vernimm wahrheitsgemäß, dass Gott der Vater ist und dass das einzige Kind . Christus bezeichnet.'
(Otfrid, Evangelienbuch 55r, II 9, 75; ID 9697)

Auch Notker verwendet diese Formel mit Vorliebe in seinen Schultexten. In der Bearbeitung des auf Aristoteles zurückgehenden Werkes *Categoriae* erklärt Notker die Unterscheidung der ontologisch selbstständigen und der sekundären Substanzen:

(8) *Et cu(m) aliqua(m) ar|bore(m) reddideris. man¡festius assignabis cu(m) ar|bore(m) assignabis qua(m) arbustu(m)· Zéigôst tû uuáz* | *éin réba sî. táz tuôst tû báz póum chédendo.* | *tánne dáz in érdo stât· An érdo stât oúh chrûit* | *unde speid· Amplius· Ferním nóh mêr· Prime* | *substantie p(ro)pterea q(uo)d aliis om(n)ib(us) subiacent. (et)* | *alia om(n)ia dehis om(n)ibus p(re)dicent(ur). aut in eis s(unt). idcir|co maxime substantie d(icu)n(tur)* ·
,*Und wenn du irgendeinen Baum wiedergibst, wirst du ihn deutlicher bezeichnen, wenn du ,Baum' sagst, als wenn du ,baumartig' sagst. Zeigst du, was ein Weinstock sei, dann tust du es besser, indem du ,Baum' sagst, als (indem du sagst), das, (was) auf der Erde steht'. Auf der Erde steht auch Kraut und Busch. Ferner: Vernimm noch mehr: Die prime substantie (die ersten Substanzen) werden so genannt, weil sie allen Dingen zu Grunde liegen und alles andere von ihnen ausgesagt wird oder in ihnen ist. Deshalb werden sie maxime substantie (oberste Substanzen) genannt.*'
(Notker, Categoriae (Hs. B, CSg 818) 23, 1; ID 5140)

Auch hier wird die Formel *fernim nóh mêr* eingesetzt, um den Rezipienten anzusprechen, seine Aufmerksamkeit weiter in Anspruch zu nehmen, aber darüber hinaus, um eine vertiefende Information einzuführen, die sich direkt auf das Vorausgehende bezieht und dieses ergänzt. Damit wird der Rezipient aufgefordert, sich diese Informationen zu merken.

Zudem kann diese Formel auch eine belehrende Funktion aufweisen, wenn sie etwa als Einleitung einer Zusammenfassung der vorausgehenden Aussagen verwendet wird und hier noch einmal ganz dezidiert auf die wichtigen Lehrinhalte verweist, wie etwa in folgendem Beispiel:

(9) *keméinlîcho uernín uóne állen daz óuh fóre ge|ságet ist. daz tu e(ss)e unde non esse háben sólt fúre | subiecta. unde affirmatione(m) ih méino est . ioh ne|gatione(m) ih méino no(n) est . sólt tu légen zû demo mo|do.*
‚Gemeinhin vernimm von allen, was auch vorher gesagt wurde, dass du *esse* und *non esse* für *subiecta* halten sollst und die *affirmatio*, ich meine *est* und die *negatio*, ich meine *non est*, sollst du zu dem *modus* hinzusetzen.'
(Notker, De interpretatione 219, 12; ID 13086)

Die Formel *firnemet/firnim* mitsamt ihrer Varianten ist für das Althochdeutsche bislang[13] 43 Mal in der HiFoS-Datenbank belegt, wobei sie in all diesen Belegen eine vergleichbare Funktionalität aufweist: Ihren Einsatz findet die Formel in erster Linie in wissensvermittelnden Kontexten, in denen die Aufmerksamkeit des Rezipienten errungen wird bzw. er dazu aufgefordert werden muss, sich wichtiges Wissen zu merken. Vor allem für Notker und Otfrid ist die Verstärkung durch die Wahrheitsbeteuerung kennzeichnend. Williram hingegen kennt diesen Einsatz nicht und benutzt die Routineformel allgemein seltener (auf ihn gehen nur drei Belege zurück). Die Struktur der Wendung ist auf *nu uernemet, nv uernim* bzw. *nu uernemet diu mâre* reduziert und bezieht sich in ihrer Funktionalität verstärkt auf Aufmerksamkeitssteuerung und Einleitung. Die zurückhaltendere Verwendung der Formel bei Williram ist möglicherweise durch den Rezipientenkreis, an den sich der Autor wendet, bedingt: Anders als bei Notker richtet sich Williram in erster Linie an ein Fachpublikum, an ausgebildete Theologen, die mit der Exegese des Hoheliedes vertraut sind. Die Aufforderung, sich eine Information im Sinne einer schulischen Lektion zu merken, tritt hier eher in den Hintergrund.

6.2. *Belehrende Routineformeln*

Belehrende Funktion hat die Formel *ih sagen dir*, die verwendet wird, um einer Aussage Nachdruck zu verleihen, um zu zeigen, dass das Nachfolgende von hoher Bedeutung ist und daher vom Rezipienten mit besonderer Umsicht zur Kenntnis genommen werden soll. So erklärt Otfrid in Rekurs auf Joh. 1,8, dass Johannes der Täufer nicht mit dem Messias verwechselt werden dürfe, sondern als dessen Vorbote zu verstehen sei:

(10) *Ni uuas er thaz lioht <u>ih sagen thir ein</u>. thaz thar liutin irskein | suntar quam sie manoti . ioh thanana in gisag(et)i*
‚Nicht war er [Johannes] das Licht, ich sage dir nur, welches den Leuten da erschien, sondern er kam, um sie zu mahnen und um ihnen davon zu sagen.'

(Otfrid, Evangelienbuch 43r, II 2, 11; ID 9611)

Mit der Formel *ih sagen thir ein* unterstreicht Otfrid die Aussage und belehrt seinen Rezipienten, indem er sich direkt an ihn wendet. Durch diese direkte Ansprache wird aber wiederum die Aufmerksamkeit des Rezipienten auf das Nachfolgende gesteuert und der Kontakt zwischen Rezipienten und Vermittler erneuert. Somit hat die Formel auch eine Kontakt sichernde Funktion. In diesem Funktionsspektrum tritt die Formel auch in Notkers Bearbeitung von *De interpretatione* auf:

(11) *dico (et)ia(m) no(n) fieri una(m) affirmatione(m) (ue)l ne|gatione(m). si unu(m) nom(en) co(m)mune positu(m) sit mult|is rebus. (et) si ex illis n(on) sit unu(m). <u>Íh ságo dir</u> daz | ouh tánnan ûz ein affirmatio alde ein nega|tio neuuírdet. ube éin nome(n) gemeíne fúnde | ist mánigen díngen diu éin specie(m) nîeht ke|uuúrchen nemúgen*
‚Ich behaupte auch, dass es nicht eine *affirmatio* (Bejahung) oder *negatio* (Verneinung) geben wird, wenn ein gemeinsamer Name vielen Dingen gegeben wird und aus diesen nicht eines existiert. Ich sage Dir, dass daraus nicht eine *affirmatio* (Bejahung) oder eine *negatio* (Verneinung) wird, wenn ein gemeinsames *nomen* (Name) mehreren Dingen gegeben wird, die nicht eine *specie* (Gattung) bilden können.'

(Notker, De interpretatione 201, 11; ID 4030)

Notker wendet sich hier direkt an den Rezipienten, womit sich ein Unterschied zur lateinischen Stelle, die er übersetzt, ergibt, die lediglich *dico* ‚ich sage, ich benenne' aufweist, also keine Routineformel mit explizit dialogischer Funktion verwendet. Dadurch verstärkt Notker die belehrende Funktion der Routineformel.

Die Form *ih sago dir* und ihre Varianten sind insgesamt 82 Mal für die althochdeutsche Überlieferung in der HiFoS-Datenbank belegt. In den narrativen Texten wie dem Evangelienbuch Otfrids ist sie einerseits in der Erzählerrede verwendet und dient dem Erzähler in seiner Funktion als Vermittler der direkten Hinwendung an den Leser/Hörer. Andererseits wird sie aber auch in der Figurenrede eingesetzt, in erster Linie, wenn es um die Einleitung einer wichtigen Aussage geht. In den meisten Fällen wird diese Formel verwendet, wenn sich Jesus an seine Jünger wendet und ist somit eine Übernahme der im Neuen Testament sehr häufigen Formel *amen dico vobis* (vgl. Matth. 6,2; 6,5; 6,16 u.ö.). In ihrer pragmatischen Verwendung ist die Formel weitgehend konstant. Interessanterweise wird sie in anderen hier nicht berücksichtigten Texten (so z.B. im althochdeutschen Tatian) konsequent durch die Routineformel *uuâr uuâr quidu ih iu* ersetzt. Es bleibt zu untersuchen, ob dies nicht auf einen semantischen Unterschied zwischen den Verben *quedan* und *sagên* zumindest im Bereich der formelhaften Sprachen hindeutet.

Otfrid führt in einem Spiritualiter-Kapitel seine Überlegungen zur Nächstenliebe als die höchste Form der Liebe aus:

(12) *Nist thiu minna sumirih . kreftin anderen gilih* | *giuuisso uuizist thu thaz. thia uuir heizen karitas*
   ‚Diese Liebe ist wahrlich nicht anderen Kräften gleich, wisse das gewiss, die wir *Caritas* nennen.'

(Otfrid, Evangelienbuch 168r, V 12, 80; ID 11838)

Mit Hilfe der Routineformel *giuuisso uuizist thu thaz* belehrt Otfrid seinen Rezipienten, indem er bekräftigend darauf hinweist, dass es sich um eine wichtige Information handle. Durch die direkte Ansprache des Hörers/Lesers sichert Otfrid einerseits den Kontakt zu diesem und betont zusätzlich die Bedeutung der Aussage. Die Formel inklusive ihrer Varianten ist in der HiFoS-Datenbank 63 Mal belegt. Sie kommt hierbei in Kontexten vor, in denen der Rezipient über einen wichtigen Umstand belehrt werden soll. Bei Notker und besonders Otfrid wird diese Routineformel wie das oben gezeigte Beispiel *uernemet/uernim* mit den Wahrheitsbeteuerungen *giuuisso, giuuisso [...] âna uuân, gimuato, in alauuâr, ana zuiual, zi uuâre, in uuâra, giuuâro* kombiniert.

Von diesen primär an den Rezipienten gerichteten Verwendungssituationen sind Stellen zu unterscheiden, in denen die Routineformel innerhalb der Figurenrede in den narrativen Passagen in der Form *ih uueiz uuola* vorkommt. Sie drückt die Belehrung durch den Rekurs auf den autoritären Status des Autors aus, signalisiert die Übernahme der Sprecherrolle durch ihn und leitet Wissensinhalte ein, denen eine besondere Wichtigkeit zugesprochen wird. Diese Verwendung ist vor allen für Williram kennzeichnet, obwohl er auch hier nach wie vor zurückhaltend ist: Die Formel ist bei ihm 6 Mal in der invarianten oben angeführten Form belegt.

6.3. Hinweisende Routineformeln

Ebenfalls belehrende, aber im Wesentlichen auch hinweisende Funktion haben die Formeln *hier ist ze uuizzen* und *hier ist ze merchene*, die sowohl von Notker als auch von Williram eingesetzt werden. Diese Formeln machen auf einen bemerkenswerten Aspekt im Text aufmerksam. So beispielsweise in der Hoheliedparaphrase Willirams, in der ein Vers zweimal im Bibeltext vorkommt, aber je nach Kontext eine andere Interpretation erfährt, worauf Williram mit der Formel hinweist:

(13)   *DAZ sélba uérs stêt oûh | da uora . ad tale signv(m). | Daz ęina íst ábo hîe ze | mérchene . daz daz êrera | uérs hôret ad primitiua(m) êccl(esi)am | de iudęis collecta(m)!*
,Derselbe Vers steht auch davor, bei einem solchen Zeichen. Das eine ist aber hier anzumerken, dass sich der erste Vers auf die *erste versammelte Kirche der Juden* bezieht.'
(Williram, Hoheliedkommentar 21v, 33c; ID 3018)

Diese Formel ist für das Althochdeutsche in der HiFoS-Datenbank zwar nur einmal belegt, wird aber im Frühneuhochdeutschen sehr häufig in wissensvermittelnden Texten wie beispielsweise in der Historiographie eingesetzt. Bislang sind 17 Belege dieser Formel und ihrer Varianten für das Frühneuhochdeutsche in der Datenbank verzeichnet.

In einem sternenkundlichen Exkurs, in Notkers Martianus Capella-Bearbeitung, wird das Sternbild des Bärenhüters (Boötes) beschrieben. Um hier wissenswerte Hintergrundinformationen anzufügen, die es dem Rezipienten ermöglichen, das Sternbild einzuordnen, verwendet Notker die Routineformel *hier ist ze uuîzenne*.

(14)   *Sî rûor(et) boote(m) án dien | áhselon . hárto skîmbariu éinahálb . únde áber ánderhálb tún|cheliu . Híer íst ze uuîzenne . dáz er (ét)elichiu nórd zéichen | únde (ét)elichiu súnt zéichen némmendo álliu zéichen ferfá|h(et) ·*
,Sie [das Sternbild der nördlichen Himmelskrone] berührt Boötes an den Achseln, sehr Leuchtende auf der einen Seite und aber eine Dunkle auf der anderen Seite. Hier ist zu wissen, dass er [Boötes] etliche nördliche Sternbilder und etliche südliche Sternbilder nennend alle Sternbilder umfasst.'
(Notker, Martianus Capella 87, 13; ID 3532)

Die Wendung fungiert hier somit als hinweisende Einleitungsformel, mit der der Rezipient über einen weiteren Wissensaspekt belehrt wird. Sie ist insgesamt

4 Mal in der HiFoS-Datenbank belegt. Alle Belege stammen aus den Schultexten Notkers und weisen eine ähnliche Funktionalität wie im hier beschriebenen Beleg auf.

6.4. Erklärende/ausdeutende Routineformeln

Die exegetischen wie auch die philosophischen Texte weisen immer wieder schwer verständliche Passagen auf, die eine große Herausforderung an die Rezipienten stellen. Die Bearbeiter dieser Texte wie Notker und Williram sind daher bemüht, solche Stellen zu erklären oder durch veranschaulichende Beispiele nachvollziehbar zu machen, unbekannte lateinische Wendungen, Fachwortschatz für den Rezipienten zu übersetzen oder aber zu paraphrasieren. Um solche erklärenden Zusätze einzuleiten, werden wiederum Routineformeln wie *daz chît* oder *ich meino* verwendet.

Der sehr bildhafte Text des Hoheliedes muss beispielsweise von Williram in seiner Auslegung immer wieder mit konkreten Bedeutungen verbunden werden, damit der Rezipient die Aussage des Bibeltextes versteht. So auch in folgendem Beispiel, in dem es um einen Vergleich der Haare des Bräutigams mit aufrecht stehenden Palmenwedeln geht. In der folgenden Auslegung lässt Williram den Bräutigam, der mit einer christlichen Auslegungstradition folgend als Christus interpretiert wird,[14] vom ewigen Heil sprechen, das erst erfüllt werden kann, nachdem Christus die Passion auf sich genommen habe:

(15) *Alle dîu gnâda. | díe íh dír hában gehêiz|zan . dîu neuuírdet ê nîeth | uólliclîcho gelêistet! ê íh | gestîgon ûffe dén pálm|bôum . íh mêino daz crûce.*
    ‚Alle Gnade, die ich [= Christus] dir habe verheißen, die wird nicht eher völlig geleistet, bevor ich auf den Palmbaum gestiegen bin, ich meine das Kreuz.'

(Williram, Hoheliedkommentar 53v, 27c; ID 3079)

Die Routineformel *ich meino* leitet hier also die Auslegung des metaphorisch verwendeten Begriffs *palmbôum* ‚Palme' ein und stellt den Bezug zwischen der alttestamentarischen Hoheliedstelle zur Passion Christi her.

Auch Notker verwendet sehr häufig in seinen schuldidaktischen Texten erklärende Formeln, um genauer auszudrücken, was mit einer bestimmten vorausgehenden Wendung gemeint ist. Im folgenden Beispiel aus der Martianus Capella-Bearbeitung wird die Göttin Diana – für das christlich geprägte Frühmittelalter keine geläufige mythologische Person – eingeführt und ihr Name mit Hilfe einer im Mittelalter beliebten Form der etymologischen Herleitung erklärt:

(16) *Áber luna héizet diana . sámo so du|ana . uuánda sî duob(us) te(m)porib (us) . ih méino dieb(us) ac noctib(us) | zeóugon íst ·*
,Aber Luna heißt Diana, gleichsam Duana, weil sie <u>duobus temporis</u> (zu zwei Zeiten), ich meine tagsüber und nachts, zu sehen ist.'
(Notker, Martianus Capella 146, 16; ID 4672)

Mit der Formel *ih meino* wird hier erklärt, welche zwei Zeiten gemeint sind, um dem Rezipienten das Verständnis dieser etymologischen Herleitung zu erleichtern. *Ih meino* zählt zu den hochfrequenten Formeln, die zur Wissensvermittlung im Althochdeutschen genutzt werden. Sie weist auch kaum Varianten auf, nur in sehr wenigen Fällen ist ein Akkusativobjekt (*ih meino des*) hinzugefügt. Sie ist bislang 92 Mal für das Althochdeutsche in der HiFoS-Datenbank belegt.

Eine ähnliche Funktion wie *ih meino* weist die Formel *daz chît* auf, die sowohl bei Notker als auch bei Williram zur Einleitung einer Erklärung oder einer Übersetzung verwendet wird. So leitet *daz chît* in folgendem Beleg aus der Psalterbearbeitung Notkers eine Auslegung des Bibeltextes ein:

(17) *DOMINE DEVS MEVS IN TE | speraui. saluum me fac ex omnibus p(er)sequenti|bus me . et libera me. An dih trúhten gedíngta ih | iêo . halt mih . daz chît . nére mih fóne mînen fienden . unde | lôse mih.*
,Herr, mein Gott, auf dich hoffte ich. Mache mich heil von allen Verfolgern und befreie mich. Auf dich, Herr, habe ich stets gehofft, bewahre mich, das heißt: Rette mich von meinen Feinden und erlöse mich.'
(Notker, Psalmenauslegung 21,13 (Psalm 7,2); ID 3937)

Durch die Routineformel *daz chît* wird noch einmal genau erklärt, was mit dem althochdeutschen Wort *haltan* in der Bedeutung ,bewahren, beschützen' gemeint ist. Hier wird also ein quasi-synonymer Begriff durch die Formel *daz chît* eingeführt, der das Verständnis dieser Textstelle erleichtern soll.

In folgendem Beleg aus der Hoheliedparaphrase Willirams leitet die Formel eine Übersetzung aus dem Lateinischen ein, die ihrerseits eine Übersetzung aus dem Hebräischen ist. Es geht um die etymologisierende Herleitung von biblischen Personennamen, in diesem Fall des Namens David:

(18) *Dauîdis námo | uuírt gántfrístet . manu for|tis! daz quît . ármstrénger.*
,Davids Name wird gedeutet starke Hand, das heißt Starkarmiger.'
(Williram, Hoheliedkommentar 27v, 18c; ID 3028)

Auch Notker nutzt diese Formel, um Übersetzungen einzuleiten, beispielsweise in seiner Martianus Capella-Bearbeitung, u.a. wenn er Begriffe, die bei Martinus griechisch wiedergegeben sind ins Lateinische übersetzt. In den meisten Fällen unterlässt er jedoch eine weitere Übersetzung ins Deutsche. Umso bemerkenswerter ist die Verwendung der volkssprachigen Routineformel *daz chît* für den Transfer vom Griechischen ins Lateinische:

(19) *Téro sláhto sínt | óuh egipani . dîe fóne egea gehéizen sint . táz chît capra*
,Dieser Art sind auch die Egipanen, die nach Egea benannt sind, das heißt *capra* (Ziege).'

(Notker, Martianus Capella 144, 11; ID 4669)

Diese Formel, die ebenso wie *ih meino* fast ohne Varianz auftritt, ist gegenwärtig insgesamt 122 Mal in der HiFoS-Datenbank belegt. Auffällig ist, dass sie fast ausschließlich von Notker und Williram verwendet wird, also in den erklärenden, deutenden und auslegenden Kontext der Schul- und Exegeseliteratur verweist.

7. Fazit

Die hier aufgeführten Routineformeln stellen nur einen Bruchteil der im Althochdeutschen vorhandenen und gebräuchlichen pragmatischen Formeln da, die zur Wissensaufbereitung und -vermittlung dienten.

Es zeigt sich, dass die althochdeutschen Autoren ganz gezielt Routineformeln einsetzten, um Wissensinhalte aufzubereiten und ihren Rezipienten nahezubringen. Dabei dienen die Routineformeln auch in lateinisch-deutschen Textensembles wie den Notkerschen Schultexten oder der Hoheliedparaphrase Willirams dazu, zwischen den ursprünglich lateinischen Auctortexten und der althochdeutschen Bearbeitung zu vermitteln. Die polyfunktionalen Formeln lassen sich unter Berücksichtigung ihres Funktionsspektrums auf einige dominante pragmatische Funktionen beschränken: Eine Gruppe von Routineformeln hat die Funktion, die Aufmerksamkeit der Leser/Hörer auf einen neuen Inhalt zu lenken, wodurch gleichzeitig auch Neues eingeführt und die Textstruktur gegliedert wird. Bei einer weiteren Gruppe steht die belehrende Funktion im Vordergrund, sie soll Wichtiges und Wissenswertes hervorheben. Bei einer dritten Gruppe ist der hinweisende Charakter der Formeln dominant. Sie haben zwar auch aufmerksamkeitssteuernde und belehrende Funktion, wollen aber in erster Linie auf Bemerkenswertes verweisen. Eine vierte Gruppe hat vornehmlich die Funktion, Vorausgegangenes auszudeuten, zu erklären oder zu übersetzen. Die belehrende Funktion tritt bei dieser vierten Gruppe gegenüber der erklärenden, veranschaulichenden deutlich in den Hintergrund, während bei den ersten drei Gruppen eine eindeutig differenzierende Zuordnung Schwierigkeiten bereitet.

Hier wirkt sich die Polyfunktionalität der Formeln stärker aus, eine angemessene Beschreibung dieser Formeln erfordert daher die Berücksichtigung eines Funktionsspektrums.
Bislang ist dieser insgesamt sehr ergiebige Bereich von der phraseologischen Forschung jedoch wenig beachtet worden. Innerhalb der Nachwuchsforschergruppe „Historische Formelhafte Sprache und Traditionen des Formulierens (HiFoS)" soll diese Forschungslücke quellennah, kontextbezogen und systematisch geschlossen werden.

Universität Trier

Anmerkungen

Kontaktadresse: filatkin@uni-trier.de

1. Der Begriff *Althochdeutsch* bezieht sich auf den dialektalen Raum des Hochdeutschen in der Zeit zwischen ca. 750 bis ca. 1050 und umfasst den ältesten Überlieferungsstand des Hochdeutschen.
2. Das Projekt wird dort seit Juli 2007 im Fachteil Ältere deutsche Philologie (Wissenschaftliche Gastgeberin: Prof. Dr. Claudine Moulin) und im Historisch-Kulturwissenschaftlichen Forschungszentrum (HKFZ) Trier (http://www.hkfz.uni-trier.de) mit finanzieller Unterstützung der Alexander von Humboldt-Stiftung (Sofja Kovalevskaja-Preis 2006; Stifter: Bundesministerium für Bildung und Forschung) durchgeführt. Vgl. weitere Informationen zum Projekt unter: http://www.hifos.uni-trier.de.
3. Vgl. den Überblick in Filatkina (2009: 76–77).
4. Einen aktuellen Überblick über die relevante Forschungsliteratur bietet Lüger (2007: 445–447).
5. Diese vorläufigen Ergebnisse basieren auf den systematischen Auswertungen der althochdeutschen Segenssprüche in der HiFoS-Nachwuchsforschergruppe, die demnächst veröffentlicht werden sollen.
6. Wenngleich die Klosterkultur diese Funktionserweiterung erst ab dem 8./9. Jahrhundert erfährt (Haubrichs 1995: 53).
7. Die von Karl dem Großen initiierte Bildungsoffensive hatte dabei auch zum Ziel, Bildung und Wissenschaft als Voraussetzungen für die Übernahme politischer Aufgaben im Reich zu funktionalisieren (Goetz 2003: 253).
8. Vgl. dazu grundlegend Glauche (1970).
9. Einen konzentrierten Überblick über Bildung und Wissenschaft im Frühmittelalter bietet Hans-Werner Goetz (2003) in seiner Monographie *Europa im frühen Mittelalter 500–1050* auf den Seiten 250–260.
10. Grotans (1998: 38) führt hierzu aus: "The revolutionary aspect of Notker's work is not so much that he used the vernacular – interlinear vernacular glosses were already

old hat by the year 1000 – but the way in which he structured his classroom texts and the extent to which he wove the vernacular into the Latin commentative discourse."
11. Die spärliche Überlieferung volkssprachiger Texte zwischen dem 10. und 11. Jahrhundert lässt den Schluss zu, dass eine gewollte Abkehr von der volkssprachigen Schriftlichkeit vollzogen wurde. Vgl. hierzu auch de Boor (1979: 79).
12. Die Belege sowie ihre Übersetzungen sind der HiFoS-Datenbank (http://www.hifos. uni-trier.de) entnommen. Die jeweilige Beleg-ID findet sich in Klammern nach der Belegstelle. Die einzelnen Belege sind nach der Handschrift bzw. nach einer rezenten diplomatischen Edition erfasst. Abbreviaturen, die in den Handschriftentexten vorhanden waren, wurden aufgelöst und durch Klammern markiert. Die jeweilige Routineformel ist im Belegkontext unterstrichen.
13. Gesicherte Angaben lassen sich noch nicht machen, da das Korpus des Althochdeutschen gegenwärtig noch in Bearbeitung ist.
14. Überblickartig fasst Zerfaß (1995: 62–77) die Entwicklung und Tendenzen der Hoheliedexegese im Mittelalter zusammen. Grundlegend hierzu sind die Hoheliedstudien Ohlys (1958).

Literatur

Primärliteratur

Notker der Deutsche. 1995. De Interpretatione. Boethius' Bearbeitung von Aristoteles' Schrift Peri Hermeneias: Konkordanzen, Wortlisten und Abdruck des Textes nach dem Codex Sangallensis 818. Evelyn Scherabon Firchow (Hrsg.). Berlin: de Gruyter.
Notker der Deutsche. 1995. Categoriae. Boethius' Bearbeitung von Aristoteles' Schrift ,kategoriai'. Konkordanzen, Wortlisten und Abdruck der Texte nach den Codices Sangallensis 818 und 825. Evelyn Scherabon Firchow (Hrsg.), unter Mitarbeit von Richard Hotchkiss. Berlin: de Gruyter.
Notker der Deutsche. Martianus Capella, de Nuptiis Philologiae et Mercurii. Cod. Sang. 872 der Stiftsbibliothek St. Gallen.
Notker der Deutsche. Psalmenauslegung. Cod. 21 der Stiftsbibliothek St. Gallen.
Otfrid von Weißenburg : Evangelienbuch. Edition nach dem Wiener Codex 2687. Bd. I, Teil 1: Text. Wolfgang Kleiber (Hrsg.). Tübingen: Niemeyer.
Williram von Ebersberg. 2001. Expositio in Cantica Canticorum. Die älteste Überlieferung von Willirams Kommentar des Hohen Liedes. Edition, Übersetzung, Glossar. Rudolf Schützeichel und Birgit Meinecke (Hrsg.). Göttingen: Vandenhoeck & Ruprecht.

Sekundärliteratur

Álvarez de la Granja, María (ed.). 2008. *Fixed expressions in cross-linguistic perspective: A multilingual and multidisciplinary approach*. Hamburg: Kovac.
Baldzuhn, Michael. 2002. Schulunterricht und Verschriftlichungsprozess: Forschungsansätze und Forschungsergebnisse. In Christel Meier et al. (eds.), *Pragmatische*

Dimensionen mittelalterlicher Schriftkultur (Akten des Internationalen Kolloquiums, 26.–29. Mai 1999), 161–175. Munich: Wilhelm Fink.

Büge, Oskar. 1908. *Die Beteuerungsformeln in Otfrids Evangelienbuch.* Greifswald: Greifswald University dissertation.

Burger, Harald. 1977. Probleme einer historischen Phraseologie des Deutschen. *PBB* 99. 1–24.

Burger, Harald. 1983. Neue Aspekte der Semantik und Pragmatik phraseologischer Wortverbindungen. In Josip Matešič (ed.), *Phraseologie und ihre Aufgaben: Beiträge zum 1. Internationalen Phraseologie-Symposium vom 12. bis 14. Oktober 1981 in Mannheim.* Band 3, 24–34. Heidelberg: Groos.

Burger, Harald. 1998. Problembereiche einer historischen Phraseologie. In Wolfgang Eismann (ed.), *Europhras 95. Europäische Phraseologie im Vergleich: Gemeinsames Erbe und kulturelle Vielfalt* (Studien zur Phraseologie und Parömiologie 15), 79–108. Graz & Leibnitz: N. Brockmeyer.

Burger, Harald. 2007. *Phraseologie: Eine Einführung am Beispiel des Deutschen.* 3rd edn. Berlin: Schmidt.

Burger, Harald, Annelies Buhofer & Ambros Sialm. 1982. *Handbuch der Phraseologie.* Berlin: de Gruyter.

Coulmas, Florian. 1981. *Routine im Gespräch: Zur pragmatischen Fundierung der Idiomatik.* Wiesbaden: Akademische Verlagsgesellschaft Athenaion.

de Boor, Helmut. 1979. *Die deutsche Literatur: Von Karl dem Großen bis zum Beginn der höfischen Dichtung, 770–1170.* Band I. Munich: Beck.

Eikelmann, Manfred. 1999. Altsprochen wort: Sentenz und Sprichwort im Kontext der mittelalterlichen Gnomik. In Sieglinde Hartmann & Ulrich Müller (eds.), *Jahrbuch der Oswald von Wolkenstein Gesellschaft.* Band 11, 299–315. Frankfurt/Main: Dr. Ludwig Reichert Verlag.

Eikelmann, Manfred. 2002. Zur historischen Pragmatik des Sprichworts im Mittelalter. In Dietrich Hartmann & Jan Wirrer (eds.), *Wer a sägt, muss auch B sägen: Beiträge zur Phraseologie und Sprichwortforschung aus dem Westfälischen Arbeitskreis,* 95–105. Baltmannsweiler: Schneider Verlag Hohengehren.

Feilke, Helmuth. 1994. *Common-sense-Kompetenz: Überlegungen zu einer Theorie des „sympathischen" und „natürlichen" Meinens und Verstehens.* Frankfurt/Main: Suhrkamp.

Fellbaum, Christiane. 2007. *Idioms and collocations: Corpus-based linguistic and lexicographic studies.* London: Continuum.

Filatkina, Natalia. 2007. Pragmatische Beschreibungsansätze. In Harald Burger, Dmitrij Dobrovol'skij, Peter Kühn & Neal R. Norrick (eds.), *Phraseologie: Ein internationales Handbuch der zeitgenössischen Forschung. An International Handbook of Contemporary Research.* Band 1 (Handbücher zur Sprach- und Kommunikationswissenschaft / Handbooks of Linguistics and Communication Science [HSK] 28), 132–158. Berlin & New York: de Gruyter.

Filatkina, Natalia. 2009. Historische Formelhafte Sprache als „harte Nuss" der Korpus- und Computerlinguistik: Ihre Annotation und Analyse im HiFoS-Projekt. *linguistik-online* 39. http://www.linguistik-online.de/ (accessed 9 December 2009).

Filatkina, Natalia. 2009. Und es duencket einem noch/wann man euch ansiehet / daß ihr Sand in den Augen habt. Phraseologismen in ausgewählten historischen Grammatiken des Deutschen. In Csaba Földes (ed.), *Europhras 2006: Phraseologie disziplinär und interdisziplinär*.

Filatkina, Natalia, Johannes Gottwald, Monika Hanauska & Carolin Rößger. 2009. Formelhafte Sprache im schulischen Unterricht im Frühen Mittelalter: Am Beispiel der sogenannten ,Sprichwörter' in den Schriften Notkers des Deutschen von St. Gallen. *Sprachwissenschaft* 34(4). 341–397.

Friedrich, Jesko. 2006. *Phraseologisches Wörterbuch des Mittelhochdeutschen: Redensarten, Sprichwörter und andere feste Wortverbindungen in Texten von 1050–1350*. Tübingen: Niemeyer.

Friedrich, Jesko. 2007. Historische Phraseologie des Deutschen. In Harald Burger, Dmitrij Dobrovol'skij, Peter Kühn & Neal R. Norrick (eds.), *Phraseologie/Phraseology: Ein internationales Handbuch der zeitgenössischen Forschung: An International Handbook of Contemporary Research*. Band 2 (Handbücher zur Sprach- und Kommunikationswissenschaft / Handbooks of Linguistics and Communication Science [HSK] 28), 1092–1106. Berlin & New York: de Gruyter.

Glauche, Günther. 1970. *Schullektüre im Mittelalter: Entstehung und Wandlungen des Lektürekanons bis 1200 nach den Quellen dargestellt* (Münchener Beiträge zur Mediävistik und Renaissance-Forschung 5). Munich: Olms.

Goetz, Hans-Werner. 2003. *Europa im frühen Mittelalter 500–1050*. Stuttgart: Ulmer.

Grabmeyer, Bernhard. 1976. *Die Mischsprache in Willirams Paraphrase des Hohen Liedes* (Göppinger Arbeiten zur Germanistik 179). Göppingen: Kümmerle.

Green, Dennis. 1987. Zur primären Rezeption von Otfrids Evangelienbuch. In Rolf Bergmann (ed.), *Althochdeutsch*, Vol. 1, 737–771. Heidelberg: Winter.

Grotans, Anne. 1998. Simplifying Latin in Notkers classroom: Tradition and innovation. *Journal of Germanic Language and Literature* 10(1). 1–43.

Gülich, Elisabeth. 1997. Routineformeln und Formulierungsroutinen. In Rainer Wimmer & F.-J. Berens (eds.), *Wortbildung und Phraseologie* (Studien zur deutschen Sprache 9), 131–175. Tübingen: Narr Francke Attempto.

Gülich, Elisabeth & E. Henke. 1979/1980. Sprachliche Routine in der Alltagskommunikation. *Die Neueren Sprachen* 78. 513–530; 79. 2–33.

Haubrichs, Wolfgang. 1995. *Geschichte der deutschen Literatur von den Anfängen bis zum Beginn der Neuzeit. Band. I/1: Die Anfänge: Versuche volkssprachiger Schriftlichkeit im frühen Mittelalter*, 2nd edn. Tübingen: Niemeyer.

Haubrichs, Wolfgang & Max Pfister. 1990. *In Francia fui. Studien zu den germanisch-romanischen Interferenzen und zur Grundsprache der althochdeutschen „Pariser" (Altdeutschen) Gespräche*. Stuttgart: Steiner Franz.

Hellgardt, Ernst. 1979. Notkers des Deutschen Brief an Bischof Hugo von Sitten. In Klaus Grubmüller & Ernst Hellgardt (eds.), *Befund und Deutung: Zum Verhältnis von Empirie und Interpretation in Sprach- und Literaturwissenschaft*. Festschrift für Hans Fromm, 169–192. Tübingen: Niemeyer.

Hellgardt, Ernst. 1981. *Die exegetischen Quellen von Otfrids Evangelienbuch* (Hermaea 41). Tübingen: Niemeyer.

Kahl, Hans-Dietrich. 2000. ‚Mission, II. Missionsgeschichte'. In *Lexikon des Mittelalters CD-Rom-Ausgabe*, Vol. 7, 669–670. Stuttgart.

Kühn, Peter. 1984. Pragmatische und lexikographische Beschreibung phraseologischer Einheiten: Phraseologismen und Routineformeln. In H.E. Wiegand (ed.), *Studien zur neuhochdeutschen Lexikographie IV*, 175–235. Hildesheim: Olms.

Linke, Angelika. 1996. *Sprachkultur und Bürgertum: Zur Mentalitätsgeschichte des 19. Jahrhunderts*. Stuttgart: Metzler.

Lorenz-Bourjot, Martine & Heinz-Helmut Lüger. 2001. *Phraseologie und Phraseodidaktik*. Vienna: Praesens.

Lüger, Heinz-Helmut. 2007. Pragmatische Phraseme: Routineformeln. In Harald Burger, Dmitrij Dobrovol'skij, Peter Kühn & Neal R. Norrick (eds.), *Phraseologie: Ein internationales Handbuch der zeitgenössischen Forschung. An International Handbook of Contemporary Research*. Band 1 (Handbücher zur Sprach- und Kommunikationswissenschaft / Handbooks of Linguistics and Communication Science [HSK] 28), 444–459. Berlin & New York: de Gruyter.

Ochsenbein, Peter. 1991. L'enseignement et l'étude. In Werner Vogler (ed.), *L'Abbaye de Saint-Gall. Rayonnement spirituel et culturel*, 133–144. St. Gallen: Stiftsarchiv St. Gallen.

Ohly, Friedrich. 1958. *Hohelied-Studien: Grundzüge einer Geschichte der Hoheliedauslegung des Abendlandes bis um 1200*. Wiesbaden: F. Steiner.

Penzl, Herbert. 1984. Gimer min ros. *German Quarterly* 57. 392–401.

Riecke, Jörg. 2004. *Die Frühgeschichte der medizinischen Fachsprache im Deutschen. Band 1: Untersuchungen*. Berlin: de Gruyter.

Schröder, W. 1981. Glossae Cassellanae. In Kurt Ruh (ed.), *Die deutsche Literatur des Mittelalters – Verfasserlexikon. Band 3*, 2nd rev. edn., 61–63. Berlin: de Gruyter.

Schulz, Monika. 2000. *Magie und Wiederherstellung der Ordnung*. Frankfurt/Main: Lang.

Schulz, Monika. 2003. *Beschwörungen im Mittelalter: Einführung und Überblick*. Heidelberg: Winter.

Sonderegger, Stefan. 1978. ‚Altdeutsche Gespräche'. In Kurt Ruh (ed.), *Die deutsche Literatur des Mittelalters – Verfasserlexikon. Band 1*, 2nd rev. edn., 284–285. Berlin: de Gruyter.

Stein, Stephan. 1995. *Formelhafte Sprache. Untersuchungen zu ihren pragmatischen und kognitiven Funktionen im gegenwärtigen Deutsch*. Frankfurt/Main: Lang.

Zerfaß, Christiane. 1995. *Die Allegorese zwischen Latinität und Volkssprache. Willirams von Ebersberg „Expositio in cantica canticorum"*. Göppingen: Kümmerle.

Idioms: Motivation and etymology

DMITRIJ DOBROVOL'SKIJ and ELISABETH PIIRAINEN

Abstract

One of the questions in idiom research is the extent to which the image component of a figurative idiom fixed in its inner form reaches into its lexicalized meaning and consequently its pragmatics. This paper explores two hypotheses: that traces of the image component of idiom semantics can have an effect on the usage of the given idiom, and that, in certain cases, its etymology (as a contributor to its imagery) can thus influence an idiom's usage conditions. To test these hypotheses we will use data drawn from large text corpora.

Keywords: idiom motivation; etymology of idioms; image component; intertextuality; usage restrictions.

1. Preliminary remarks, aims and key questions

In this paper we will discuss some of the problems of idiom motivation with regard to its relationship with etymology.[1] As is well-known, the synchronic motivation of an idiom often does not coincide with the "true" etymology of that idiom, and sometimes the two can contradict each other. In such cases, the question arises whether it is the synchronic motivation or the etymology that is more important for the functioning of an idiom. This involves examining the external combinatorial restrictions of a given idiom. For any idiom this then becomes the question of whether any such restrictions can be explained by addressing the idiom's conceptual basis. If so, what are the motivational "bridges"? These could involve how most speakers intuitively construct such bridges (which often takes the form of folk etymology), or it could involve the true etymology of the idiom. Both possibilities are plausible, the latter on the assumption that an idiom's figurative past may be accessible in the present in the form of traces of an "etymological memory" so that even where speakers do not know the etymology, the idiom is not used in combinatorial surroundings that would violate a historically relevant type of context. The former possibility predicts that speakers use idioms according to the idiom's personal associations for the speaker, which need not have anything in common with the idiom's true etymology.

Let us make these proposals more specific. Psycholinguistic and cognitive-semantic research suggests that speakers, when processing an idiom, map the conceptual domain evoked by the idiom's lexical structure (source) onto another conceptual domain (target) that underlies that idiom's lexicalized meaning. The target concept can then be structured according to the structure of the source concept, so that the source can influence the lexicalized meaning (cf. examples in Lakoff 1990). These are more or less plausible hypotheses about the ways in which motivation can influence the processing of an idiom. It may be that, consequently, such processing can also influence an idiom's use. The usage of idioms and its relationship to idiom processing can be investigated on the basis of empirical data drawn from sufficiently large text corpora (see Section 4.2 below). That is what will be done in this paper.

Our investigation uses *Conventional Figurative Language Theory* (CFLT) developed by Dobrovol'skij and Piirainen (2005) as an appropriate theoretical framework. Central to this theory is the idea that figurative lexical units (prototypical idioms and conventional figurative one-word metaphors) differ from non-figurative units (i.e. from "normal" words, collocations etc.) in their semantics since their content plane consists not only of the lexicalized meaning of the conventional figurative unit, but also of the linguistically relevant traces of the underlying image. Dobrovol'skij and Piirainen (2009) have developed initial stages of a theory of phraseology, which can be considered a specific implementation of CFLT. The main postulates of CFTL are as follows: *idioms* are a subset of phrasal lexemes, on the one hand, because of their constitutive characteristics: *polylexicality* (i.e. they consist of more than one word) and *stability* (i.e. they are not produced, but reproduced with approximately the same form and meaning). Because of their *idiomaticity*, on the other hand, idioms have much in common with other figurative units in the lexicon. The prototypical idiom (the *figurative idiom*) can be interpreted on two different conceptual levels: on a primary level, i.e. on the level of its "literal" meaning which underlies its inner form, and on a second level, i.e. on the level of its figurative meaning. The latter is also called the *lexicalized meaning* which is the term we use in this paper. The so-called *image component* of an idiom takes the role of a semantic bridge between the two levels. What is meant by *image component* is neither the etymology nor the original image, but linguistically relevant traces of an image that are comprehensible for the majority of speakers. It is an additional conceptual link that mediates between the literal reading (fixed in the idiom's lexical structure) and the lexicalized meaning of an idiom, cf. similar ideas in Baranov and Dobrovol'skij (2008).

There are also certain points of intersection between CFLT and Conceptual Metaphor Theory. However, CMT is designed to capture fundamental properties of all possible metaphoric expressions, primarily, novel or dynamic metaphors. This makes CMT not quite adequate for describing idioms or conventional metaphors because conventional figurative expressions are mostly based on different principles. Patrick Hanks (2006: 17) points out "that the distinction between conventional metaphors and literal meanings is less important than the distinction between dynamic metaphors and conventional metaphors. Dynamic metaphors are coined ad hoc to express some new insight; conventional metaphors are just one more kind of normal use of language." Moreover, many conventional metaphors and idioms are products of their time, so they cannot be accounted for without addressing elements of concrete, basic level images which are mostly culture-specific, cf. also Allan 2006 on this issue.

Motivation, which is the part of the inner form, involves the possibility of interpreting the underlying mental image in a way that makes sense of the meaning conventionally ascribed to it. Thus the conceptual structure of a motivated lexical unit includes not only the lexicalized figurative meaning and the relevant traces of the mental image (i.e. the inner form) but also the conceptual links between them. However, since it is difficult to investigate how individual speakers process a given lexical unit, only trends can be revealed by means of psycholinguistic experiments.[2] There are various types of idiom motivation which we will now outline.

2. Types of motivation

The relevant traces of the mental image of a motivated idiom must be regarded as part of its content plane in a broad sense. As a rule, the image component is involved in the cognitive processing of the particular idiom. This means that relevant elements of the inner form have to be included in the structure of the semantic explication of idioms. Since the majority of idioms are semantically motivated, we need to distinguish between two principal types of semantic motivation: the *metaphoric motivation* type and the *symbol-based motivation* type. Both types can additionally be affected by a third, not purely semantic type of motivation, namely *intertextuality*. We will concentrate on these three major types of motivation.[3]

2.1. Metaphoric type of motivation

The motivational links that are relevant to *metaphorically motivated* idioms can most adequately be explained either on the superordinate level of the *conceptual metaphor*, i.e. on the level of the abstract *metaphoric model* (cf. Lakoff and Johnson 1980; Lakoff 1987) or on the *basic level of categorization* (following Rosch 1975, 1978) that is encoded in the lexical structure of an idiom. We call such "basic level cases" of motivation *frame-based metaphors*, cf. (1–2).

(1) *to throw dust in someone's eyes*
 'to mislead or betray someone willfully'

(2) *to be a red rag to the bull*
 'to be the cause for making someone very angry all the time'

Idiom (1) is motivated by the abstract conceptual metaphor DECEPTION IS DISTURBANCE OF SEEING. Together with other figurative units (e.g. *to pull the wool over someone's eyes* 'to deceive, mislead someone', *to muddy the waters* 'to make things more confused by obscuring them', *to cover up something*, etc.), it forms a well-developed metaphoric model. For idiom (2), no such metaphoric model can be found. This idiom can be best described within the theoretical framework of the *cognitive modeling of idiom semantics*, developed by Baranov and Dobrovol'skij (cf. Baranov and Dobrovol'skij 1996, 2000, 2008). Idiom (2) is motivated by fragments of world knowledge about the frame BULLFIGHT. The meaningful elements that are significant for the lexicalized meaning are slots of this frame: TORERO, BULL, INSTRUMENTS USED BY THE TORERO, although not all of them are explicitly expressed in the lexical structure of the idiom. So, the motivation is based here on the conceptual correspondence between the source frame BULLFIGHT and the target frame CAUSE TO GET ANGRY, rather than on a kind of superordinate conceptual metaphor. From a purely linguistic point of view, it is not important under which conceptual metaphor idioms like (2) should be subsumed. We take it that this is a classification task rather than being of theoretical significance.

It is, however, crucial to determine how the image component contributes to the actual meaning in each instance, and how it determines the contextual behavior of a given idiom. Thus, corpus examples containing the idioms *hit the ceiling, go through the roof, blow your stack, flip your lid* are not interchangeable in all contexts, though they are regarded as instantiations of the same conceptual metaphor, namely ANGER IS HOT FLUID IN A CONTAINER, cf. also Gibbs (1993). It is one task of linguistic research to discover the relevant semantic differences and correlate them (where possible) with the image components, which we suppose to be encoded in the lexical structure on the level of concrete frames rather than on the abstract level of conceptual metaphors. Doing this seems more promising than constructing conceptual metaphors to cover groups of idioms whose image components have something in common. Compare also (Deignan 2006: 121) on this issue: "[...] it is time to work more directly with the individual linguistic metaphors from naturally-occurring texts, searching back for theoretical implications, rather than proceeding from the theory to find linguistic examples that are needed in order to support it."

To this end let us analyze one example taken from Longman 1998. Idiom (3) is interesting because it shows that the image component is not necessarily identical with the idiom's literal meaning.

(3) *to throw in the towel* (also *to throw in the sponge* BrE)
'to stop trying to achieve something because it has been too difficult'

The present-day TOWEL variant is a truncation from *to throw the towel into the ring*. This earlier form still exists in some loan translations in other languages (e.g. Dutch *de handdoek in de ring werpen*). The idiom derives from modern professional boxing and its rules, which were established at the end of the 19th century. It was common practice for the contestant's trainer to throw the towel into the ring as a signal during an ongoing round for the referee to stop the attack and in order to admit defeat and give up the fight. The (mainly BrE) version *to throw in the sponge* (originally *to throw up the sponge*) is not merely a lexical variant but, strictly speaking, refers to a different frame. This idiom goes back to the days of prize-fighting in the mid-nineteenth century. When a contestant had taken enough of a beating and was ready to admit defeat, his second admitted the defeat by tossing the sponge, otherwise used to refresh the fighter, into the air (Brewer 2005: 1383; Flavell and Flavell 2006: 278). According to conventional lexicographic practice, these two different mental images are combined into one entry.

From a cross-linguistic viewpoint, idioms using the SPONGE variant, e.g. French *jeter l'éponge* (which is probably a loan translation of the BrE idiom), are "fully equivalent" only to the British, not to the AmE version. However, the images behind both versions have lost their significance except for those who are knowledgeable about boxing. The contemporary motivation is based on the symbolic action of throwing a towel into the ring or possibly a sponge into the air. Idioms of this type can be regarded as borderline cases between metaphoric and symbolic motivation. On the one hand, the lexicalized meaning is based on a metaphoric mapping of a source domain (BOXING or FIGHTING) onto a target domain. On the other hand, the source frame contains a symbolically motivated slot, therefore *towel* and *sponge* themselves can be considered to be symbols of defeat (or, more precisely, concession of defeat) – however, only within the conceptual field of BOXING or FIGHTING. As a whole, the idiom's lexicalized meaning came about in two steps. First, the physical action of throwing the towel or the sponge was metonymically reinterpreted as a symbolic action indicating the concession of defeat. Second, this conceptual structure was metaphorically reinterpreted in the sense of 'abandoning further attempts to achieve something because it has been too difficult'.

This example shows that the linguistically relevant image component is neither identical with the literal reading of the underlying word chain nor with the etymologically reconstructed "primary" image. Only certain motivating traces of this image survive and are taken over by the idiom's content plane. In the case of *throw in the towel* and *throw in/up the sponge* these traces are identical, so that the differences in the "primary" image do not play any role for the use of the idiom.

2.2. Symbol-based type of motivation

In idioms with *symbol-based motivation*,[4] the relevant cultural knowledge mainly extends to one constituent (or more precisely, to the concept behind it) and not to the idiom as a whole (as is the case with the metaphoric type of motivation). The key constituents of "symbolic" idioms have clear semantic autonomy.[5] The motivational link between the literal and figurative readings of these constituents is established by semiotic knowledge about the cultural symbol in question, especially its meaning in culturally relevant sign systems other than language, cf. (4).

(4) *to keep the wolf from the door*
 'to ward off starvation or financial ruin; to maintain oneself at a minimal level'

The concept WOLF with its symbolic functions 'hunger and greediness' and 'economic despair' plays the principal part in the semantic motivation of idiom (4). This agrees with the symbolic functions of WOLF that are anchored in various cultural codes, ranging from fairy tales and folk tales of the dangerous, people-devouring wolf to folk beliefs about werewolves, and throughout Western history from antiquity to Christian exegesis up to present-day nursery rhymes, cartoons or film animations. Thus, in order to process idiom (4), other pieces of knowledge must be activated: the knowledge of the symbolization behind the constituent *wolf*. In most cases, the semantic procedures that underlie symbol-based motivation constitute a *metonymical shift*.

The difference between metaphoric motivation and symbol-based motivation is that the former involves the idea of some kind of similarity between the entity encoded in the inner form and the entity denoted by the idiom taken in its lexicalized meaning, whereas the latter exploits certain cultural conventions based on the ability of material objects to "stand for" some non-material entity.

2.3. *Intertextuality as factor of motivation*

Intertextuality is of the utmost importance given the cultural foundation of idioms. In this article, *intertextuality* is understood as the relationship of a conventional figurative unit (such as an idiom) with an already existing text as its cultural historical origin.[6] There are a great number of figurative units whose image components can be traced back to an existing (mostly identifiable) textual source. Intertextuality is a result of the etymology of idioms (e.g. idioms taken from the Bible, Shakespeare, classical literature etc.), rather than a question of motivation. Nevertheless, in certain cases, intertextuality must be accounted for as a special type of motivation. Therefore, we will look at this phenomenon more closely both within this section (where we try to answer the question as to what extent intertextuality provides motivating links synchronically) and below within Section 3.4 where we will be dealing with etymological aspects of intertextual connections.

Several idioms can be regarded as motivated by intertextuality and by a certain frame or cultural symbol at the same time. However, there is a small group of idioms where we may assume that the intertextual motivation offers the only possibility for making sense of the idiom, i.e. for establishing the motivational link between the inner form and the lexicalized meaning of the idiom. Let us first consider such an idiom, (5).

(5)   *a/the Trojan Horse*
      'a deception, a concealed danger; an enemy concealed within someone or something that attacks the group or organization he/she/it belongs to'

Idiom (5) is currently very well-known in computing, as a program with a concealed function that damages other programs on the computer to which it is downloaded. The idiom is either opaque to speakers or motivated by intertextuality. A semantic motivation can be excluded. It is motivated by knowledge that there is a story behind it, even if this story may not be mentally present with all its details to every speaker. Homer reports in his *Odyssey* (and Virgil in his *Aeneid*) that, after Hector's death, Ulysses had a huge wooden horse made and declared that it was an offering to the gods to secure a safe voyage back to Greece. The Trojans dragged the horse within their city, but it was filled with Greek soldiers, including Menelaus, who stole out of the horse at night, slew the guards, opened the city gates and set fire to the city. This phrase, in the sense of an imminent and great danger, became proverbial as early as in Roman antiquity (Pohlke 2008: 219).

Other idioms of intertextual origin can also be motivated for speakers by different knowledge structures (e.g. metaphors or symbols), cf. (6–7).

(6) *to run/approach with seven-league boots*
 'to run/approach very quickly'

(7) *a snake in the grass*
 'a secretly untrustworthy or treacherous person; a great danger'

Idiom (6) seems to be motivated intertextually for people who are familiar with the tales of the seven-league boots, which magically enable a giant to take great strides and approach very fast. They are a motif in folktales, cf. the fairy tale "The Seven-leagued Boots" and various literary treatments of the theme (for German, e.g. by Wilhelm Hauff and Adalbert von Chamisso). The lexicalized meaning then would be 'to run/approach very quickly, as if someone was the giant of the tale whose boots carry him/her seven leagues at a step'. For people who are unfamiliar with the textual source, the idiom may be motivated in part by their symbolic knowledge of the number SEVEN which has, among others, the symbolic meaning 'many, much' ('intensification'). The ability to make strides of *seven* leagues clearly results in great speed.

Similarly, idiom (7) has its origin in classical literature (it is a quotation from Virgil's "Eclogues": *latet anguis in herba* 'there is a snake hiding in the grass', 37 BC). Its motivation for the average speakers, however, is likely based on knowledge about snakes (they actually hide in tall grass, and their bite is dangerous), on the one hand, and symbolic knowledge (SNAKE is a strong cultural symbol signifying 'danger', 'evil', 'malice'), on the other. Thus, idioms that have roots in works of literature, fables, fairy tales etc. may be motivated by their "true" etymological origin for speakers who are familiar with the textual source, while other speakers can often activate other knowledge structures to make sense of the idiom. In what follows we will look at the issue of idiom etymology in more detail.

3. Aspects of etymology

3.1. *Historical and etymological research on phraseology*

The aims of historical comparative approaches to phraseology are many, ranging from uncovering the etymological origin or the initial form of single phrasemes to reconstructing former stages in the development of a phraseological system or entire domains that were previously culturally significant. This branch of research has to rely on cooperation with culturally-oriented academic disciplines other than linguistics (e.g. folklore, mythology research, ecclesiastical history) and to incorporate dialectal and historical language varieties as well as comprehensive extra-linguistic material.

First, it is crucial to discriminate between historical research and etymological analysis. As for historical research, there is such a tradition in Slavic languages. Since the 1960s, several studies have analyzed dialectal and ethnographic material in order to reconstruct the phraseology of a Proto-Slavic variety (Tolstoj 1973) and aspects of early religious and mythological concepts of folk culture. Using variants or (quasi)-synonyms of a given phraseme in many dialects and related languages as a starting point, Mokienko (1989) develops structural semantic models. This approach finds expression in further diachronic studies, above all in the historical-etymological dictionary of phrasemes (Bierich et al. 2005).

In contrast to that, other significant etymological studies start from the particular phrasemes themselves in order to advance to their real origins or sources. Recently, Wanzeck (2003) has given a coherent description of the etymology of idioms containing color words in historical and current use. Starting from the lexicalized meaning of the phrasemes, the study centers on the question of how the color adjectives took on their phraseologically bound meanings. Exhausting the written sources from the very beginning and considering their cultural and historical contexts, the author succeeds in clarifying the true etymology of many phrasemes that became obscure in the course of history. For example, she was able to illuminate how the German idiom (8), completely opaque until then, came into being.

(8) German *einen blauen Montag machen*
"to make a blue Monday"
'to skip work on Monday'

Since medieval times there was a "blue mass" (German *blaue Messe*) that was said for the deceased of a craftsmen's guild on a particular Monday. It was also named *blauer Montag*, after the priest's blue vestment, since with regard to ecclesiastical history, *blue* was the color of fasting and mourning. Through various social historical circumstances, the meaning shifted from 'requiem mass on a Monday' to 'Monday off' (Wanzeck 2003: 156–211).

This example shows that knowledge of its etymology mostly has no effect on the way speakers deal with an idiom. Unlike with idioms that are obviously transparent (e.g. because of a well-known underlying source frame), play on words with the historical meaning of *blue* (the color of the priest's vestment, ecclesiastical color of mourning) would not be possible.

Important for our research are the questions: what is the true etymology in each individual case? How does this "true" etymology correlate with the synchronic motivation? And what is the role of folk etymology in those cases in which the true etymology does not work?

3.2. Folk etymology

Motivation exists only in those cases where the image component is alive. This can be the (historically) true etymology, but it can also be a reinterpretation of the original concept, a "modernized" folk etymology, brought into line with the extra-linguistic facts that are encoded in the inner form. This can be illustrated by the idiom *to give someone the green light* 'to give someone permission to do something that they were planning'. It originates historically in the signals used in early *railroad systems* and not in urban *traffic lights*, although, from a contemporary view, the image component seems to be grounded in the regulation of road traffic, when the light switches to green signaling road users to proceed. Compare also idiom (9).

(9) *to hit the nail on the head*
    'to describe something in exactly the right way, to find exactly the right answer to a problem in one or two words'

The idiom is clearly motivated (for the average speaker) by fragments of world knowledge about the function of nails (as a tool). The allusion is to an accurate blow with a hammer on the head of a nail, which requires some skill. There is a homomorphic relation between the literal and figurative meaning: the *head of the nail* is the central point of a matter, while *to hit* correlates with 'to grasp, capture something concisely and appropriately'. Thus, the idiom is semantically decomposable (in the sense of Dobrovol'skij 1982; Nunberg et al. 1994 or Langlotz 2006). When historical correspondences are taken into account, however, the correlation is different, resulting in a complete shift of the image. The true etymology is based on medieval knighthood and archery, where a target was fixed to the wall with a nail, exactly in its center. The best bowman was able to hit precisely on the nail. This true etymology can be proven by historical evidence. We find a clear reference to the bowman in a German equivalent in one of Martin Luther's texts (1541): *das ein guter schütze den pflock odder nagel treffe* ["that a good archer may hit the tack or nail"] (Cornette 1997: 88). Presumably, the earliest English pieces of evidence were also used with reference to the archery frame (cf. *Thou hittest the nayle on the head*, ca. 1520, Apperson 1969: 435). It is impossible to say at what time the shift of the mental image (in the direction of the hand tool) took place.

These examples show that shifts from true to folk etymology do not have clear consequences for the usage of an idiom. The crucial factor is whether speakers perceive the idiom as motivated or opaque.

3.3. *Cultural history*

Phraseology is a linguistic domain that, due to its interrelation with culture, can be better explored and understood in a cultural and historical context than merely in a synchronic perspective. Every idiom has its history or "biography" and can be categorized according to its *culture-boundness* (cf. Sabban 2008). In the course of history, an idiom may undergo various influences. The impact of cultural and historical features is evident in the evolution of an idiom. It is unpredictable how its outward structure and figurative meanings will develop. In addition to that, the interpretation of the underlying mental image can be subject to historical transformations, as example (9) has shown. This must especially be kept in mind when looking at the etymology. Let us illustrate this point with idiom (10).

(10) *to look for a needle in a haystack*
'to try to find something very small that is lost among many other things; to struggle with searching for something without any prospect of success'

Taylor (1962: 190) assigns the idiom to the domain "household", based on the constituent *needle* (together with the idiom *to be on pins and needles*), although the domain "country life", which is also mentioned by Taylor, would probably be more adequate (because of the constituent *haystack*). However, there is an entirely different way in which the idiom can be assigned to a certain cultural domain. There are many folktales involving futile searches for objects. Most probably, the idiom refers to one of them, the jester's tale of a fool who is hunting for a needle in a haystack. The Grimms' fairy tale No. 32, *Clever Hans*, tells us about a fool who puts a needle into a hay cart where the needle later must be found

(Aarne/Thompson 1961 No. 1685). If there is a synchronically relevant connection to this once well-known narrative motif, the cultural domain in question must be defined in different terms. It is no longer an aspect of "material culture" but a fragment of the knowledge domain of "intertextuality". At the same time, idiom (10) is connected to a group of narrations which have been well-known since ancient or medieval times and live on as short forms in modern idioms.

3.4. Intertextuality from the etymological perspective

There are thousands of idioms that go back to an identifiable textual source (originally either direct quotations from an author's work or allusions to an entire text passage). A large set of idioms is traceable to classical antiquity, to the Bible or narrative traditions. Even film productions are a modern textual source. Some of these idioms belong to the motivation type of "intertextuality" (cf. Section 2.3).

Out of the different strands of intertextual tradition, only one has been studied in more detail so far: idioms of biblical origin. Many idioms date from translations of the Bible. Larger, however, is the proportion of idioms in contemporary languages that were already very popular with classical authors (including many inconspicuous idioms with nothing to suggest their classical origin). This strand of tradition is not as well researched as the phenomenon of biblical idioms. The works of Erasmus of Rotterdam alone contain hundreds of expressions that live on to this day in modern languages.

Further sources that should be mentioned when discussing the intertextual origins of idioms include idioms going back to fables of the Aesopic type like *to bell the cat* 'to undertake a dangerous mission at great risk to oneself for the sake of others', *the lion's share* 'the biggest part of something that is taken or done by one person instead of being shared fairly with other people'), to fairy tales (cf. idiom (6) or, for example, *to be a bird in a gilded cage* 'to live in affluence, prosperity but lacking freedom', to animal tales (*as poor as a church mouse* 'very poor, possessing nothing', *to fight like cat and dog* 'to frequently have violent arguments with each other, to keep quarrelling with each other all the time') and all the other kinds of folk tales, jests and comical tales that once were well-known but fell into oblivion in the course of history and survive in idioms of the present day, as is supposedly the case with idiom (11) above.

These examples clearly show that no generalizations can be made in this field because every idiom has undergone its own development in the course of its history. What these examples make evident is that the task of describing true etymology must be strictly separated from the task of revealing productive motivating links that influence the idiom's functioning in discourse.

4. Image component and usage restrictions

4.1. *Traces of the image component in the lexicalized meaning of idioms*

Two idioms that share a nearly identical lexicalized meaning but have different literal meanings can almost never be considered "equivalent". This holds true for *intra-linguistic* as well as for *cross-linguistic quasi-synonymous idioms*. An idiom with a different lexical structure often cannot be replaced or translated by a "similar" one without consequences for the meaning of the given text passage.

Cross-linguistic quasi-synonyms, i.e. quasi-equivalents are idioms of two or more different languages that show almost the same image component and very similar, but not identical, lexicalized meanings. Their lexicalized meanings may even coincide in the core. However, they show different nuances. This means that they can function as equivalents in many contexts but not in all of them. There are certain contexts that highlight these subtle differences. These can barely be noticed in an isolated presentation and, for this reason, corpus-based data is necessary to be able to properly describe the meanings of partly equivalent idioms from various languages. Compare the idioms (11–12) and the contexts (13–14), drawn from large German and Russian text corpora: from DeReKo Mannheim, RNC (Russian National Corpus) and from the Corpora of the Department of Experimental Lexicography of the Russian Language Institute of the Russian Academy of Sciences.

(11) German *schwarz auf weiß*
 "black on white"
 'in writing or print, therefore official'

(12) Russian *черным по белому*
 "in black on white"
 'clear, plain (only with regard to something in writing, mostly officially printed matters)'

(13) Damit bekämen sportliche Aktivitäten einen verbindlicheren Charakter. Was einmal *schwarz auf weiß festgehalten sei*, werde nicht so schnell umgestoßen, sagt Mayrhofer.
 ["By this, sporting activities would get a more obliging character. What once *has been recorded black on white*, would not be upset as quickly, says Mayrhofer."]

(14) Читай внимательней! Там же черным по белому написано, что на что влияет.

["Read more attentively! There it *stands written in black on white* what has an effect on what things."]

Both idioms (11–12) have seemingly the same underlying knowledge structures as their image components (fragments of frame knowledge about printed and written material). The lexicalized meanings show little divergence. The semantic component "printed" is a presupposition of the Russian idiom (12). The assertive part of its meaning (as contrasted with presupposition and implication consists of the semantic components "clearness, clarity". However, the semantics of the German idiom (11) highlights the "official character" (of a printed or written document) so that everything recorded black on white can be used as a piece of evidence. This idea is a part of its assertion whereas in the semantic structure of (12) it is only a possible inference.

This leads to differences in the combinatorial profile of these two idioms. The German idiom (11) tends to be found in contexts such as "*to give/show* someone something in writing (official)" or "*to (want to) have/record* something in writing (official)" whereas the Russian idiom (12) is mostly used in co-occurrences such as "something *stands* clearly in writing or print". These differences can be deduced from the usage of the idioms by means of analyzing text corpora. In RNC, idiom (12) has been encountered in 165 contexts which can be used for our purposes. Only 16 contexts are semantically ambivalent in the sense that they are either autonomous or deal with official documents so that the semantic component "official" can be ascribed to the semantic structure of the idiom as a kind of implication.

In DeReKo Mannheim, idiom (11) has been encountered in 223 contexts which can be used for our purposes. 192 text passages use the idiom quite similarly to that of example (13). The idiom highlights the official character of the documents printed or written in black and white.

Can these semantic differences be explained in terms of relevant traces of the image component? At first glance, it seems that it is not the case because the image components of (11) and (12) appear to be identical. However, the lexical structures of the two idioms point to correlating slots of two different frames. The frame within which idiom (11) has to be interpreted is a kind of OFFICIAL DOCUMENT. As for (12), it goes back to the frame of every possible WRITTEN OR PRINTED TEXT. That is the reason why the idea of being approved by an authority is highlighted in the image component of (11) whereas the image component of (12) focuses the semantic feature 'clearly readable'. So, in (11) and (12) we are dealing with the case where nearly the same lexical structure evokes different frames and, therefore, not identical image components. In many cases, text corpora can provide evidence for illustrating the subtle differences between seemingly similar idioms of two languages.

Traditionally, cross-linguistic quasi-synonyms have been regarded as "absolute equivalents". Older bilingual dictionaries like Taylor and Gottschalk (1966) or Binovič and Grišin (1975) are full of such examples. Therefore, it is important to examine their functional characteristics in more detail. This is significant for semantic theory as well for solving several practically oriented tasks.

4.2. *Case study: German gender-specific idioms*

This section shows that there exist traces of the image component in the figurative lexicalized meaning and pragmatic features of idioms. It follows that the image component may have an effect on the use of an idiom in such a way as to restrict its usage. For instance an idiom might contain elements of a mental image which impede certain kinds of usage. There are convincing examples from gender-specific idioms, which show such restrictions. Some idioms of this type show traces of an "etymological memory", i.e. the idiom in question "memorizes" its history and does not allow it to be used in combinatorial surroundings which are incompatible with that history. Idiom (15) serves to demonstrate how this "etymological memory" of an idiom can determine its behavior in discourse. The idiom passes on an old symbolic concept which came into being in the Middle Ages and still has an effect on this idiom in its present-day usage.

(15) German *die Hosen anhaben* "to wear the trousers"
'to be the dominant partner in a marriage; it is the wife rather than the husband or partner who makes decisions in the family'

The origins of this idiom lie in the "Battle for the Trousers", which was treated frequently in disputes, literature and paintings of the Early Modern times. The figure of the virago, the domineering woman whose unfeminine aggressiveness was perceived as a direct threat to male authority, was a widespread stereotype at that time and treated explicitly in iconography. The "Battle for the Trousers", women's attempt to try to steal their husband's breeches which symbolized the man's supremacy and power, is the topic of numerous proverb anthology paintings and illustrations since early fifteenth-century art, especially in Flanders, the Netherlands, Germany and adjoining regions.[7] The idiom itself was already well-known in pamphlets and moralizing texts of various languages.

At first, this idiom was only applied to a female person, or more precisely to a woman who was married or lived in a partnership. In a case study which will be briefly summarized here, it was discovered that a restriction to women is still part of the semantic structure of idiom (15) (Dobrovol'skij and Piirainen 2009: 125–130). Corpus analyses based on DeReKo (above all, its written language parts) show that the hit rate for the idiom amounts to 157 texts, 46 of which can be used for our purposes (see below for more detail). 44 texts refer to a female person; only two texts refer to a male person. This gender-specific character is due to the image component of BREECHES, which still has the symbolic function to represent men's power, although different ideas are connected with trousers (breeches, pants) today and women wear trousers just like men. The image component has remained constant. It is the symbolic character of the garment, despite the fact that the source frame fixing the underlying mental image has undergone a shift towards a "modernized" concept.

Below we would like to briefly outline the approaches of how the data of analyzing gender-specifics in German idioms (Dobrovol'skij and Piirainen 2009: 116–141) have been collected. Investigations into questions concerning idiom semantics by means of corpus analyses are still rare. As Deignan (2005) emphasizes, the researcher is faced with an enormously rich resource which is too large to be processed manually. However, semantically adequate results can be obtained only on the basis of a thorough analysis of rich empirical data.

> The corpus researcher who attempts to develop valid generalizations about language meaning and use has to sift through a large amount of linguistic data, looking for regularities and patterns. It follows that corpus analysis of semantic issues such as metaphor must be bottom-up rather than top-down.
>
> (Deignan 2005: 92)

In view of this fact, we have developed a method of capturing the gender-specific idioms from text corpora, which consists of five steps. The *first step* was to compile a list of potential gender-specific idioms, based on preliminary knowledge and later completed by systematically checking many idiom dictionaries. This list consists of 107 German idioms (cf. Piirainen 2001). In a *second step*, these idioms were pre-tested on the base of a smaller part of the corpora of written language from the Mannheim German corpus DeReKo (with half a billion words), which is available to any user. These preliminary tests have shown that 39 of the idioms in question did not appear in the corpora at all, and another set of 22 idioms was represented only by a too small number of texts. Idioms with fewer than three hits in the corpora were removed from the list.[8]

The *third step* consisted of checking the remaining 46 "gender-specific idiom candidates" against the full data of DeReKo (with approx. 3.5 billion words). The average number of hits was 349, ranging from 3410 to five.

Our task (*step four*) was therefore, to check 12,558 texts manually for the occurrence of the idioms in question. We refrained from analyzing the idiom *mit einer weißen Weste/eine weiße Weste* '(with) a white vest', documented in 3410 contexts, because this number of texts is too large to be processed manually at the present time following Deignan (2005).[9] The remaining 9,148 contexts then have been worked through in the following way:

We marked those contexts (i) where the idiom refers to a male person, (ii) where the idiom refers to a female person and (iii) those contexts which cannot be used for our purposes because the reference of a given idiom in such context is gender-nonspecific; cf. concepts such as government, company, party etc. or expressions like *people, everyone, they, the students, the Germans*. Texts where the idiom was used only for the purpose of play on words were also excluded. It turned out that the third group makes up the vast majority of all texts. Again, 36 idioms had to be removed from our list because the contexts did not provide enough information on potential gender-specific features, i.e. most relevant contexts belonged to group (iii).

Step five consisted of a careful analysis of the texts in which the remaining ten idioms occurred. It produced unambiguous results, as has already been shown with idiom (15). The other nine idioms show a similar pattern; all are gender restricted. The idioms (16–24) have image components which restrict their use to a male person so that traces of an "etymological memory" become evident. The image component can include a male animal concept (COCK in (16), evoked by the constituent meaning 'comb'), a concept of a garment, never worn by women in the past (NECKTIE, VEST (17–18)), a part of such garment (TROUSERS POCKET, VEST POCKET (19–21)) or equipment possessed exclusively by men (BILLFOLD, (22)), and, finally, an anatomic peculiarity of men (BEARD (23)). Idiom (24) is a special case. Here responsible for the usage restriction is not the image component but a kind of folk etymology, based on the polysemy of the German word *Schwanz*: 1. 'tail (e.g. of a dog)' and 2. 'male member'.

On the basis of this data set we can now ask how far the image component of an idiom's meaning contributes to the restrictions on its use. Coding of the data below uses the following schema: **H** number of *hits* in the corpora; **U** *usable* text passages, **M** number of texts with a *male* person and **F** number of texts with a *female* person.

(16) *jmdm. schwillt der Kamm* "sb.'s comb swells"
  1. 'sb. gets very angry'; 2. 'sb. gets very proud, conceited'
  H 89, U 48, M 47, F 1.

(17) *sich auf den Schlips getreten fühlen* "to feel (like being) stepped on one's necktie"
'to feel insulted, offended, injured'
H 227, U 111, M 107, F 4.

(18) *sich einen hinter die Binde kippen/gießen* "to tip/pour one behind one's tie"
'to drink much alcohol'
H 197, U 147, M 139, F 8.

(19a) *eine/keine reine Weste haben* "to have a/no pure vest"
'to have done nothing/something dishonorable'
H 323, U 142, M 141, F 1.

(19b) *eine/keine saubere Weste haben* "to have a/no clean vest"
'to have done nothing/something dishonorable'
H 237, U 94, M 92, F 2.

(20) *etwas wie seine Hosentasche kennen* "to know something like one's trousers pocket"
'to know something very well'
H 84, U 70, M 69, F 1.

(21) *etwas wie seine Westentasche kennen* "to know something like one's vest pocket"
'to know something very well'
H 590, U 477, M 440, F 34.

(22a) *eine dicke Brieftasche haben* "to have a fat billfold"
'to have much money'

(22b) *mit einer dicken Brieftasche* "with a fat billfold"
'possessing much money, very rich'
H 256, U 45, M 45, F 0.

(23) *sich etwas in den Bart murmeln/brummen* "to mutter/mumble something in one's beard"
'to speak (unwillingly) quietly or indistinctly to oneself'
H 64, U 55, M 55, F 0.

(24) *den Schwanz einziehen* "to retract one's tail (informal also: penis)"
'to have feelings of despondency and humiliation or surrender, to be embarrassed or ashamed because you have failed at something'
H 95, U 33, M 33, F 0.

Our corpus-analysis has shown that the idioms (16–24) have clear usage restrictions which are correlated with the image component of the idiom and in one case also with its folk etymology. In summary, we are not supposing that all motivation is based on the knowledge of the idiom's true etymology.[10] But we do argue against the postulate that it never is and that only "folk etymology" and/or such interpretation of the underlying image which is consistent with the present-day world knowledge can be relevant to the processing and usage of conventional figurative language. The result of these considerations is that the study of motivation must include an etymological description. Only at the next stage of analysis can it be determined whether the data obtained via etymological analysis are consistent with the usage conditions of a given lexical unit and whether the "etymological memory" is, therefore, a part of the image component.

5. Summary

Most idioms are motivated in some way. The study of idiom motivation is an important linguistic issue because motivation may influence the way an idiom is used. Motivation is neither a purely psychological nor an etymological phenomenon. The motivational basis of an idiom consists of linguistically relevant traces of the underlying image rather than of the image itself. Some of these traces are part of the conceptual basis of the idiom. This kind of image trace makes up the so-called image component of idiom semantics, and, in this sense, they are part of the content plane of the idiom. As for etymology, it rarely forms the motivational basis of an idiom. But as our case study shows, there are occasional cases where it may. Sometimes idioms are motivated by the knowledge of texts that served as the idioms' origin sources, i.e. by factors of intertextuality. However, speakers are mostly not aware of these textual sources, i.e. intertextuality is a part of an idiom's etymological description, rather than a relevant motivational factor. Idioms which have textual sources are perceived as motivated only because speakers address their metaphoric or symbolic basis, i.e. speakers interpret the underlying concept that is fixed in the metaphor or in the cultural symbol contained in the lexical structure of the idiom and correlate the results of their interpretation with the lexicalized meaning of the idiom. This does not mean that the true etymology of an idiom may not play any role in linguistic research. First, it is a significant task to compare the true etymology with the synchronically relevant motivational basis. And second, in the case of some idioms "etymological memory" (compare Section 4.2) may have a role to play in motivation. In these cases, a given idiom may exhibit restrictions on its use that can only be explained by addressing its history, i.e. these idioms cannot be used in contexts that are not compatible with their etymological origins.

University of Vienna
Steinfurt, Germany

Notes

Correspondence address: piirainen@t-online.de

1. We use the term *idiom* in the European tradition. The consensus here is that idioms are the central and most irregular group of phrasemes. For the discussion of idiom motivation see among others: Vinogradov 1947; Burger et al. 1982; Gréciano 2002; Dobrovol'skij 1995, 1997, 2007: 790–795; Burger 2007a; Burger 2007b; Baranov and Dobrovol'skij 2008.
2. For results of psycholinguistic experiments on *idiom processing* compare overview papers, such as Häcki Buhofer 2007; Gibbs and Colston 2007; Skoufaki 2009.
3. There are also a few minor motivation types (e.g. so-called *kinetic idioms, play on words* or *indexal motivation*); for more detail, see Langlotz 2006: 120–170; Burger 1976, 2007a: 62–67, 2007b: 101; Burger et al. 1982: 56–60; Dobrovol'skij and Piirainen 2005: 87–101, 2009: 19–38.
4. For the discussion of this term in the phraseological literature see among others Dobrovol'skij and Piirainen 1997, 2005, 2009; Piirainen 1998; Burger 2007b: 93–94; Ďurčo 2007: 731–732; Dobrovol'skij 2007: 794–795.
5. On the notion of semantic analyzability or decomposability of idioms, cf. Rajxštejn 1980; Dobrovol'skij 1982, 2004, 2007; Nunberg et al. 1994; Langlotz 2006; Dobrovol'skij and Piirainen 2009: 43–60.
6. Phraseology researchers use it with different meanings, often in the sense of *interdiscursivity*. For example, Burger 1991 applies it to the availability of pre-fabricated text fragments (aphorisms, slogans, book titles etc.) and their interweaving in a text. See also Piirainen 2005, 2010: 17–22.
7. These depictions have often been discussed in works on history of painting. For an overview, see Metken 1996; Jaritz 1997.
8. Similar experiences are reported by Yu (1995: 161–163) when he attempted to confirm the well-known ANGER IS HEAT metaphors by means of the large Bank of English corpus. Various metaphoric expressions turned out to be rare or did not occur at all in the corpus.

9. In text corpora it appears, for the main part, in newspaper sport reports on football and similar kinds of sport where it is used in the sense of 'to be winning, superior to the opponent', chiefly said about the teams and clubs. These texts do not help in answering the question whether the idiom is gender-restricted or not. In everyday language, the meaning of the idiom is close to that of idiom (19a,b).
10. The exhaustive description of an idiom should include its motivating links as well as an etymological comment. Langacker (2005) points to the fact that dictionaries should make it clear that lexemes give access to domains of independent knowledge, instead of just providing a concise definition.

References

Aarne, Antti & Stith Thompson. 1961. *The types of the folktale: A classification and bibliography.* Helsinki: Suomalainen Tiedeakatemia.
Allan, Kathryn. 2006. On groutnolls and nog-heads: A case study of the interaction between culture and cognition in intelligence metaphors. In Anatol Stefanowitsch & Stefan Th. Gries (eds.), *Corpus-based approaches to metaphor and metonymy*, 175–190. Berlin & New York: Mouton de Gruyter.
Apperson, George Latimer. 1969 [1929]. *English proverbs and proverbial phrases: A historical dictionary.* London & Toronto: Dent.
Baranov, Anatolj & Dmitrij Dobrovol'skij. 1996. Cognitive modeling of actual meaning in the field of phraseology. *Journal of Pragmatics* 25. 409–429.
Baranov, Anatolj & Dmitrij Dobrovol'skij. 2000. Tipologija formal'nyx operacij pri poroždenii aktual'nogo značenija idiomy. [Typology of formal operations at generation of idioms' actual meaning] *Linguistische Arbeitsberichte* 7. 7–20.
Baranov, Anatolj & Dmitrij Dobrovol'skij. 2008. *Aspekty teorii frazeologii.* [Aspects of a theory of phraseology] Moscow: Znak.
Bierich, Alexander, Valerij M. Mokienko & Ljudmila I. Stepanova. 2005. *Russkaja frazeologija. Istoriko-ëtimologičeskij slovar'* [Russian phraseology. Historical-etymological dictionary]. Moscow: Astrel'.
Binovič, Leonid E. & Nikolaj N. Grišin. 1975. *Nemecko-russkij frazeologičeskij slovar' = Deutsch-russisches phraseologisches Wörterbuch.* Moscow: Russkij jazyk.
Brewer's dictionary of phrase & fable. 2005. 17th edn. Revised by John Ayto. London: Weidenfeld & Nicolson.
Burger, Harald. 1976. "Die achseln zucken". – Zur sprachlichen Kodierung nichtsprachlicher Kommunikation. *Wirkendes Wort* 26. 311–334.
Burger, Harald. 1991. Phraseologie und Intertextualität. In Christine Palm (ed.), *EUROPHRAS 90: Akten der internationalen Tagung der germanistischen Phraseologieforschung, Aske/Schweden, 12.–15. Juni 1990*, 13–27. Uppsala: Almquist & Wiksell International.
Burger, Harald. 2007a [1998]. *Phraseologie: Eine Einführung am Beispiel des Deutschen.* Berlin: Erich Schmidt.

Burger, Harald. 2007b. Semantic aspects of phrasemes. In Harald Burger, Dmitrij Dobrovol'skij, Peter Kühn & Neal R. Norrick (eds.), *Phraseology: An international handbook of contemporary research*, 90–109. Berlin & New York: de Gruyter.

Burger, Harald, Annelies Buhofer & Ambros Sialm. 1982. *Handbuch der Phraseologie*. Berlin & New York: Walter de Gruyter.

Burger, Harald, Dmitrij Dobrovol'skij, Peter Kühn & Neal R. Norrick (eds.). 2007. *Phraseology: An international handbook of contemporary research*. Berlin & New York: de Gruyter.

Cornette, James. 1997. *Proverbs and proverbial expressions in the German works of Martin Luther*. Bern et al.: Peter Lang.

Deignan, Alice. 2005. *Metaphor and corpus linguistics*. Amsterdam & Philadelphia: Benjamins.

Deignan, Alice. 2006. The grammar of linguistic metaphors. In Anatol Stefanowitsch & Stefan Th. Gries (eds.), *Corpus-based approaches to metaphor and metonymy*, 106–122. Berlin & New York: Mouton de Gruyter.

Dobrovol'skij, Dmitrij O. 1982. Zum Problem der phraseologisch gebundenen Bedeutung. *Beiträge zur Erforschung der deutschen Sprache* 2. 52–67.

Dobrovol'skij, Dmitrij O. 1995. *Kognitive Aspekte der Idiom-Semantik: Studien zum Thesaurus deutscher Idiome*. Tübingen: Narr.

Dobrovol'skij, Dmitrij O. 1997. *Idiome im mentalen Lexikon: Ziele und Methoden der kognitivbasierten Phraseologieforschung*. Trier: WVT.

Dobrovol'skij, Dmitrij O. 2004. Idiome aus kognitiver Sicht. In Kathrin Steyer (ed.), *Wortverbindungen – mehr oder weniger fest*, 117–143. Berlin & New York: de Gruyter.

Dobrovol'skij, Dmitrij O. 2007. Cognitive approaches to idiom analysis. In Burger, Harald, Dmitrij Dobrovol'skij, Peter Kühn & Neal R. Norrick (eds.), *Phraseology: An international handbook of contemporary research*, 789–818. Berlin & New York: de Gruyter.

Dobrovol'skij, Dmitrij O. & Elisabeth Piirainen. 1997. *Symbole in Sprache und Kultur. Studien zur Phraseologie aus kultursemiotischer Perspektive*. Bochum: Brockmeyer.

Dobrovol'skij, Dmitrij O. & Elisabeth Piirainen. 2005. *Figurative language: Cross-cultural and cross-linguistic perspectives*. Amsterdam et al.: Elsevier.

Dobrovol'skij, Dmitrij O. & Elisabeth Piirainen. 2009. *Zur Theorie der Phraseologie: Kognitive und kulturelle Aspekte*. Tübingen: Stauffenburg.

Ďurčo, Peter. 2007. Slovak phraseology. In Burger, Harald, Dmitrij Dobrovol'skij, Peter Kühn & Neal R. Norrick (eds.), *Phraseology: An international handbook of contemporary research*, 728–736. Berlin & New York: de Gruyter.

Flavell, Linda & Roger Flavell. 2006. *Dictionary of idioms and their origins*. London: Kyle Cathie.

Gibbs, Raymond W. 1993. Why idioms are not dead metaphors. In Christina Cacciari & Patrizia Tabossi (eds.), *Idioms: Processing, structure, and interpretation*, 57–77. Hillsdale, NJ: Lawrence Erlbaum.

Gibbs, Raymond W. & Herbert L. Colston. 2007. Psycholinguistic aspects of phraseology: American tradition. In Burger, Harald, Dmitrij Dobrovol'skij, Peter Kühn & Neal R.

Norrick (eds.), *Phraseology: An international handbook of contemporary research*, 319–336. Berlin & New York: de Gruyter.

Gréciano, Gertrud. 2002. Semantik und Herkunftserklärungen von Phraseologismen. In Alan Cruse, Franz Hundsnurscher, Michael Job & Peter Rolf Lutzeier (eds.), *Lexicology: An International handbook on the nature and structure of words and vocabularies*, 433–441. Berlin: de Gruyter.

Häcki Buhofer, Annelies. 2007. Psycholinguistic aspects of phraseology: European tradition. In Burger, Harald, Dmitrij Dobrovol'skij, Peter Kühn & Neal R. Norrick (eds.), *Phraseology: An international handbook of contemporary research*, 836–853. Berlin & New York: de Gruyter.

Hanks, Patrick. 2006. Metaphoricity is gradable. In Anatol Stefanowitsch & Stefan Th. Gries (eds.), *Corpus-based approaches to metaphor and metonymy*, 17–35. Berlin & New York: Mouton de Gruyter.

Jaritz, Gerhard. 1997. Die Bruoch. In Gertrud Blaschitz, Helmut Hundsbichler, Gerhard Jaritz & Elisabeth Vavra (eds.), *Symbole des Alltag: Alltag der Symbole. Festschrift für Harry Kühnel zum 65. Geburtstag*, 395–416. Graz: Akad. Dr.- und Verl.-Anst.

Lakoff, George. 1987. *Women, fire, and dangerous things: What categories reveal about the mind*. Chicago & London: Chicago University Press.

Lakoff, George. 1990. The invariance hypothesis: Is abstract reason based on image-schemas? *Cognitive Linguistics* 1. 39–74.

Lakoff, George & Mark Johnson. 1980. *Metaphors we live by*. Chicago & London: Chicago University Press.

Langacker, Ronald W. 2005. Cognitive grammar: The state of the art and related issues. An interview with Ronald Langacker, by Jozsef Andor. *Acta Linguistica Hungarica*, 52(4). 341–366.

Langlotz, Andreas. 2006. *Idiomatic creativity: A cognitive-linguistic model of idiom-representation and idiom-variation in English*. Amsterdam: Benjamins.

Longman. 1998. *Longman idiom dictionary*. Harlow: Addison Wesley Longman.

Metken, Sigrid. 1996. *Der Kampf um die Hose. Geschlechterstreit und die Macht im Haus: Die Geschichte eines Symbols*. Frankfurt/M et al.: Campus.

Mokienko Valerij M. 1989 [1980]. *Slavjanskaja frazeologija* [Slavic phraseology]. Moscow: Vysšaja škola.

Nunberg, Geoffrey, Ivan A. Sag & Thomas Wasow. 1994. Idioms. *Language* 70. 491–538.

Piirainen, Elisabeth. 1998. Phraseology and research on symbols. In Peter Ďurčo (ed.), *International symposium Europhras '97. September 2–5, 1997, Liptovský Ján: Phraseology and paremiology*, 280–287. Bratislava: Akadémia PZ.

Piirainen, Elisabeth. 2001. Der hat aber Haare auf den Zähnen! Geschlechtsspezifik in der deutschen Phraseologie. In Rudolf Hoberg (ed.), *Sprache-Erotik-Sexualität*, 283–307. Berlin: Erich Schmidt.

Piirainen, Elisabeth. 2005. Colorless green ideas oder Am Anfang war der Prätext. "Bildungstrümmer" und Streitkultur in wissenschaftlichen Titeln. In Ulla Kleinberger Günther, Annelies Häcki Buhofer & Elisabeth Piirainen (eds.), *"Krieg und Frieden": Auseinandersetzung und Versöhnung in Diskursen*, 175–193.Tübingen: Francke.

Piirainen, Elisabeth. 2010. Common features in the phraseology of European languages: Cultural and areal perspectives. In Jarmo Korhonen, Wolfgang Mieder, Elisabeth Piirainen & Rosa Piñel (eds.), *Phraseologie global – areal – regional: Akten der Konferenz EUROPHRAS 2008 vom 13.–16.8.2008 in Helsinki*, 15–27. Tübingen: Gunter Narr.

Pohlke, Reinhard. 2008. *Das wissen nur die Götter: Deutsche Redensarten aus dem Griechischen*. Düsseldorf: Patmos.

Rajxštejn, Aleksandr D. 1980. *Sopostavitel'nyj analiz nemeckoj i russkoj frazeologii* [Contrastive analysis of German and Russian phraseology]. Moscow: Vysšaja škola.

Rosch, Eleanor. 1975. Cognitive representations of semantic categories. *Journal of Experimental Psychology: General* 104. 192–233.

Rosch, Eleanor. 1978. Principles of categorization. In Eleanor Rosch & Barbara B. Lloyd (eds.), *Cognition and categorization*, 27–48. Hillsdale NJ: Erlbaum.

Sabban, Annette. 2008. Critical observations on the culture-boundness of phraseology. In Sylviane Granger & Fanny Meunier (eds.), *Phraseology: An interdisciplinary perspective*, 229–241. Amsterdam & Philadelphia: Benjamins.

Skoufaki, Sophia. 2009. Investigating the source of idiom transparency intuitions. *Metaphor and Symbol* 24. 20–41.

Taylor, Archer. 1962 [1931]. *The proverb and an index to the proverb*. Hartbo: Folklore Associates.

Taylor, Ronald & Walter Gottschalk 1966. *A German-English dictionary of idioms*. Munich: Hueber.

Tolstoj, Nikita I. 1973. O rekonstrukcii praslavjanskoj frazeologii. [On reconstruction of the Proto-Slavic phraseology]. In *Slavjanskoe jazykoznanie. VIII Meždunarodnyj s'ezd slavistov. Doklady sovetskoi delegacii*, 272–294. Moskva: Nauka.

Vinogradov, Viktor V. 1947. Ob osnovnych tipach frazeologičeskich edinic v sovremennom russkom jazyke [Basic types of phraseological units in present-day Russian]. In *Izbrannye trudy. Leksikologija i leksikografija* (V. V. Vinogradov, 1977), 140–162. Moscow: Nauka.

Wanzeck, Christiane. 2003. *Zur Etymologie lexikalisierter Farbverbindungen. Untersuchungen anhand der Farben Rot, Gelb, Grün und Blau*. Amsterdam & New York: Rodopi.

Yu, Ning. 1995. Metaphorical expressions of anger and happiness in English and Chinese. *Metaphor and Symbolic Activity* 10. 59–92.

Ist ein idiomatischer Ausdruck immer expressiv? Korpusbasierte und fragebogengestützte Beobachtungen zu einer verbreiteten Prämisse

GÜNTER SCHMALE

Abstract

The proposition that all idiomatic expressions are expressive seems to be widely assumed in different linguistic disciplines. For example, Gertud Gréciano (1983) states that – in the process of reformulation of textual development – idiomatic paraphrases tend towards greater expressivity than their non idiomatic semantic equivalents, whereas non idiomatic paraphrases of idiomatic expressions are conversely rational, matter-of-fact, unemotional. This can be taken to be a testable hypothesis. It is shown not to be corroborated and instead, the data outlined below show that Burger's (1998) and in particular Drescher's (1997) view that the (potential) expressivity of idiomatic expressions may develop within specific contexts is supported.

The present article sets out to study the hypothesis of the inherently expressive nature of idiomatic expressions using data taken from a specific context, namely a 32-hour-corpus of German television talk shows. While talk shows have an institutionalized nature, they do provide basically authentic communicative interactions. This makes it possible to study displayed[1] expressivity from a corpus-based, holistic and multimodal perspective. This, in turn, provides a number of relevant criteria for judging whether an idiom is expressive by means of empirical criteria from authentic conversational contexts rather than from made-up examples.

Unfortunately, given that the talk show corpus contains only one metadiscursive activity which has the possibility of manifesting the idiom producer's or receiver's interpretation of an idiom's expressiveness (auf gut Deutsch man ist der letzte Dreck – to say it in plain language/in so many words you are being treated like dirt), the potentially expressive character of an idiom can only be indirectly deduced from different phenomena such as topics like love, separation, violence which are a priori likely to provoke emotional behaviour; conversational phases like arguments, exaltations, quarrels involving high personal involvement; prosodic features such as strong accents, intensity, changing fundamental frequency, speed; nonverbal characteristics, e.g. intensity of gaze, smiling, sad/happy facial expression, aggressive gesture, proximity/distance. Analysis of such elements was systematically carried out within their conversational contexts, deviation from the speaker's "normal" way of speaking being an important criterion for deciding as to the contingent expressivity of an idiom.

Based on these phenomena as potential signals of expressivity, three types of reformulations involving idiomatic expressions are studied in their sequential conversational environments:

- *idiomatic paraphrases of non idiomatic constructions, e.g. ich kann ihn ja nicht zurückhalten, ich kann ihn ja nicht in Ketten legen – I can't hold him back, I can't put him in chains/fetters;*
- *idiomatic paraphrases of another phraseological expression, e.g. so einen würd ich doch laufen lassen [...] dann würd ich so einen doch in den Wind schießen – I would let him go [...] I would send him packing;*
- *non idiomatic paraphrases of idiomatic expressions, e.g. manchmal sind sie sogar wie FEU:ER und WASSE:R [...] unterschiedlicher könnten sie eigentlich nicht sein – they're like fire and water [...] they couldn't be more different.*

Detailed analyses of seven examples of the three mentioned types of paraphrases reveal that, strictly speaking, no definite, intersubjectively verifiable proof for the expressiveness of idioms exists. In many cases, none of the characteristics mentioned above apply as speakers use idioms without any deviation from their normal way of speaking. Only sporadically can one conclude – indirectly – that there is an increased degree of speaker involvement when – talking about a potentially emotionally connotated subject – a highly metaphorical and/or figurative idiom is produced using specific prosodic and nonverbal means which are not part of the normal expressive range of the speaker. However, there is no definite display of whether the participants themselves consider the idiomatic sequences in question as expressive.

The study therefore turns to folk judgements. In order to obtain information on folk judgements of the expressiveness of idioms, a questionnaire of 15 items was designed asking non-specialized subjects to rate the idiomatic or non idiomatic part of a briefly contextualized paraphrase as more or less expressive and to explain the reasons for their decision. The results were unexpected and counter to the expressiveness hypothesis being tested in this paper. In almost 50% of the presented sequences, subjects (over and under 40 years old) rated the non-idiomatic or non-figurative expression as more expressive than the idiomatic, metaphorical, figurative one, e.g. langsam und faul sein – be slow and lazy as more expressive than nicht in die Pötte kommen – never get anything done. Subjects mainly considered idioms as more expressive than their non idiomatic paraphrases when they were highly metaphorical and/or figurative as put someone in chains; treat someone like dirt/shit; be like fire and water; have butterflies in one's stomach etc. – provided they did not judge them as old-fashioned, trivializing, ironical, or "beating about the bush". Whenever this was the case, subjects judged the non-idiomatic, non figurative variant to be more precise, direct, getting straight to the point. It has to be pointed out, however, that subjects had only the written sequences at their disposal and therefore could not make judgements based on prosodic or nonverbal criteria. It is therefore likely that it is not the idiomatic nature of a phraseological expression which induces a perception of expressiveness, but particular prosodic, nonverbal, situational or contextual elements which allow an (not obsolete) idiom to develop its expressive potential within specific conversational contexts. This supports the hypothesis of Burger and Drescher.

Keywords: idiomatic expressions; expressivity; paraphrases; corpus-based study; questionnaire survey; folk beliefs.

1. Inhärente Expressivität idiomatisch-bildlich-metaphorischer Ausdrücke

Im Anschluss an Ballys (1909) These, dass spezifische sprachliche Mittel zum Ausdruck expressiver Inhalte existieren, gehen nicht nur Arbeiten aus der Stilistik, sondern auch aus der Linguistik und insbesondere der Phraseologieforschung häufig davon aus, dass idiomatische Ausdrücke aufgrund der verwendeten Metaphern und/oder Bilder[2] grundsätzlich besonders ausdrucksstark sind. So beispielsweise Riesel (1989): „Je höher die Bildkraft der Sprechweise in Lexik und Phraseologie ist, desto stärker wird ihr Gefühlswert" (Riesel 1989: 25). Auch Bardosi et al. (2003: x) sind davon überzeugt, dass der bildhafte Charakter der Redewendung „*tirer les ves du nez de qn*"[3] gegenüber seinem nicht-phraseologischen Pendant „*questionner habilement qn pour lui faire dire des choses qu'il veut cacher*"[4] einen „semantischen Mehrwert" besitzt, der in einer emotional-expressiven Färbung besteht.[5] „Je nach Einstellung des Sprechers kann hier eine gewisse Bewunderung mitschwingen oder aber auch das Gegenteil der Fall sein, nämlich Verachtung zum Ausdruck kommen" (Bardosi et al. 1989: x).

Gréciano (1983) geht ebenfalls davon aus, dass im Verlaufe der textuellen Entwicklung eine idiomatische Paraphrase eines nicht-idiomatischen Ausdrucks hin zu mehr Expressivität tendiert, während die nicht-phraseologische Paraphrase eines idiomatischen Ausdrucks mehr Rationalität oder Sachlichkeit impliziert als dieser. „Si l'E I (= expression idiomatique; GS) précède le terme impliqué, sa définition ou sa glose, la progression est perçue comme évoluant vers une synthèse rationnelle. Si l'idiotisme, au contraire, suit les paraphrases en question, le texte développe son pouvoir expressif, jouant sur les symbolisations possibles. Il déploie alors son impact sur l'imagination et l'émotion du lecteur. [...]" (Gréciano 1983: 235).[6]

Im Gegensatz dazu postuliert Drescher (1997), dass Expressivität nur im Rahmen eines interaktiven und holistischen Ansatzes bestimmt werden kann. „Phraseologismen werden häufig mit der expressiven Färbung der Rede in Verbindung gebracht. [...] Nicht ein sprachliches Zeichen ist expressiv, sondern seine Verwendung in einer bestimmten Interaktionssituation. Daher muss sich der Akzent der Analysen verschieben von der Betrachtung isolierter Phänomene hin zu einer holistischen Sicht von Interaktionssequenzen" (Drescher 1997: 67, 70).

Ähnlich wie Drescher (1997) plädiert Burger (1998) für ein differenzierteres Verständnis von Expressivität, indem er diesen Begriff durch den des „konnotativen Mehrwertes" zu ersetzen vorschlägt. „Viele Phraseologismen haben unter konnotativen Aspekten ein Plus gegenüber entsprechenden einfachen Wörtern bzw. gegenüber einer nicht-phraseologischen äquivalenten Formulierung. Zum Teil handelt es sich dabei um latente Eigenschaften, die erst in bestimmten Kontexten wirksam werden" (Burger 1998: 78).

Dieser von Burger (1998) formulierte Grundsatz findet sich i.Ü. schon bei Drescher (1997), die im Rahmen ihres ganzheitlichen interaktiven Ansatzes weitere Annahmen expliziert:

– kein sprachliches Mittel ist *a priori* expressiv, diese Qualität erhält es erst in bestimmten kommunikativen Kontexten, was bedeutet, dass eine kommunikative Sequenz nicht allein durch die Präsenz eines idiomatischen Ausdrucks expressiven Charakter erhält, sondern dass noch andere Faktoren hinzukommen müssen;
– die Existenz von Gefühlen oder Emotionen ist keine *conditio sine qua non* für die Produktion expressiver Äußerungen;
– die Expressiviät einer Äußerung ist Folge des Zusammenspiels segmentaler, suprasegmentaler, non-verbaler, sequentieller, situationeller und sozialer Faktoren in spezifischen konversationellen Kontexten.

Diese Prinzipien eines holistischen interaktiven Ansatzes sollen nun im Anschluss an Grécianos (1983) Aussagen zur Expressivität idiomatischer

Paraphrasen bei der Analyse unterschiedlicher Typen derartiger Reformulierungen, die in einem Talkshow-Korpus erhoben wurden, zugrunde gelegt werden. Im Anschluss an eine kurze Darstellung des Korpus und der darin untersuchten phraseologischen Aspekte (Pkt. 2) sowie Vorüberlegungen zu Phänomenen des Ausdrucks von Expressivität (Pkt. 3) sollen im Hauptabschnitt des vorliegenden Beitrags drei verschiedene Typen idiomatischer Paraphrasen auf Spuren von Expressivität auf verschiedenen Ebenen der multimodalen Kommunikation untersucht werden (Pkt. 4). Angesichts der kaum endgültigen Aufschluss erbringenden Ergebnisse, was die verbalen und nonverbalen Spuren von Expressivität idiomatischer Paraphrasen angeht, sollen in Punkt 5. die Ergebnisse einer Fragebogenstudie unter Muttersprachlern des Deutschen diskutiert werden, in der diese gefragt wurden, welchen Ausdruck sie aus welchen Gründen für expressiver halten, den phraseologisch-idiomatischen oder den nicht-phraseologischen. Abschließend werden im Punkt 6. Überlegungen zu „folk beliefs" über die Expressivität idiomatischer Ausdrücke und deren Kontextabhängigkeit angestellt.

2. Untersuchung der Expressivität idiomatischer Ausdrücke auf der Grundlage eines Talkshow-Korpus

Bei der Untersuchung der Präsenz, Verwendung und Funktion phraseologischer Ausdrücke in einem 32-stündigen Korpus[7] sämtlicher zu der Zeit existierenden deutschen Talkshows aus den Jahren 1998 und 1999 fiel auf, dass idiomatische Ausdrücke, insbesondere dann, wenn diese metaphorisch und/oder bildlich sind, in unterschiedlicher Weise konversationell bearbeitet werden.

Der Begriff der konversationellen Bearbeitung impliziert, dass Interaktionsbeteiligte vor, während oder nach der Äußerung idiomatischer Phraseme verbale oder non-verbale Aktivitäten vollziehen, die sich unmittelbar auf die betreffenden Idiome beziehen. Neben sehr häufig vorkommenden Reormulierungen[8] von Phrasemen (vgl. Schmale 2001b, 2007) oder durch solche findet man auch, allerdings weniger häufig, metadiskursive Aktivitäten (vgl. Schmale 2009), Wortspiele (vgl. Schmale 2005a), begleitende nonverbale Aktivitäten (vgl. Schmale 2005b), die idiomatische Ausdrücke in unterschiedlicher Weise konversationell bearbeiten.

Im Anschluss an die oben zitierte Aussage Grécianos (1983) soll es im vorliegenden Aufsatz allein um Paraphrasen *von* Idiomen oder *durch* sie gehen, um zu untersuchen, ob tatsächlich konversationelle Indikatoren dafür vorliegen, dass idiomatische Paraphrasen in bestimmten Kontexten hin zu mehr Ausdrucksstärke tendieren, während bei nicht-idiomatischen Paraphrasen idiomatischer Ausdrücke das Gegenteil eintritt, nämlich ein Verlust von Expressivität.

Im Anschluss an Gülich und Kotschi (1987) wird unter einer Paraphrase eine semantische Äquivalenz im weiteren Sinne vom Typ „x R y" verstanden, wobei R Äquivalenz der Signifikate von X und Y bezeichnet, deren Signifikanten allerdings unterschiedlich sind.[9] Drei Typen phraseologischer Paraphrasen wurden anhand des Korpus untersucht:

1. idiomatische Paraphrasen nicht-idiomatischer Bezugsausdrücke: „$x_{nicht-PHR}$ R y_{PHR}" vom Typ *sehr gerne essen – kein Kostverächter sein;*
2. idiomatische und/oder phraseologische Paraphrasen bereits idiomatischer bzw. phraseologischer Bezugsausdrücke: „x_{PHR-1} R y_{PHR-2}" vom Typ *klar Tisch machen*[10] *– ein klärendes Gespräch führen;*
3. nicht-idiomatische Paraphrasen idiomatischer Bezugsausdrücke: „x_{PHR} R $y_{nicht-PHR}$" vom Typ *jedem Tierchen sein Pläsierchen – jeder soll so leben wie er es für richtig hält.*

3. Hinweise auf die Expressivität idiomatischer Paraphrasen

Welche verbalen und nonverbalen Phänome könnten nun darauf schließen lassen, dass in einer Sequenz verbaler Interaktion ein Expressivitätszuwachs bzw. -verlust vorliegt? Im Sinne „konversationsanalytischer Mentalität" läge dann ein „idealer" Indikator vor, wenn Interaktionsbeteiligte selbst, der Produzent der Paraphrase oder noch besser: der interpretierende Gesprächspartner, im Verlaufe der konversationellen Aushandlung durch metadiskursive Aktivitäten mehr oder weniger explizit ausdrücken, dass sie eine Äußerung oder einen Bestandteil davon für *expressiv* halten, wie dies im folgenden Beispiel der Fall ist (vgl. auch Schmale/in Vorb.).

(1) HM saß wegen Pädophilieverdachts unschuldig über ein Jahr im Gefängnis[11]
Bio: man is man **is** in der Hierarchie der Gefangenen **ganz unten**;
HM: ja *auf gut Deutsch man man is der letzte Dreck*.

Hier wird die idiomatische Paraphrase *man is der letzte Dreck* des Phrasems *ganz unten sein* durch die metakommunikative Routineformel *auf gut Deutsch* eingeleitet, die laut Duden 11 (1998) einen Sachverhalt „unverblümt, beschönigend" Duden 11, 1998: 151) ausdrückt, in der Regel jedoch dann gebraucht zu werden scheint, wenn der Produzent einer Äußerung diese für besonders derb oder vulgär, also aufgrund der Abweichung von einer in der vorliegenden Situation angemessenen lexikalen Norm für expressiv hält.[12]

Leider handelt es sich hier um das einzige Beispiel dieses Typs im vorhandenen Korpus; der Konversationsanalytiker muss sich deshalb mit weniger eindeutigen Spuren der Expressivität, die er auf der Gesprächsoberfläche vorfindet, begnügen. Derartige Spuren, die auf die besondere Expressivität einer Aktivität oder Sequenz, die eine idiomatische Wendung enthält, hinweisen mögen, können suprasegmentaler oder nonverbaler, aber auch thematischer und situativer Natur, d.h. insbesondere in bestimmten Kontexten oder Gesprächssequenzen auftreten, vor allem wenn es um *a priori* emotional besetzte Themen wie Liebe, Trennung, Konflikte oder auch spezifische konversationelle Phasen wie Exaltation, Streit, Argumentation geht, bei denen Beteiligte ein besonders hohes Maß an Sprecherbeteiligung demonstrieren, wobei es für die Konversationsanalyse gleichgültig ist, ob diese echt ist oder nur vorgegeben wird.[13]

Auf prosodischer Ebene können starke Akzentuierung von Äußerungsteilen, Sprechgeschwindigkeit, Lautstärke, Tonhöhe/Grundfrequenz, Intonation usw. in bestimmten Ko- und Kontexten auf Expressivität hindeuten.

Auf nonverbaler Ebene können es Intensität und Dauer des Blickkontakts, Mimik: Lächeln, trauriger oder glücklicher Gesichtsausdruck, Gestik: agressive Gesten wie der Stinkefinger oder besonders intensive Hand- und Armbewegungen, Körperhaltungen: Distanz/Nähe, fallende Schultern sein, die auf Expressivität des Sprechers hinweisen.

Bei der Analyse derartiger Elemente, die grundsätzlich in ihrem sequentiellen Kontext zu erfolgen hat, spielt der Begriff der Abweichung eine wesentliche Rolle. Er impliziert, dass die Form bestimmter segmentaler, suprasegmentaler oder nonverbaler Phänomene von einer Grundform, die für den Produzenten der betreffenden Äußerung als eine Art Norm gelten kann, in derartiger Weise abweicht, dass man auf deren Expressivität in der vorgängigen Kommunikationssituation schließen kann. Der Produzent einer idiomatischen Wendung könnte diese demzufolge schneller, lauter, stärker akzentuierend, in einer anderen Tonlage artikulieren als üblich oder aber nonverbal in seiner Mimik (Ausdruck von Wut oder Freude) oder Gestik (Erregung, Akzentuierung bestimmter Lexeme) von seinem „normalen" sprachlichen Handeln abweichend agieren.

Im folgenden Abschnitt soll nun anhand der drei skizzierten idiomatischen Paraphrasetypen untersucht werden, inwieweit die angeführten suprasegmentalen und/oder nonverbalen Mittel die Produktion idiomatischer Ausdrücke in spezifischen Ko- und Kontexten begleiten und so auf die Expressivität der betreffenden Idiome enthaltenden Sequenzen schließen lassen könnten. Um es noch einmal zu wiederholen: angesichts fehlender expliziter Aktivitäten der Beteiligten, die direkt oder auch indirekt die Expressivität eines idiomatischen Ausdrucks thematisieren, kann es nicht darum gehen, anhand bestimmter Faktoren auf die inhärente Expressivität bestimmter idiomatischer Ausdrücke zu schließen. Vielmehr muss das Ziel der folgenden Korpusanalysen sein, expressive Elemente bestimmter Sequenzen, in denen idiomatische Paraphrasen vorhanden sind, herauszuarbeiten, um so mit aller gebotenen Vorsicht auf eine mögliche sequentielle Expressivität von Idiomen zu schließen.

4. Expressivität idiomatischer Paraphrasen

Vorausgeschickt sei, dass bei der folgenden Analyse idiomatische Ausdrücke unberücksichtigt bleiben, die direkt oder indirekt[14] Gefühle oder Emotionen ausdrücken, wie z.B. *die Schnauze voll haben* oder *sich vor Angst in die Hose machen*. Hier soll es vielmehr um „neutrale" Idiome gehen, z.B. *kein Kostverächter sein* oder *reinen Tisch machen*, die nicht schon per se bestimmte Einstellungen thematisieren. Bei der Untersuchung der unterschiedlichen Paraphrasetypen sollen nun zunächst idiomatische Paraphrasen nicht-phraseologischer Ausdrücke bzw. anderer Phraseme behandelt werden, im Anschluss daran nicht-phraseologische Paraphrasen idiomatischer Ausdrücke, d.h. von einer potentiellen Zunahme an Expressivität hin zu einem Verlust bzw. einer Abnahme derselben.

Eine kurze Vorbemerkung zu den in den nachstehenden Analysen verwendeten Begriffen *idiomatisch, metaphorisch, bildlich und bildhaft* im Anschluss an Burger (1989) und (1998). Idiomatisch ist ein Phrasem, dessen Gesamtbedeutung nicht durch spezifische semantische Verfahren kompositionell erschließbar ist und/oder bestimmte syntaktische und/oder semantische Abweichungen von der modernen Standardnorm (z.B. veraltete Genitivkonstruktionen oder unikale Komponenten) bzw. stilistische Merkmale wie Reim oder Rhythmus usw. enthalten.

Einen Phraseologismus, der *metaphorisch* bzw. *bildhaft/bildlich* ist, definiert Burger (1989) wie folgt: „Ein metaphorischer Phraseologismus stellt einen abstrakten Sachverhalt in einem konkret vorstellbaren Modell dar." (Burger 1989: 26) Ein abstrakter Sachverhalt ist dann konkret vorstellbar und folglich metaphorisch, wenn er *bildlich* ist, d.h. einen abstrakten Vorgang durch einen konkret vorstellbaren, wie z.B. bei *Öl ins Feuer gießen* oder *das fünfte Rad am Wagen (sein)*, konzeptualisiert. Andererseits können phraseologische Ausdrücke zwar *bildhaft* sein, d.h. konkrete visuelle Vorstellungen hervorrufen, wie z.B. *jmdm. einen Korb geben* oder *jmdm. Zucker in den Arsch blasen*, die aber nicht bildlich sind, da sie streng genommen keinen abstrakten Sachverhalt konzeptualisieren. Aufgrund der häufig schwierigen Abgrenzbarkeit beider Begriffe schlägt Burger (1998: 92) allerdings vor, sie durch das einheitliche Konzept des „bildkräftigen Ausdruckes" zu ersetzen.

4.1. Idiomatische Paraphrasen nicht-phraseologischer Ausdrücke: "$x_{nicht-PHR}$ R y_{PHR}"

Entsprechend der zitierten These Grécianos (1983) müsste in den folgenden Konversationssequenzen die idiomatische Paraphrase jeweils expressiver sein als der paraphrasierte nicht-idiomatische Bezugsausdruck, folglich auch im nachstehenden Ausschnitt aus einem Talkshow-Gespräch.

(2) Jörg Pilawa fragt Gast Patrizia nach den Gründen für ihr starkes Übergewicht
P: aber auch n großer Grund is eigentlich dass ich **sehr gerne esse** auch Essen zubereite- Gäste einlade- (.) und **kein Kostverächter** bin also:-

Hier müsste die idiomatische Paraphrase *(dass ich) kein Kostverächter bin* expressiver sein als der durch sie paraphrasierte Bezugsausdruck *(dass ich) sehr gerne esse*.

Allerdings gibt es für diese Annahme in der verbalen und nonverbalen Kommunikationsstruktur der Sequenz keinerlei konkrete Indizien, weder auf prosodischer noch auf mimisch-gestischer Ebene, da die Sprecherin P das idiomatische Phrasem in sehr ruhiger, gelassener und völlig unaufgeregter Redeweise verwendet. Zudem ist *kein Kostverächter sein* wenn überhaupt, dann nur sehr schwach metaphorisch-bildlich oder bildhaft, so dass ko- und kontextuell betrachtet keinerlei Indiz für eine eventuelle Expressivität der Sequenz und somit auch nicht des idiomatischen Ausdrucks vorliegt.

Im Gegensatz dazu lassen sich den folgenden beiden Sequenzen (3) und (4) gewisse Spuren expressiver Sprecherbeteiligung feststellen.

(3) Vera fasst die Gefühle übergewichtiger Menschen zusammen
V: wenn man dick is **is man langsam, is man faul, kommt man nich in die Pötte**;

Während hinsichtlich der Prosodie keinerlei Abweichung von der normalen Sprechweise der Talkmasterin Vera zu verzeichnen ist, wird die Produktion der idiomatischen Paraphrase *kommt man nich in die Pötte* von starker Mimik begleitet: Vera verzieht nämlich das Gesicht und sieht aus, als ob sie leidet. Zudem ist der hier verwendete idiomatische Ausdruck bildhaft, möglicherweise auch bildlich-metaphorisch.

Keinerlei Zweifel am bildlich-metaphorischen Charakter der paraphrasierenden Idiome besteht in der Sequenz (4).

(4) Die Talkmasterin fragt J nach ihrer Reaktion, wenn ihr Partner sie verließe
J: (lacht etwas) ich lieb ihn; aber **ich kann ihn ja auch nich festhalten; ich kann ihn ja nich in KETTEN legen.**

Hier wird die idiomatisch-bildlich-metaphorische Paraphrase *nicht in KETTEN legen können* des nicht-phraseologischen Bezugsausdrucks *nicht festhalten können* mit starker Akzentuierung des Substantivs *KETTEN* geäußert. Gleichzeitig lächelt die Sprecherin J etwas verlegen, was jedoch kaum kein Anzeichen für die Expressivität des produzierten Idioms sein kann. Allerdings könnte man aufgrund der Bildstärke des Idioms und der starken Akzentuierung eines seiner Konstituenten, i.e. *KETTEN*,[15] auf eine erhöhte Sprecherbeteiligung und damit auf das Vorhandensein einer gewissen Expressivität in der vorliegenden Sequenz schließen.

4.2. Idiomatische Paraphrasen idiomatischer Ausdrücke: „x_{PHR-1} R y_{PHR-2}"

Wenn nun ein idiomatischer Ausdruck einen bereits phraseologischen, aber nicht oder nur teilweise idiomatischen (z.B. ein Teil-Idiom oder eine Kollokation) bzw. einen schon voll-idiomatischen paraphrasiert, ist dann der zweite im Rahmen der textuellen Entwicklung expressiver als der erste oder sind beide gleich ausdrucksstark? Dieser Frage soll anhand der zwei X nachstehenden Beispiele (5) und (6) beantwortet werden.

(5) HM war zwei Jahre unschuldig im Gefängnis
Bio: **man is** in der Hierarchie der Gefangenen **ganz unten.**
HM: ja **auf gut Deutsch** man **man is der letzte DRECK.**

HMs bildhafte bzw. metaphorisch-bildliche Paraphrase[16] *man is der letzte Dreck* des metaphorisch-bildlichen Phrasems *ganz unten sein* wird durch die ebenfalls idiomatische metakommunikative Routineformel *auf gut Deutsch* eingeleitet, die auf Abweichung von einer lexikalen Norm schließen lässt und folglich als – expressiv? – markiert gelten kann. Da HMs Hetero-Paraphrase, in der *der letzte Dreck (sein)* zweifellos als bildkräftiger gelten kann als *ganz unten (sein)*, zudem noch mit starker Akzentuierung von *DRECK* realisiert wird, angesichts einer ansonsten sehr ruhigen, völlig unaufgeregten Sprechweise dieses Talkgastes, kann in diesem Fall nicht nur auf eine stärkere Expressivität von HMs Turn i.A., sondern auch der idiomatisch-bildhaften Paraphase gegenüber dem Bezugsausdruck i.B. geschlossen werden.

Für die folgende Sequenz könnte die gleiche Aussage zutreffen.

(6) Die Talkmasterin über einen untreuen Ehemann
BS: **so einen** würd ich doch **LAUfen lassen**; [...] ja aber dann würd ich so einen doch **in=nen WIND schießen** und laufen lassen;

Sowohl der Bezugsausdruck *jmdn. LAUfen lassen* als auch seine Paraphrase *jmdn. in den WIND schießen* sind im vorliegenden Beispiel – zumindest für deren Produzentin – metaphorisch-bildlich.[17] Bei beiden Idiomen wird ein Konstituent des Phrasems stark akzentuiert, nämlich *LAUfen* einerseits und *WIND* andererseits, allerdings ist das paraphrasierenden zweite *jmdn. in den WIND schießen* durch das verwendete Bild und vor allem das Verb *schießen* potentiell bild- und damit ausdrucksstärker als das paraphrasierte *jmdn. laufen lassen*. Überdies wird das zweite Idiom von einer illustrierenden Geste begleitet: BS macht nämlich mit der linken Hand eine von sich selbst wegweisende Bewegung, die die Aussage des Phrasems noch verstärken könnte.

4.3. *Nicht-phraseologische Paraphrasen idiomatischer Ausdrücke: „x_{PHR} R $y_{nicht-PHR}$"*

Entwickelt die phraseologische Paraphrase laut Gréciano (1983) im Text Expressivität, müsste folglich die nicht-phraseologische Paraphrase eines Idioms, hin zu mehr Rationalität und Nüchternheit tendierend, mit einem Expressivitätsverlust einhergehen. Diese Vermutung soll in den Sequenzen (7) und (8) untersucht werden.

(7) F fragt einen jugendlichen Straftäter, ob er nachts gut schläft
F: dann sacht ma:n- ähm **(n?) schlechtes Gewissen is nich n gutes Ruhekissen** also- **geht die:se Geschichte mit einem in die Nacht rein,** [...] **also träumst du davon,**

Weder das stark deformierte[18] Sprichwort *ein gutes Gewissen ist ein sanftes Ruhekissen* noch der paraphrasierende nicht-phraseologische Ausdruck werden mit auf erhöhte Sprecherbeteiligung hinweisenden prosodischen oder nonverbalen kommunikativen Mitteln geäußert. Nichts scheint deshalb *a priori* darauf hinzudeuten, dass das bildstarke Sprichwort expressiver ist als seine folgende nicht-phraseologische Paraphrase. Es wäre allerdings möglich, dass dies an der starken Deformation des Sprichwortes liegt, die dem Sprecher F selbst auffällt, woraufhin er erst die erklärende Paraphrase produziert.

Im folgenden Gesprächsausschnitt (8) sind demgegenüber alle Merkmale einer erhöhten Sprecherbeteiligung bei der Äußerung des metaphorisch-bildlichen Idioms *wie Feuer und Wasser (sein)* versammelt.

(8) A beschreibt ein äußerst unterschiedliches junges Paar
A: manchmal sind sie sogar **wie FEU:ER und WASSE:R**; und da bin ich bei Angelika, die bei ihren Freunden Jörg und Martina sich auch denkt, naja **unterschiedlicher könnten sie eigentlich (.) nicht sein**;

Dieser idiomatische phraseologische Vergleich ist äußerst bildstark, wird zudem mit starker Akzentuierung der Nomina *FEU:ER* und *WASSE:R*[19] geäußert; außerdem schaut die Talkmasterin Arabelle bei der Äußerung ihres Turns sehr intensiv ihrem Gesprächspartner in die Augen und ballt obendrein noch die rechte Hand zur Faust. Es ist deshalb kaum überraschend, dass die den Freunden Jörg und Martina zugeschriebene nicht-phraseologische Paraphrase, ohne jegliche prosodische oder nonverbale Mittel der erhöhten Sprecherbeteiligung geäußert, *a priori* weniger ausdrucksstark erscheint.

4.4. Idiomatische Paraphrasen – Expressivitätszuwachs oder Expressivitätsabnahme?

Die Analyse der Korpus-Beispiele (1) bis (8) hat ergeben, dass nur in einem einzigen Fall, nämlich dann, wenn eine metadiskursive Aktivität vorliegt (vgl. Bsp. (1)), tatsächlich von einem intersubjektiv nachvollziehbaren Nachweis der Expressivität eines idiomatischen Ausdrucks ausgegangen werden kann. Hier schreibt nämlich ein Interaktionsbeteiligter, der Produzent des betreffenden Idioms selbst, diesem durch die Formel *auf gut Deutsch* explizit einen von der Norm des „guten Deutsch" abweichenden Status und damit eine gewisse Expressivität zu. In allen anderen Fällen kann man – mangels expliziter Aktivitäten der Beteiligten – lediglich auf eine expressive Markierung der idiomatische Ausdrücke enthaltenden Turns oder Sequenzen schließen. In den seltensten Fällen – bei ausgeprägter Bildstärke des Idioms und gleichzeitigen prosodischen und nonverbalen Mitteln erhöhter Sprecherbeteiligung – jedoch, und auch dann nur potentiell, auf expressive Konnotationen des idiomatischen Ausdrucks selbst. Deshalb kann auch nur mit äußerster Vorsicht auf eine potentielle größere Expressivität bestimmter paraphrasierter oder paraphrasierender idiomatischer Ausdrücke geschlossen werden; aufgrund ihrer Bildstärke mag dies insbesondere auf die idiomatischen Ausdrücke in den Sequenzen (4), (5), (6) und (8) zutreffen. Diese Bildstärke bzw. Bildlichkeit und eine daraus folgende Expressivität wird hier allerdings vom Analysten des vorliegenden Artikels im Anschluss an eine eingehende Analyse der betreffen Sequenzn angenommen, was noch nichts darüber aussagt, wie Interaktionsbeteiligte in vorgängigen Interaktionssituationen diese beurteilen würden. Um dennoch Einstellungen von Beteiligten zur Expressivität der diskutierten Idiome zu erheben, da es aber unmöglich ist, die Verwendung idiomatischer Ausdrücke und insbesondere deren Paraphrasen in authentischen Situationen zu simulieren, wurde eine Fragebogenaktion unter Muttersprachlern des Deutschen durchgeführt, deren Ergebnisse im folgenden Abschnitt dargestellt werden.

5. Was ist für Sie expressiver? – Resultate einer Fragebogen-Untersuchung unter Muttersprachlern

Auch wenn es sich von selbst versteht, dass eine Fragebogenumfrage nicht die konversationelle Aushandlung authentischer kommunikativer Interaktionssituationen ersetzen kann, so bieten die Meinungen unterschiedlicher Probanden doch ein repräsentativeres Bild als die alleinige Meinung des analysierenden Linguisten ungeachtet all seiner Kenntnisse und Erfahrungen, die diesen jedoch keineswegs zu einem „allwissenden" Teilnehmer aller nur denkbaren Kommunikationssituationen machen. Bei aller Skepsis gegenüber Laienbefragungen, die Anweisungen oder Situationen missverstehen können, (zu) schnell oder unüberlegt antworten oder vielleicht die zu beurteilenden idiomatischen Ausdrücke gar nicht kennen, und der daraus folgenden gebotenen Vorsicht bei der Verwendung derart gewonnener Erkenntnisse, misst die Volkslinguistik[20] den Einstellungen, Meinungen und Kenntnissen von „folk" bzw. Teilnehmern am gesellschaftlichen Kommunikationsprozess eine nicht zu unterschätzende Bedeutung bzw. Rolle im Hinblick auf das Erreichen wissenschaftlicher Erkenntnisse bei. "We use *folk* to refer to those who are not trained professionals in the area under investigation [...]. We definitely do not use *folk* to refer to rustic, ignorant, uneducated, backward, primitive, minority, isolated, marginalized, or lower status groups or individuals. [...] folk belief is simply belief, its folk character being no indication of its truth or falsity." (Niedzielsi & Preston 2000: viii) Mit dieser Definition befinden sich Niedzielsi & Preston (2000) im direkten Gegensatz zur Haltung Leonard Bloomfields gegenüber den Meinungen von Nicht-Linguisten, die er als „stankos"[21] bezeichnete. Niedzielsi und Preston (2000) sind vielmehr aus folgenden, kurz angerissenen Gründen von der nicht zu vernachlässigenden Rolle der „folk beliefs" überzeugt:

We have sought out and encouraged stankos, for we believe what the folk believe about language deserves careful consideration. This is justified along several lines:

1. The study of folk beliefs about language is one of the ethnographies of a culture. [...]
2. In the general area of applied linguistics, folk linguistics surely plays a most important role. When professionals want to have influence, they are,

we believe, ill-advised to ignore popular belief, and, [...], popular belief about language is both ubiquitous and strong. [...]
3. Finally, folk linguistic beliefs may help determine the shape of language itself. It would be unusual to discover that what nonlinguists believe about language has nothing to do with linguistic change [...]. (Niedzielski und Preston 2000: vii–viii)

Ausgehend von diesen Prämissen der Volkslinguistik wurde ein Fragebogen entwickelt, um die „beliefs", die Meinungen und Einstellungen zur Ausdrucksstärke idiomatischer Wendungen von „normalen" Teilnehmern zu erforschen, nicht um diese als wahr oder falsch den Überzeugungen der Stilistik oder Phraseologie gegenüberzustellen, sondern vielmehr um diesen wissenschaftlichen Ansätzen eine Art Hilfestellung bei ihren oft wenig oder gar nicht empirisch abgesicherten Hypothesenbildungen zu geben.[22]

Der Fragebogen enthielt im Anschluss an eine kurze Situationsbeschreibung fünfzehn idiomatische Paraphrasen der drei zuvor diskutierten Typen (s. Anhang 1 zum vorliegenden Artikel) und wurde von insgesamt 68 deutschsprachigen Probanden beantwortet. Diese sollten unter Kenntnis der kurz beschriebenen Kommunikationssituation entscheiden, welcher von zwei Ausdrücken ihrer Ansicht nach der ausdrucksstärkere ist und dies auch begründen. Hier die Situation Nr. 1 aus dem Fragebogen als Beispiel:

(1) In der TS „Zu dick, so will ich nicht weiterleben" sagt eine stark übergewichtige Frau:	
(1a) Ich esse sehr gerne.	(1b) Ich bin kein Kostverächter.

Abbildung 1. *Auszug aus dem Fragebogen*

5.1. *Gesamtergebnisse der Fragebogenstudie*

Aus der Zusammenfassung der Ergebnisse (s. Anhang 2) sind zwei wesentliche Schlüsse hinsichtlich der Einschätzung der Expressivität idiomatischer Ausdrücke durch linguistisch und insbesondere phraseologisch nicht spezialisierte Probanden[23] zu ziehen:

Zum einen, dass in fast 50% aller Fälle (7/15) der nicht-phraseologische bzw. nicht-bildhafte[24] Ausdruck von der Gesamtheit der befragten Personen (unter und über 40 Jahren) für expressiver gehalten wird als das idiomatisch-metaphorisch-bildliche oder bildhafte semantisch mehr oder weniger äquivalente Phrasem. Dies gilt für Nr. 1: *sehr gerne essen*; Nr. 2: *langsam und faul sein*; Nr. 5: *offen miteinander reden*; Nr. 6: *man gibt zurück, was man bekommt*;

Nr. 7: *tot sein*; Nr. 10: *jeder soll so leben, wie er es für richtig hält*; Nr. 14: *irgendwas wird da schon dran sein*.
Zum anderen, dass die Ergebnisse für die unter und über 40-jährigen in sieben Fällen variieren (vgl. die Nummern 3, 5, 6, 9, 11, 14 und 15). Dabei ist besonders auffällig, dass gerade die unter 40-jährigen Befragten, von denen man eher hätte erwarten können, dass sie die bildstarken Ausdrücke vielleicht nicht kennen oder für veraltet halten, in diesen Fällen gerade die idiomatische Variante wählen, während die über 40-jährigen für die nicht-phraseologische bzw. nicht-bildhafte optieren. Nach Erklärungen für diesen Tatbestand zu suchen, ist kaum möglich, da häufig keine Begründung für die getroffene Wahl angegeben wurde. Generell scheint es aber so, dass ältere Probanden die angebotenen Alternativen – semantisch – genauer analysieren als die jüngeren und allgemein die nicht-phraseologischen Ausdrücke für konkreter, direkter, ehrlicher halten als ihre semantisch betrachtet bildstärkeren Paraphrasen.

5.2. *Probanden-Präferenzen und Begründungen bezüglich der Expressivität in den analysierten Sequenzen*

Am Beispiel der im vorliegenden Beitrag im Detail analysierten Sequenzen (cf. Pkt. 4. des vorliegenden Aufsatzes), die auch Bestandteil des Fragebogens waren,[25] soll nun beleuchtet werden, welche Gründe die Probanden für die Wahl des idiomatischen Ausdrucks oder des nicht-phraseologischen als der für sie expressiveren Variante angeben. Es geht um die folgenden fünf Paraphrasen.[26]

Bsp. in Pkt. 4	Frageb.	Bezugsausdruck	Paraphrase
2	1	**sehr gerne essen (65.63%)**	kein Kostverächter sein
3	2	**langsam und faul sein (54.69%)**	nicht in die Pötte kommen
4	3	nicht festhalten können	**nicht in Ketten legen können (67.19%)**
5	13	ganz unten sein	**der letzte Dreck sein (81.25%)**
8	11	**wie Feuer und Wasser sein (75.38%)**	unterschiedlicher könnten sie nicht sein

Abbildung 2. *Bewertung der in Punkt 4. analysierten Beispiele in der Fragebogenstudie*

Es fällt auf, dass lediglich die idiomatischen Ausdrücke der analysierten Sequenzen (4), (5) und (8) von den Befragten für expressiver gehalten werden als ihre nicht-phraseologische Variante, bei (2) und (3) ist genau das Gegenteil der Fall. Der idiomatische Ausdruck *kein Kostverächter sein* in Sequenz (2) ist allerdings nicht bildhaft, wohingegen *nicht in die Pötte kommen* in (3) für den

Hörer nur dann bildhaft bzw. metaphorisch-bildlich ist, wenn er ein konkretes Modell mit dem ausgedrückten abstrakten Sachverhalt verbinden kann. Demgegenüber sind die idiomatischen Ausdrücke in (4), (5) und (8), die die Befragten für expressiver halten als ihr nicht-phraseologisches Pendant, äußerst bildstark und – vielleicht mit Abstrichen bei (5) – eindeutig metaphorisch-bildlich. Diese Einschätzung wird durch die Kommentare der Befragten gestützt:[27]

- *sehr gerne essen* wird von 64.7% der Probanden für expressiver gehalten als *kein Kostverächter sein*, weil der Ausdruck „konkret, einfach, verständlich, ehrlich, klar und deutlich" ist, „auf den Punkt kommt", wohingegen das Idiom in b als „geschwollen, ironisch, altmodisch, verharmlosend, gekünstelt, veraltet, literarisch" eingestuft wird; es „zieht ins Lächerliche, spricht durch die Blume, verniedlicht den Tatbestand, redet um den heißen Brei herum, passt nicht in eine Alltagssituation". Nur sehr wenige Probanden halten Variante a für „sachlich und banal" und deshalb die „übertragene Bedeutung" von b für ausdrucksstärker, dies vor allem aufgrund der „doppelten Verneinung".
- *langsam und faul sein* wird von (nur) 54.4 % aus ähnlichen Gründen für ausdrucksstärker gehalten als seine idiomatische Paraphrase *nicht in die Pötte kommen*: „die Adjektive [in a] verstärken sich gegenseitig und unterstreichen Negatives, sind expressiver (sic!) als Pötte; [a] drückt den [gemeinten] Sachverhalt deutlicher aus; ist konkret; eindeutig und klar; drastisch, aber konkret; direkt; bringt es auf den Punkt; ist beleidigend"[28]. Die Paraphrase b ist dagegen in den Augen der Probanden „schwach; verharmlosend; zu unernst; das harmlose Bild schwächt den Sachverhalt ab". Andererseits wird aus folgenden Gründen für Variante b optiert: „hört sich sprachgewandter an; ist nicht so direkt und plump; eine bekannte Floskel; metaphorisch".

Wird den idiomatischen Ausdrücken in den beiden vorstehenden Fällen gerade aufgrund ihrer Vorgeformtheit eine geringere Ausdrucksstärke als ihren nicht-phraseologischen Paraphrasen zugeschrieben, ist in der folgenden Sequenz genau das Gegenteil der Fall:

- *jmdn. nicht in Ketten legen können* wird nämlich von 66.2% für expressiver gehalten als *jmdn. nicht festhalten können* – und zwar gerade deshalb, weil „das Bild [...] sprechender, phantasievoller [ist]" aufgrund der „bildliche[n] Vorstellung: Gefängnis mit Eisenkugel am Fuß" und weil „Ketten stärker als Hände [sind]" und die „Metapher die Aussage vervielfacht".

Genau diese metaphorische Bildstärke wird direkt oder indirekt auch in den Begründungen für die Wahl von *wie Feuer und Wasser sein* (77.9% der Befragten) und *der letzte Dreck sein* (76.5%) als des expressiveren Ausdrucks der angebotenen Alternativen angeführt. Ganz offensichtlich spielt *Bildstärke* bei der Zuschreibung von Expressivität also eine entscheidende Rolle!

5.3. Expressivitätszuschreibungen in den restlichen Fragebogenitems

Die weiteren im Fragebogen bewerteten idiomatischen Paraphrasen bestätigen die Vermutung jedoch nicht, dass metaphorisch-bildliche idiomatische Wendungen prinzipiell als bildstark und somit als expressiver als eine nicht-phraseologische Formulierung eingeschätzt werden. Die folgende Tabelle, in der nicht-phraseologische Ausdrücke als expressiver eingeschätzt werden, belegt dies:

Frageb.	nicht-PHR: + expressiv	Idiom: − expressiv
5	offen miteinander reden (56.25%)	klar Schiff machen
6	man gibt zurück, was man bekommt (57.81%)	wie man in den Wald hineinruft …
7	tot sein (60.94%)	das Zeitliche segnen
10	jeder soll so leben, wie er es für richtig hält (62.5%)	jedem Tierchen sein Pläsierchen
14	irgendwas wird da schon dran sein (51.56%)	wo Rauch ist, ist auch Feuer

Abbildung 3. *Von Befragten als expressiver eingeschätzte nicht-phraseologische Wendungen*

In der Tat werden hier, wie schon zuvor bei *kein Kostverächter sein* und *nicht in die Pötte kommen*, die nicht-phraseologischen Bezugsäußerungen bzw. Paraphrasen für expressiver gehalten als die idiomatischen Wendungen. In den Fragebögen wird dies wie folgt begründet:

ad (5): *offen miteinander reden* ist die „klarere, konkretere, eindeutigere, besser verständliche, explizitere Aussage". Diejenigen, die minderheitlich *klar Schiff machen* gewählt haben, weisen allerdings darauf hin, dass der „bildhafte Ausdruck aus der Seemannssprache besonders ausdrucksstark" ist, und dass die Metapher zudem „den Neuanfang stärker zum Ausdruck" bringt.

ad (6): *man gibt zurück was man bekommt* wird ebenfalls als für „klarer, verständlicher, neutraler, eindeutiger, direkter" als das paraphrasierende Sprichwort gehalten. Dieses erscheint Befragten eher „unpersönlich, abgehoben, lächerlich, deplatziert, eher negativ besetzt, unpassend (Frau nicht gleich Wald), nicht zum Kontext passend".

ad (7): Während *das Zeitliche segnen* den Sachverhalt als Euphemismus verharmlost, beschreibt *tot sein* denselben „klar und unmissverständlich", gar „brutal, endgültig, hart, nicht so beschönigend, klar und deutlich" und ist deshalb für die Befragten mehrheitlich expressiver als die idiomatische Variante, die aber allgemein als „schöner, taktvoller, feiner, nicht so grob, brutal" eingestuft wird.

ad (10): *jeder soll so leben wie er es für richtig hält* „bringt es auf den Punkt" und „drückt genau das aus, was gemeint ist", ist „wertneutral, rücksichtsloser, toleranter, ernsthafter, präziser, klar und deutlich". *jedem Tierchen sein Pläsierchen* ist dagegen „abschwächend, mehr ausschmückend, zu harmlos, veraltet, verniedlichend, ironisch, frivol und verachtend, eher abwertend, lächerlich machend".

ad (14): Die Paraphrase *irgendwas wird da schon dran sein* wird insbesondere von den über vierzigjährigen Probanden für expressiver gehalten, weil diese Formulierung „deutlicher, verständlicher, eindeutiger" ist, und weil der „rationale Satz die Vorverurteilung noch deutlicher macht", „es auf den Punkt bringt". Die Bildsprache von *wo Rauch ist (da) ist auch Feuer* wird demgegenüber für „unangemessen, zu oberflächlich, unspontan, aufgepropft, gewählt" gehalten. Gerade die unter 40-jährigen Befragten sind jedoch der Ansicht, dass die „Metapher den Kausalzusammenhand Rauch-Feuer eindrucksvoll und bildhaft" darstellt.

Bleiben noch die Fragebogenitems, bei denen die Probanden der idiomatischen Variante eine expressivere Bedeutung zuschreiben.

Frageb.	Idiom/PHR: + expressiv	nicht-PHR: − expressiv
4	schware Zahlen schreiben (60.94%)	keine Schulden haben
8	ein Versprechen halten (60.94%)	zuverlässig
9	(s)ein blaues Wunder erleben (54.69%)	eine Überraschung erleben
12	Schmetterlinge im Bauch haben (67.19%)	verliebt sein
15	reinen Tisch machen (56.25%)	ein klärendes Gespräch führen

Abbildung 4. *Von Befragten als expressiver eingeschätzte phraseologische bzw. idiomatische Wendungen*

Wenn in den vorstehenden Fällen die phraseologische bzw. idiomatische Variante gegenüber der nicht-phraseologischen für ausdrucksstärker gehalten wird, dann begründen die Befragten dies wie folgt:

Ist ein idiomatischer Ausdruck immer expressiv? 115

ad (4): Die Paraphrase *schwarze Zahlen schreiben* wird hier von der Mehrheit für expressiver gehalten, weil sie „bildhafter und einprägsamer, besser vorstellbar, stärker, interessanter formuliert und geläufiger, positiver" usw. ist.

ad (8): Auch die nicht-idiomatische Kollokation *ein Versprechen halten* ist für die Befragten „stärker und präziser, konkreter, genauer, deutlicher, mit höherer Emotionalität [behaftet]" als die „zu allgemeine" und „ungenaue" nicht-phraseologische Paraphrase *zuverlässig sein*.

ad (9): Das Idiom *(s)ein blaues Wunder erleben* wird von einer knappen Mehrheit der Probanden aufgrund des verwendeten „Bildes"[29] für expressiver gehalten, weil es den Sachverhalt dadurch „stärker, negativer, eindeutiger, präziser, bedrohlicher" ausdrückt.

ad (12): Der von mehreren Befragten als „Metapher" eingestufte Ausdruck *Schmetterlinge im Bauch haben* wird aufgrund des „schönen, allen bekannten Bildes", das „die Vorstellungskraft weckt" und „zeigt, was in einem vorgeht" sowie aufgrund „seiner emotionellen Wirkung" für expressiver gehalten als *verliebt sein*, das allerdings als „konkreter" und „verständlicher" eingestuft wird.

ad (15): Während im Item (5) noch die nicht-phraseologische Variante *offen miteinander reden* der idiomatisch-bildlichen *klar Schiff machen* vorgezogen wurde, halten die Probanden nun mehrheitlich den metaphorischen Ausdruck *reinen Tisch machen* für expressiver als *ein klärendes Gespräch führen*, denn er ist für sie „bildlicher, deutlicher, endgültiger, radikaler, pragmatischer", „bezieht sich auf die emotionale Ebene" und „verdeutlicht den Frust der Situation".

6. Überlegungen zu „folk beliefs" über die Expressivität idiomatischer Ausdrücke und deren Kontextabhängigkeit

Es versteht sich von selbst, dass die Erkenntnisse einer Fragebogenstudie nicht die multimodale Analyse authentischer verbaler Interaktionen ersetzen können. Angesichts der Tatsache, dass *in situ*-Aushandlungen der „Bedeutung" idiomatischer Ausdrücke nur selten oder gar nicht zur Verfügung stehen, können „folk beliefs" jedoch wichtige und interessante Anhaltspunkte für den Linguisten und Phraseologieforscher liefern (vgl. auch Schmale 2008).

Sehr aufschlussreich ist in jedem Fall, dass im Gegensatz zur häufig in der einschlägigen Literatur angetroffenen Behauptung, idiomatische, insbesondere bildstarke Ausdrücke seien prinzipiell expressiv bzw. expressiver als ihre nicht-phraseologischen Äquivalente, Befragte in fast 50% der beurteilten

Paraphrase-Fälle meinen, der nicht-idiomatische Bezugsausdruck sei *expressiver*. Begründet wird dies von den Probanden in der Regel damit, dass der entsprechende nicht-phraseologische Ausdruck, z.B. *tot sein*, „es besser auf den Punkt bringt", d.h. „klarer, deutlicher, präziser, direkter" usw. als ein idiomatisch-bildhafter Ausdruck wie *das Zeitliche segnen*, der den anvisierten Sachverhalt weniger direkt und weniger präzise benennt, „durch die Blume spricht, den Tatbestand verniedlicht, um den heißen Brei herum redet"[30]. Gelegentlich ziehen bestimmte Bilder den gemeinten Sachverhalt laut Probanden-Einschätzungen sogar ins Lächliche, was dann als das Gegenteil von Expressivität eingeschätzt wird. Teilweise wird auch explizit ausgedrückt, dass man Idiome, vor allem Sprichwörter, für veraltet hält.

Ganz offensichtlich stufen die Befragten idiomatische Ausdrücke nur dann als expressiver ein als ihre nicht-phraseologischen Bezugsausdrücke bzw. Paraphrasen, wenn sie ein besonders starkes, einfach zu durchschauendes Bild enthalten, z.B. *wie Feuer und Wasser sein, jmdn. in Ketten legen oder der letzte Dreck (sein)*, was bei *klar Schiff machen* oder *wie man in den Wald hineinruft...* offenbar nicht (mehr) der Fall ist. Und vorausgesetzt, die betreffenden Idiome werden nicht für veraltet und abgenutzt gehalten, was beim letztgenannten Sprichwort noch erschwerend hinzukommt.

Nun darf allerdings nicht vergessen werden, dass die Probanden auf den von ihnen bearbeiteten Fragebögen zwar über kurzgefasste Situationsbeschreibungen verfügten, neben der aufs Segmentale beschränkten Angabe der Bezugs- und paraphrasierenden Ausdrücke jedoch über keinerlei prosodische und/oder nonverbale Informationen der multimodal abgelaufenen Kommunikationssituation. Sie konnten folglich allein aufgrund der verbalen Form der Ausdrücke auf deren eventuelle Expressivität schließen. Es wäre vorstellbar, dass sie anders entschieden hätten, wenn sie die Videoaufnahme, die alle Phänomene der multimodalen Kommunikation gezeigt hätte, angeschaut hätten. Dies wiederum würde aber implizieren, dass nicht allein die segmentale Form eines idiomatischen Ausdrucks, gleichgültig ob bildstark, metaphorisch-bildlich oder nicht, für seine Expressivität verantwortlich ist, sondern vielmehr auch oder insbesondere suprasegmentale, nonverbale, sequentielle, situative und kontextuelle Faktoren (vgl. Drescher 1997). Nicht der idiomatische Ausdruck an sich wäre also expressiv, sondern die konversationelle Sequenz, in der er als Turnkonstruktionseinheit fungiert. Nur in ihr kann das bildstarke, nicht als veraltet geltende und situationsangemessene Idiom sein gesamtes Expressivitätspotential enwickeln.

Université Paul Verlaine

Anhang 1: Der Fragebogen zur Expressivität

Ihr Alter: _____ Geschlecht: _____ Beruf: _____
Woher stammen Sie? _____
Welchen Ausdruck der folgenden Ausdruckspaare aus deutschen Talkshows halten Sie für ausdrucksstärker bzw. expressiver? Begründen Sie bitte warum. Die in (a) und (b) angegebenen Ausdrücke wurden übrigens vom gleichen Sprecher in der gleichen Äußerung, meist aufeinander folgend verwendet (b drückt in der Situation also im Prinzip das Gleiche wie a aus).

(1) In der TS " Zu dick, so will ich nicht weiterleben " sagt eine stark übergewichtige Frau :			
	(1a) Ich esse sehr gerne.		(1b) Ich bin kein Kostverächter.

(2) Die gleiche Frau wie in (1):			
	(2a) Dicke sind langsam und faul.		(2b) Dicke kommen nicht in die Pötte.

(3) Eine sehr junge Frau sagt über den Vater ihres Kindes, der sie vielleicht verlassen will:			
	(3a) Ich kann ihn ja nicht festhalten.		(3b) Ich kann ihn ja nicht in Ketten legen.

(4) Im " DSF-Doppelpass " über den FC Bayern München.			
	(4a) Bayern hat keine Schulden.		(4b) Bayern schreibt schwarze Zahlen.

(5) Veras Rat für ein Paar mit schwerwiegenden Eheproblemen:			
	(5a) Setzt euch hin und redet über alles.		(5b) Ihr solltet klar Schiff machen.

(6) Ein Mann spricht über die sehr gute Beziehung zu seiner Frau:			
	(6a) Man gibt zurück, was man bekommt.		(6b) Wie man in den Wald hineinruft, so schallt es heraus.

(7) Es geht um das Maskottchen, den Geißbock Hennes, des 1. FC Köln:			
	(7a) Den Geißbock hat das Zeitliche gesegnet.		(7b) Der Geißbock ist tot.

(8) Ein Jugendlicher über das Verhalten einer unzuverlässigen Freundin:			
	(8a) Sie soll ihre Versprechen halten.		(8b) Sie soll zuverlässig sein.

(9) Arabella über die Transsexuelle Jasmina, deren Geschlechtsumwandlung aber noch nicht vollständig vollzogen ist:	
(9a) Man kann sein blaues Wunder erleben.	(9b) Man kann eine Überraschung erleben.

(10) Ein Zuschauer über einen Talkgast, der zu Prostituierten geht:	
(10a) Jedem Tierchen sein Pläsierchen.	(10b) Jeder soll so leben, wie er es für richtig hält.

(11) Arabella über ein junges Paar, das Probleme hat.	
(11a) Sie sind wie Feuer und Wasser.	(11b) Unterschiedlicher könnten sie nicht sein.

(12) Meisers Frage an ein Paar, das ein arrangiertes " blind date " hatte:	
(12a) Hatten Sie Schmetterlinge im Bauch?	(12b) Haben Sie sich verliebt?

(13) Ein Talkgast, der unschuldig wegen Kindesmissbrauchs im Gefängnis war:	
(13a) Man ist in der Hierarchie ganz unten.	(13b) Man ist der letzte Dreck.

(14) Der gleiche Mann wie in (13) über die Reaktion der Bewohner seines Dorfes:	
(14a) Wo Rauch ist, ist auch Feuer.	(14b) Irgendwas wird da schon dran sein.

(15) Rat eines Talkmasters an ein Paar mit großen Problemen:	
(15a) Ihr solltet reinen Tisch machen.	(15b) Ihr solltet ein klärendes Gespräch führen.

Anhang 2: Gesamtergebnisse der Umfrage nach Alter
(fettgedruckt die meistgewählte Variante)

Nr	a	b	x < 40 J. (n = 43)		x = > 40 J. (n = 25)		Total (N = 68)	
			a (%)	b (%)	a (%)	b (%)	a (%)	b (%)
1	sehr gerne essen	kein Kostverächter sein	62.8	34.9	68.0	32.0	**64.7**	33.8
2	langsam und faul sein	nicht in die Pötte kommen	53.5	41.9	56.0	36.0	**54.4**	39.7
3	jm. nicht festhalten können	**jm. nicht in Ketten legen können**	16.3	83.7	64.0	36.0	33.8	**66.2**
4	keine Schulden haben	**schwarze Zahlen schreiben**	37.2	62.8	36.0	60.0	36.8	**61.8**
5	offen miteinander reden	klar Schiff machen	46.5	51.2	64.0	36.0	**52.9**	45.6
6	**man gibt zurück, was man bekommt**	wie man in den Wald hineinruft...	46.5	51.2	80.0	20.0	**58.8**	39.7
7	das Zeitliche gesegnet haben	tot sein	39.5	58.1	32.0	68.0	36.8	**61.8**
8	**ein Versprechen halten**	zuverlässig sein	62.8	30.2	64.0	40.0	**63.2**	33.8
9	**ein blaues Wunder erleben**	eine Überraschung erleben	65.1	32.6	40.0	60.0	**55.9**	42.6
10	jedem Tierchen sein Pläsierchen	**jeder soll so leben, wie er es für richtig hält**	32.6	62.8	36.0	64.0	33.8	**63.2**
11	**wie Feuer und Wasser sein**	unterschiedlicher könnten sie nicht sein	95.3	7.0	48.0	52.0	**77.9**	23.5
12	**Schmetterlinge im Bauch haben**	verliebt sein	62.8	34.9	72.0	24.0	**66.2**	30.9
13	in der Hierarchie ganz unten sein	**der letzte Dreck sein**	11.6	88.4	40.0	56.0	22.1	**76.5**
14	wo Rauch ist, ist auch Feuer	irgendwas wird da schon dran sein	53.5	34.9	24.0	68.0	42.6	**44.1**
15	**reinen Tisch machen**	ein klärendes Gespräch führen	72.1	20.3	32.0	68.0	**57.4**	42.6

Anhang 3: Begründungen zur Wahl des für expressiver gehaltenen Ausdrucks

2 – langsam und faul sein/nicht in die Pötte kommen (54.4%)

a	b
„langsam u faul" verstärken sich gegenseitig; drückt Sachverhalt deutlicher aus; netter; konkreter; eindeutig und klar; drastisch, aber konkreter; direkter; bringt es auf den Punkt; farblos; liebevoller drückt klar und direkt aus, was gemeint ist; Adjektive unterstreichen Negatives; passt besser;	schwächer; bösartig, abwertend, verachtend; verharmlosend; b verweist auf Charakterisierungswillen
	Metapher verharmlost Aussage; lustiger, sehr geläufig; b nette Umschreibung (also a); übertragene Bedeutung; zu unernst (also a);
direkter; „langsam u faul" negativer als „Pötte"; sehr direkt; Adjektive expressiver als „Pötte"; beleidigend (gerade deshalb a);	hört sich sprachgewandter an; außergewöhnlicher, nicht so direkt und plump; das harmlose Bild schwächt den Sachverhalt ab; metaphorisch; bekannte Floskel (also b)

3 – jm nicht festhalten / **nicht in Ketten legen können** (66.2%)

a	b
zu harmlos; konkreter; nicht so metaphorisch; ernsthafter;	bildliche Vorstellung (Gefängnis mit Eisenkugel am Fuß); Ketten stärker als Hände; bildhafter; deutlich; provozierender, kämpferischer; Bildsprache; zu negativ (a); Bild ist sprechender, phantasievoller;
nicht agressiv; spricht Problem direkt an, ohne Umschreibung;	Bild der Ketten AS; Metapher vervielfacht die Aussage; Metapher stärker; einfach stärker; Ketten starkes Symbol; Phr mit übertragener Bedeutung; direkter u AS als „festhalten"; kann man sich besser vorstellen; Bild
direkte, intensive Bedeutung	von Gefängnis oder Hund an der Kette, dauerhafter; bildhaft; Zwang verstärkt den Ausdruck;
	hört sich brutaler an; umschreibend, nicht zu direkt, höflicher; stärkere negative Bewertung; Metapher „Ketten" stärker als Verb „festhalten"; viel bildlicher; Symbolik von Ketten ausdrucksstark; bildlich = verstärkt den Ausdruck; metaphorische Stärke

Anmerkungen

Kontaktadresse: gschmale@free.fr

1. To use an expression from conversation analysis: expressiveness which is not interpretable by participants or the observer might exist, but is not accessible to the linguist.
2. Cf. infra zu einer Klärung dieser Begriffe.
3. *jmdm. die Würmer aus der Nase ziehen* mit der gleichen phraseologischen Bedeutung.
4. *jmdn. geschickt ausfragen, so dass er/sie Dinge erzählt, die er/sie eigentlich für sich behalten wollte.*
5. Vgl. auch Fleischer (1997), Koller (1977) oder Sandig (2007) zu einer ähnlichen Aussage.
6. Vgl. auch Gréciano (1984) und (1988).
7. Das in der Monographie Schmale (2001a) verwendet wurde.
8. Nach Gülich/Kotschi (1987) können dies (mehr oder weniger wörtliche) Rephrasierungen oder Paraphrasen sein.
9. Im Gegensatz dazu die Rephrasierungen vom Typ „x R x'", bei dem Signifikat und Signifikant identisch sind, allerdings kontextuell notwendige deiktische Verschiebungen toleriert werden.
10. Selbstverständlich eine Kontamination aus *klar Schiff machen* und *reinen Tisch machen*, was aber in der Situation in keiner Weise konversationell behandelt wird.
11. Es wurden für die Transkriptionen äußerst simple Konventionen verwendet: ; = fallende Intonation / . = tief fallende Intonation / , = steigende Intonation / - = Stimme in der Schwebe / : = Längung eines Lautes / (.) = kurzes Absetzen innerhalb eines Turns / (lacht etwas) = Kommentar zu einem parasprachlichen Phänomen / [...] = Auslassung / Großbuchstaben (bei Beibehaltung der Großschreibung von Nomina) für auffällige Akzentuierung / Fettdruck = Hervorhebung der analysierten Sequenzen.
12. Vgl. z.B. im Pons-Schemann (1993: 124): „..., *auf gut deutsch: sie ist Scheiße.*"
13. Es sei denn, es liegen explizite Spuren für eine Simulation vor, z.B. eine Kanaldiskrepanz.
14. Vgl. Gréciano (1988) oder auch Fiehler (1990), der „Emotionsausdruck" und „Emotionsthematisierung" unterscheidet.
15. Wobei man allerdings nicht vergessen sollte, dass es sich um eine Verstärkung des Äußerungsakzentes handelt, der ohnehin auf *Ketten* fällt.
16. Hier zeigt sich die Schwierigkeit bildhafte und metaphorisch-bildliche Phraseme genau zu differenzieren. Insbesondere bei *der letzte Dreck sein* muss man sich fragen, vielleicht am Besten durch eine Umfrage unter Muttersprachlern erheben, ob dort wirklich ein abstrakter Sachverhalt durch ein konkret vorstellbares Modell repräsentiert wird.
17. Wären sie es nicht, könnte BS die entsprechenden Bilder nicht zur Darstellung eines abstrakten Sachverhaltes, i.e. *ich würde mich von ihm trennen* bzw. *ihn wegjagen/rausschmeißen*, verwenden.

18. Was aber interessanterweise zu keinerlei konversationellen Aktivitäten führt, z.B. einer Behandlung von Verständnisschwierigkeiten, Kommentaren, Korrekturen, Lachen usw.
19. Darüber hinaus noch mit einer Vokaldehnung in den Lexemen *Feu:er* und *Wasse:r* realisiert, die noch stärkere Akzentuierung bewirken könnte.
20. Brekles (1985) Übersetzung des amerikanischen Terminus „folk linguistics".
21. Laut Niedzielski/Preston (2000) wahrscheinlich von der Imperfektform des Verbs *stink (stinken)* abgeleitet.
22. Vgl. auch Schmale (2008), in der die gleiche „Methodik" zur Erhebung „populärer" Vorstellungen zum Begriff und Inhalt von „Konversation" angewendet wurde.
23. Es handelte sich bei den älteren Proband/inn/en vorwiegend um Teilnehmer/innen eines VHS-Kurses in der Kölner Gegend; bei den jüngeren um Student/inn/en, die das Thema *Phraseologie* und insbesondere deren *Expressivität* nicht in Kursen behandelt hatten.
24. Im Falle von *irgendwas wird da schon dran sein* (Nr. 14).
25. In Anbetracht der Tatsache, dass der Fragebogen *vor* einer eingehenden Analyse aller idiomatischen Paraphrasen konzipiert wurde, konnten leider nicht alle zehn hier verwendeten Beispiele von Probanden beurteilt werden. Wenn andererseits nicht alle Paraphrasen des Fragebogens im vorliegenden Aufsatz als Beispiele gedient haben, dann deshalb, weil sie weder prosodische noch nonverbale Merkmale potentieller Expressivität der entsprechenden Sequenzen enthielten.
26. Die von der Mehrzahl der Probanden für expressiver gehaltene Ausdruck wird jeweils fett gedruckt.
27. Vgl. Anhang 3 für eine Zusammenfassung sämtlicher Kommentare zu zwei der o.a. Paraphrase-Beispiele.
28. Und gilt gerade deshalb als besonders ausdrucksstark für den Probanden.
29. Das aber streng – semantisch – genommen weder bildlich noch bildhaft ist.
30. Um die Probanden-Kommentare zu *kein Kostverächter sein* wieder aufzunehmen.

Literatur

Bally, Charles. 1909 [1951]. *Traité de stylistique française: Volume 1*. Paris: Klincksieck.
Bardosi, Vilmos, Stefan Ettinger & Cécile Stölting. 2003 [1992]. *Redewendungen Französisch/Deutsch. Thematisches Wörter- und Übungsbuch*. 3rd edn. Tübingen & Basel: A. Francke.
Brekle, Herbert E. 1985. ‚Volkslinguistik': ein Gegenstand der Historiographie der Sprachwissenschaft? In Herbert E. Brekle (ed.), *Einführung in die Geschichte der Sprachwissenschaft*, 34–43. Darmstadt: Wissenschaftliche Buchgesellschaft.
Burger, Harald. 1998. *Phraseologie: eine Einführung am Beispiel des Deutschen* (= Grundlagen der Germanistik; 36). Berlin: Schmidt.
Burger, Harald. 1989. Bildhaft, übertragen, metaphorisch – Zur Konfusion um die semantischen Merkmale von Phraseologismen. In Gertrud Gréciano (ed.), *Europhras 1988. Phraséologie Contrastive: Actes du Colloque International, Klingenthal – Strasbourg*

12–16 mai 1988 (Collection Recherches Germaniques 2), 17–29. Strasbourg: Université des Sciences Humaines, Département d'Etudes d'Allemand.
Drescher, Martina. 1997. Wie expressiv sind Phraseologismen? In Annette Sabban (ed.), *Phraseme im Text: Beiträge aus romanistischer Sicht* (Studien zur Phraseologie und Parömiologie 14), 67–95. Bochum: Brockmeyer.
Duden 11. 1998. *Redewendungen und sprichwörtliche Redensarten: Wörterbuch der deutschen Idiomatik. Bearbeitet von Günther Drosdowski und Werner Scholze-Stubenrecht. Nach den Regeln der neuen dt. Rechtschreibung überarb. Nachdr. der 1. Auflage.* Mannheim et al.: Dudenverlag.
Fiehler, Reinhard. 1990. *Kommunikation und Emotion: Theoretische und empirische Untersuchungen zur Rolle von Emotionen in der verbalen Interaktion.* Berlin: de Gruyter.
Fleischer, Wolfgang. 1997. *Phraseologie der deutschen Gegenwartssprache. 2., durchgesehene und ergänzte Auflage.* Tübingen: Niemeyer.
Gréciano, Gertrud. 1983. *Signification et dénotation en allemand: La sémantique des expressions idiomatiques* (Recherches Linguistiques IX). Paris & Metz: Klinksieck.
Gréciano, Gertrud. 1984. L'irréductibilité de l'expression idiomatique vivante à sa paraphrase: indice de la pluralité de ses dimensions sémantiques et de l'appel à une étude pragmatique de son contenu. In Georges Kleiber (ed.), *Recherches en pragma-sémantique* (Recherches Linguistiques X), 107–122. Paris & Metz: Klincksieck.
Gréciano Gertrud. 1988. Affektbedingter Idiomgebrauch. In Barbara Sandig (ed.), *Stilistisch-rhetorische Diskursanalyse* (Forum Angewandte Linguistik 14), 49–61. Tübingen: Narr.
Gülich, Elisabeth & Thomas Kotschi. 1987. Les actes de reformulation dans la consultation: La dame de Caluire. In Pierre Bange (ed.), *L'analyse des interactions verbales: La dame de Caluire: une consultation. Actes du Colloque tenu à l'Université Lyon 2 du 13 au 15 décembre 1985* (Sciences pour la Communication 18), 15–81. Bern et al.: Lang.
Koller, Werner. 1977. *Redensarten: Linguistische Aspekte, Vorkommensanalysen, Sprachspiel.* Tübingen: Niemeyer.
Niedzielski, Nancy A. & Dennis R. Preston. 2000. *Folk linguistics.* Berlin & New York: de Gruyter.
Riesel, Elise. 1970. *Der Stil der deutschen Alltagsrede.* Leipzig: Reclam.
Sandig, Barbara. 2007. Stilistische Funktionen von Phrasemen. In Harald Burger, Dmitri Dobrovol'skij, Peter Kühn & Neil R. Norrick (eds.), *Phraseologie / Phraseology. Ein internationales Handbuch der zeitgenössischen Forschung / An International Handbook of Contemporary Research*, 158–175. Berlin & New York: de Gruyter.
Schemann, Hans. 1993. *Pons Deutsche Idiomatik: Die deutschen Redewendungen im Kontext.* Stuttgart & Dresden: Ernst Klett Verlag.
Schmale, Günter. 2001a. *Le traitement conversationnel de phrasèmes dans les talk-shows de la télévision allemande.* Unveröffentlichte Monographie, Université de Nantes.
Schmale, Günter. 2001b. Rephrasages comme traitement conversationnel de phrasèmes dans les talk-shows de la télévision allemande. *Beiträge zur Fremdsprachenvermittlung* 39. 47–71.

Schmale, Günter. 2005a. Wortspiele mit phraseologischen Ausdrücken in deutschen Talkshows. *Deutsch als Fremdsprache* 4. 215–219.
Schmale, Günter. 2005b. Nonverbale Aktivitäten bei der Äußerung von Phraseologismen. *Studia Germanica Universitatis Vesprimiensis* 9(2). 159–173.
Schmale, Günter. 2007. Paraphrases phraséologiques dans la conversation. In Mohammed Kara (ed.), *Usages et analyses de la reformulation. Recherches Linguistiques* 29. 163–175.
Schmale, Günter. 2008. Conceptions populaires de la conversation. In Guy Achard-Bayle & Anne-Marie Paveau (eds.), *Linguistique populaire? Pratiques* 139/140. 58–80.
Schmale, Günter. 2009. Metalinguistic comments and evaluations of phraseological expressions in German talk shows. In *Textes & Contextes, no. 4, Varia 2009.* http://revuesshs.u-bourgogne.fr/textes& contextes/document.php?id=877 (accessed 16 May 2010).
Schmale, Günter. In Vorb. Une expression idiomatique est-elle plus expressive qu'une expression non idiomatique? Erscheint in Catherine Chauvin & Maurice Kauffer (eds.), *Actes du du colloque „Ecart et expressivité: description, discussion, théorisation". Université de Nancy 2 du 14 au 15 novembre 2008.* Besançon: PU Franche-Comté.

Interlinguale Phraseologie: Theorie, Praxis und Perspektiven

ERLA HALLSTEINSDÓTTIR and KEN FARØ

Abstract

In the following paper, several aspects of interlingual phraseology are considered. The term interlingual *should be understood as an umbrella term (unlike, e.g.* cross-linguistic *or German* kontrastiv*), covering both theoretical and applied contexts within phraseology related to more than one language, but without necessarily being typologically focused. We also believe that there is a need for a unified linguistic theory of lexical units covering both phraseology (in the following we use the term phraseme for all phraseological units) and single words (Colson 2008, 2010; Dobrovol'skij and Piirainen 2005, 2009; Gries 2008). This paper is a contribution to such a theory of lexis.*

Our definition of phrasemes, which serves to distinguish phrasemes from other lexical units in written language only, is based on the complexity and structure of the form of linguistic signs:

– *Single words and – in languages like German, Icelandic and Danish – word formations: linguistic signs with a visually continuous form (cf. word definitions and the concept of a graphemic word in Fuhrhop 2008).*
– *Phrasemes: linguistic signs with a visually non-continuous form. Due to their non-continuous form, the sign character of phrasemes is not obvious in writing. Especially if a phraseme is not known by a speaker, this can create problems in applied contexts such as foreign language acquisition and translation.*

The differentiation between graphemic words and phrasemes will result in either a need for a language specific categorization of phraseology (cf. Fleischer 1997: 249–250) or the inclusion of compound words in languages like French and English in the category phraseme. There are indeed, as Barz (2007: 27) points out, several functional, structural and semantic similarities between phrasemes and word formations (cf. also the discussion of Schwarzer Markt and Schwarzmarkt in Donalies 2009: 7–8).

Inspired by the diversity of recent phraseological research and the difficulties of describing our data with existing theoretical approaches based on the traditional linguistic dichotomy of langue-parole or performance-competence, we extend our linguistic approach to include a cognitive dimension (cf. Hallsteinsdóttir 2007: 161–162; Hallsteinsdóttir and Farø 2006). Thus we propose three approaches to phraseological research:

1. *The study of phrasemes as a part of an abstract language system. We assume that the language system is the linguistic resource for language use.*
2. *The study of phrasemes in texts, where language is manifested as a result of language production that is based on a selection from the resources of the language system and, in part, determined by the linguistic knowledge of each speaker.*
3. *The study of phrasemes as a cognitive phenomenon that is a part of an individual speaker's linguistic knowledge and underlies idiosyncratic aspects of language processing based on the abstract language system.*

This differentiation between forms of language manifestation is to some extent the base upon which the rest of the work is founded.

Functionalism is a central aspect of the way we look at phraseology in an interlingual perspective. This should be understood in two ways. First, we are interested in the functions of the phrasemes in the three manifestation forms of language and language use mentioned above. This includes discourse functions in general and the role – and communicative relevance – of iconography (images, pictures) in particular. Second, the idea of functionalism in this context involves a context specificity of many features which may seem relevant when analyzing phrasemes from a certain perspective within one linguistic discipline but which can be of no relevance in others.

We argue that all phrasemes have a complex semantic nature, which allows them to be used and understood both as compositional word sequences and as lexicalized units. This semiotic complexity provides an inherent potential for manipulations and it is a favored source for puns. Phrasemes are a part of the language system as lexicalized units. As well their constituents in most cases are also autonomous systemic units of the given language. The default textual realization of a phraseme is as a lexicalized unit since a compositional realization would automatically trigger the phraseological meaning, at least for known phrasemes. The cognitive linguistic processing of phrasemes can be either way: either based on the phraseological meaning for known phrasemes or on a com-

positional processing of the meaning of the components – or even a combination of several strategies and meaning sources (cf. Hallsteinsdóttir 2001).

We assume that all phrasemes (like all lexical units in general) are conventional linguistic signs, and thus arbitrary, that is in the non-trivial, Saussurian reading of the word. The arbitrariness is a characteristic of the form-meaning relation in the linguistic system. Motivation, on the other hand, can be seen as a purely cognitive phenomenon based on the individual linguistic competence. Thus speakers are able to motivate phrasemes by (a) creating a relation between the form and the meaning of known phraseological units (retrospective motivation) and (b) interpreting the relation between the form and the meaning of assumed, but basically unknown phraseological units (prospective motivation) (cf. Farø 2006). The often purported (and even Saussure himself is not sufficiently consequent here) idea that arbitrariness and motivation are antonyms does not hold. Instead, we are dealing with two different perspectives on the same phenomenon.

Phraseological equivalence is a central issue in interlingual phraseology. As shown in figure 1, we propose that equivalence should be examined by including

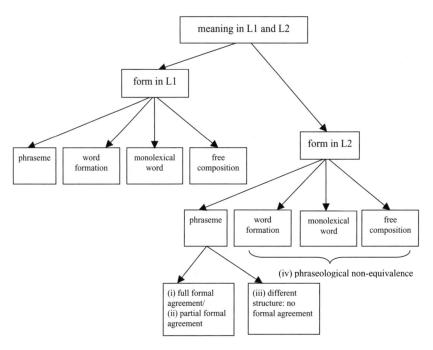

Figure 1. *A holistic approach to equivalence of lexical items based on the types of phraseological equivalence in Korhonen and Wotjak (2001: 227)*

all lexical items instead of focusing only on equivalence within the phraseology of two or more languages.

We propose that a full understanding of equivalence within phraseology should not only include all lexical items but should also differentiate in the number and granularity of equivalence aspects (cf. Farø 2006) according to the respective research context. Each research context, and by that we mean linguistic discipline, demands its own specific theory and methodological approach of phraseological equivalence. Thus phraseology should be treated differently within various "applied" and one non-applied linguistic discipline and so four different approaches to phraseological equivalence in lexicology, lexicography, translation and language acquisition respectively are illustrated.

Keywords: phraseology; lexicology, lexicography; translation studies; language acquisition; interlingual linguistics.

1. Einleitung

Dieser Beitrag beschäftigt sich mit der linguistischen Beschreibung und Definition von Phraseologismen in der geschriebenen Sprache aus einer interlingualfunktionalistischen Perspektive. Das übergeordnete Ziel unserer Ausführungen ist es, der Tradition der kontrastiven Phraseologie folgend, einen wesentlichen Beitrag zu einer allgemeinen Theorie der Phraseologie zu liefern, denn schon seit den Anfängen der Phraseologieforschung hat die kontrastive Phraseologie neue, „auch intralinguale und allgemeinlinguistische Einsichten" (Földes 2006: 11) und theoretische Erkenntnisse vermittelt.

Nach der Abgrenzung des Gegenstandsbereichs (Abschnitt 2) und einem kurzen Überblick über die interlinguale Phraseologie (Abschnitt 3) diskutieren wir grundlegende Fragen, die sowohl für die theoretische als auch die angewandte kontrastive Phraseologieforschung Relevanz haben. Unser Ausgangspunkt ist eine Differenzierung zwischen den unterschiedlichen Konstituierungsformen der Sprache als: (a) dem Resultat der Sprachverarbeitung in konkreten Texten, (b) der kognitiven Verarbeitung von Sprache und (c) dem abstrakten Sprachsystem. Wir skizzieren eine zeichentheoretische Grundlage, die auf unserer Dreiteilung basiert und die semantische Komplexität (Abschnitt 4) sowie die Rolle der Konventionalität, Arbitrarität und Motiviertheit (Abschnitt 5) in der Phraseologie mit einbezieht. Weiterhin legen wir dar, welche Aspekte die interlinguale phraseologische Äquivalenz ausmachen (Abschnitt 6) und inwieweit diese in den Disziplinen Lexikologie (Abschnitt 7.1), Translatologie (Abschnitt 7.2),

Lexikographie (Abschnitt 7.3) und Sprachdidaktik (Abschnitt 7.4) theoretisch und praktisch implementiert werden können.

2. Phraseologismen als verbale Zeichen

Über die Eigenschaften der Phraseologie herrscht in der Forschung darin Einigkeit, dass Phraseologismen systemhafte sprachliche Zeichen sind, und dass die Merkmale der Phraseologizität auf allgemeingültigen Eigenschaften der Sprache beruhen (Burger et al. 1982: 315, 323). Als allgemein anerkannt gilt die Einteilung der Phraseologie in Phraseologie im engeren und weiteren Sinne. Alle Phraseologismen weisen die Merkmale Polylexikalität und Festigkeit auf, die sich in der durch die Lexikalisierung bedingten Reproduzierbarkeit des Phraseologismus als Wortgruppe manifestieren (vgl. Burger 2010: 15). Die Phraseologismen, die zusätzlich das Merkmal der Idiomatizität aufweisen, das die Abweichung der phraseologischen Bedeutung von der Komposition der Komponentenbedeutung eines Phraseologismus beschreibt, gehören zur Phraseologie im engeren Sinne (Burger 2010: 16; Burger et al. 1982: 1; vgl. eine kritische Auseinandersetzung mit weiteren Kriterien in Donalies 2009).

Es ist unumstritten, dass der Begriff Polylexikalität die lexikalische Komplexität eines Sprachzeichens bezeichnet. Diese Komplexität gilt für Phraseologismen, die aus Einheiten bestehen, die zum großen Teil selbst als selbständige Sprachzeichen fungieren (vgl. Häcki Buhofer 2006: x). Sie gilt aber auch für Wortbildungen, und um diese eindeutig von Phraseologismen abgrenzen zu können, ist es notwendig, die Konstituierung der Komplexität zu spezifizieren (vgl. Barz 2006, 2007; Fleischer 1997: 249–250). Wir schlagen vor, die Abgrenzung anhand der Beschaffenheit der Form vorzunehmen. Phraseologismen bestehen, im Gegensatz zu Wortbildungen, aus graphematischen Wörtern (Fuhrhop 2008). Die daraus zu ziehende Konklusion wäre, dass in der geschriebenen Sprache die primäre Aufteilung des Wortschatzes in Phraseologie und Wörter durch das distinktive Merkmal „Leerzeichen" erfolgt:

1. *Wörter*: Wortbildungen und Simplizia, d.h. verbale Zeichen mit einer visuell wahrnehmbaren, einheitlichen Form.
2. *Phraseologismen*: verbale Zeichen, deren Ausdrucksseite durch Leerzeichen unterbrochen wird und die dadurch nicht unmittelbar als eine Einheit erkennbar sind.

Die Brauchbarkeit des Kriteriums Idiomatizität wurde inzwischen aufgrund seiner Subjektivität und der problematischen Operationalisierbarkeit mehrmals in Frage gestellt (vgl. die Übersicht in Donalies 2009: 20). Wir bevorzugen die Erfassung der semantischen Eigenschaften von Phraseologismen mit dem Begriff semiotische Komplexität (vgl. Abschnitt 5).

Wir gehen davon aus, dass Phaseologismen ein normales sprachliches Phänomen sind (vgl. Sinclairs „idiom principle", 1991, 2008), und dass sie als ein integrierter Bestandteil des Wortschatzes betrachtet werden sollten (vgl. Hallsteinsdóttir und Farø 2006). Unsere bisherige Forschung[1] konzentriert sich v.a. auf die Phraseologie im engeren Sinne (Idiome), die somit als Grundlage unserer Ausführungen dient. Wir sind jedoch der Auffassung, dass viele der hier diskutierten Aspekte auch generell für die Phraseologie gültig sind, geben aber zu, dass wir noch nicht den empirischen Beweis dafür liefern können.

3. Interlinguale Phraseologie

Unter kontrastiver Phraseologie[2] wird traditionell der Vergleich der Phraseologie in zwei oder mehr Sprachen verstanden. Die Ergebnisse aus kontrastiven Untersuchungen dienen sowohl zur Weiterentwicklung verschiedener Theorieansätze, z.B. der Sprachtheorie, der Erklärung der Verwendung von Phraseologismen, der Entdeckung universeller Prinzipien und der Beschreibung kultureller Muster, als auch als Grundlage von Arbeiten in angewandten sprachwissenschaftlichen Disziplinen (vgl. Colson 2008, 2010; Gries 2008; Korhonen 2007: 574–575).

Es wird zwischen diachronischen und synchronischen Dimensionen des Vergleichs unterschieden (vgl. im Folgenden Fleischer 1997: 241; Földes 2006: 11; Korhonen 2007: 574). Die historisch orientierten Arbeiten fokussieren meist auf die „Ermittlung der Herkunft, Verbreitung und Entlehnungsrichtungen phraseologischer Ausdrücke" (Korhonen 2007: 574). In der synchron ausgelegten Forschung dagegen wurden bisher bevorzugt struktur- und komponentenbezogene Untersuchungen mit ‚beschreibend-inventarisierender' Funktion durchgeführt, in denen bestimmte syntaktische und lexikalische Strukturtypen oder Sachgruppen der Komponenten, z.B. Tier-, Farb-, Körperteilbezeichnungen (Korhonen und Wotjak 2001) oder ganze phraseologische Systeme verglichen werden. Zur kontrastiven Phraseologie gehören ebenfalls Vergleiche, die sich auf die Kontrastierung anderer Phänomene wie Kultur, Symbolik und Figurativität konzentrieren, in die Phraseologismen als ein Teilbereich der Sprache einbezogen werden (vgl. Dobrovol'skij und Piirainen 2005; kurzer Überblick in Malá 2005).

Die methodische Vorgehensweise der bisherigen Untersuchungen kann grob in drei Verfahren eingeteilt werden, wobei der Komplexitätsgrad sehr unterschiedlich sein kann:

1) Der auf der Intuition des Forschers basierende Vergleich von isolierten Phraseologismen oder phraseologischen Komponenten. Dieser bezieht sich häufig zusätzlich auf Informationen in ein- oder zweisprachigen Wörterbüchern. Dazu gehören auch der metalexikographische Vergleich und die Evaluierung der Darstellung von Phraseologismen in vorhandenen Wörterbüchern.
2) Der text- und korpusbasierte Vergleich von Phraseologismen. Den Ausgangspunkt bilden einerseits Phraseologismen in Wörterbüchern, die durch Beispielanalysen auf ihre Darstellung und Äquivalentangaben im Wörterbuch überprüft werden. Andererseits werden Phraseologismen in Übersetzungen auf das angewendete Übersetzungsverfahren untersucht. Als Grundlage dienen sowohl der Vergleich von Korpusdaten aus einsprachigen Korpora als auch der Vergleich von Originaltexten und Übersetzungen. Dazu kommen Untersuchungen gesprochener Sprache, die aber gerade im interlingualen Kontext zur Seltenheit gehören.
3) Der Vergleich von empirisch gewonnenen Sprecherdaten, die sich meist auf die Bekanntheit und Existenz von Phraseologismen, ihre Verwendung oder Verstehensprozesse in der Sprachverarbeitung beziehen. Diese Untersuchungen, die sich der Werkzeuge verschiedener Disziplinen wie der Statistik, der kognitiven Linguistik oder der Sprachlehr- und Sprachlernforschung bedienen, können sowohl einsprachige als auch mehrsprachige Probanden (Földes 2007) einbeziehen.

Recht früh hat man in der interlingualen Phraseologie zwischen einer Systemebene und einer Textebene unterschieden (vgl. z.B. Földes 1997). Diese Unterscheidung bezieht sich auf eine traditionelle sprachwissenschaftliche Dichotomie, die auf de Saussures Zweiteilung von langue und parole bzw. Chomskys Kompetenz und Performanz basiert (vgl. Korhonen 2007: 575). Korhonen und Wotjak (2001: 226) fordern jedoch eine stärkere Einbeziehung „neuere[r] Erkenntnisse der kognitiven Linguistik (z.B. zu den konzeptuellen Bereichen, die durch Phraseologismen abgedeckt bzw. nicht abgedeckt werden)". Diese Forschungslücke ist auch schon z.T. geschlossen worden, denn zur kontrastiven kognitiven Linguistik gehören inzwischen empirische Untersuchungen zur Metaphorik und Figurativität, Kultursemiotik bzw. Kulturgebundenheit (vgl. Dobrovol'skij und Piirainen 2005; Malá 2005; Mellado Blanco 2010; Sabban 2007), zur Existenz, Bekanntheit und Verbreitung von Phraseologismen in verschiedenen Sprachen (Juska-Bacher 2009; Piirainen 2008[3]) und zur Phraseologie in der fremdsprachlichen Sprachverarbeitung (Hallsteinsdóttir 2001; Reder 2006, 2008).

Solchen Untersuchungen liegt meist eine Neuentwicklung von Methoden zugrunde und sie ergeben häufig ganz neue Datenmengen und Datentypen, die sich von bisherigen phraseologischen Daten deutlich unterscheiden. Die Unterschiede in der Beschaffenheit der Daten in ihren Untersuchungen nimmt Hallsteinsdóttir (2007: 161–162, vgl. auch Hallsteinsdóttir und Farø 2006) zum Anlass, die traditionelle sprachwissenschaftliche Dichotomie aufzubrechen und drei sprachliche Beschreibungsebenen anzunehmen.

Aufbauend auf dem Modell in Hallsteinsdóttir (2007; 2010) und inspiriert durch Kilian (2001) erweitern wir die Zweiteilung der Sprache in System und Text durch eine sprecherbezogene kognitive Ebene der Sprachkompetenz:

1. *Sprachsystem*: die Sprache als ein abstraktes System von Regeln und Einheiten, in dem sowohl das synchrone als auch das diachrone Potenzial einer Sprache erfasst werden können. Die Beschreibung des Sprachsystems umfasst die inhärenten Realisierungsmöglichkeiten einer Sprache in Relation zur Konstituierung dieser Möglichkeiten in der Sprachverwendung und der Sprachkompetenz der Sprecher sowie eine Antwort auf die Frage danach, welche Faktoren die Realisierung bestimmter Möglichkeiten verursachen und andere blockieren. Das abstrakte Sprachsystem wurde schon in unterschiedlichen grammatischen Theorien in verschiedenen sprachtheoretischen Paradigmen beschrieben, in denen der Fokus jedoch meist auf einzelnen Wörtern und ihren Kombinationsmöglichkeiten liegt (vgl. Gries 2008). Zum Sprachsystem gehört ebenfalls eine linguistische Metaebene der Theorie und Methodik, die durch das gewählte sprachtheoretische Paradigma vorgegeben wird. Das Sprachsystem ist die *Grundlage* des Sprachgebrauchs. Es konstituiert sich im Gebrauch als die Basis für die Interaktion zwischen der Sprachverwendung und der Sprachkompetenz. Eine alleinige Realisierung des Sprachsystems als Text kommt jedoch nur in abstrahierten Beschreibungen z.B. in Wörterbüchern und Grammatiken vor.
2. *Sprachverwendung*: die Konstituierung des abstrakten Potenzials einer Sprache im Diskurs als ein Resultat der Sprachproduktion, d.h. die tatsächlich realisierten sprachlichen Konstruktionen. In der Sprachverwendung konstituiert sich Sprache im Gebrauch als ein *Resultat* der Interaktion von Sprachsystem und Sprachkompetenz in Form von konkreten Texten.
3. *Kognitive Ebene der Sprachkompetenz*: die Konstituierung des Potenzials einer Sprache als das – bewusste und unbewusste – Wissen des einzelnen Sprechers über Sprache sowie die in der Sprachverarbeitung eingesetzten mentalen Prozesse, d.h. die individuelle Sprachkompetenz (vgl. Hallsteinsdóttir 2001). Die Sprachkompetenz konstituiert sich im Gebrauch als eine *Interaktion* zwischen Text und Sprachsystem in der mentalen Aktivierung von Sprache in der Sprachproduktion und -rezeption.

Hinter unserem Zugang verbirgt sich eine funktional-soziale Sprachauffassung, in der die Sprache als ein Gebrauchsphänomen[4] betrachtet wird (vgl. Farø 2006). Die Art und Weise der Konstituierung der Sprache im Gebrauch und somit auch die Perspektive der linguistischen Beschreibung ordnen sich in die drei Dimensionen der oben beschriebenen Dreiteilung ein.

Die drei Beschreibungsebenen ermöglichen eine differenzierte Herangehensweise an die verschiedenen Konstituierungsformen von Phraseologismen, indem nicht nur die Systemebene und die Textebene, sondern auch die kognitive Ebene berücksichtigt wird. Die Vorteile dieser Aufteilung für die interlinguale Phraseologie sind, dass die Datengrundlage und ihre Bedingungen in Relation zu den Zielen der jeweiligen Arbeit genauer erfasst und beschrieben werden können.

4. Semiotische Komplexität

Die Lexikalisierung als verbale Zeichen mit einer konventionell festgelegten, einheitlichen Bedeutung führt bei allen Phraseologismen dazu, dass die phraseologische Bedeutung nicht der Addition der Bedeutungen der einzelnen Komponenten entsprechen kann, denn durch die Lexikalisierung wird die Komponentenbedeutung prinzipiell sekundarisiert und die Zeichenbedeutung des Phraseologismus tritt an ihre Stelle. Dadurch entsteht eine Komplexität auf der Inhaltsebene, die darin besteht, dass alle Phraseologismen[5] – und nicht nur Idiome – potenziell mehrere Lesarten haben, d.h. mindestens eine kompositionelle und eine phraseologische. Es ist davon auszugehen, dass Sprecher jeder einzelnen Komponente eines Phraseologismus auch eigenes Bedeutungspotential zuweisen. Durch diese Bedeutungen haben sie die Möglichkeit, kompositionelle Bedeutungen zu konstruieren. Für Sprecher ist nicht die Zeichenhaftigkeit eines Phraseologismus, sondern die der einzelnen Komponenten visuell wahrnehmbar. Es ist daher anzunehmen, dass sowohl freie als auch phraseologische Bedeutungen in der Sprachverarbeitung potenziell verfügbar sind (vgl. ausführlich in Hallsteinsdóttir 2001: 45–52). Demnach sind auch alle Phraseologismen potenziell mehrdeutig, denn sie können potenziell kompositionell – wörtlich – verwendet und v.a. verarbeitet werden. Ersteres sieht man häufig in Sprachspielen und Letzteres dürfte nicht zuletzt bei unbekannten Phraseologismen der Fall sein.

Die Sprachkompetenz gaukelt uns zwar vor, wir verstünden bestimmte Typen von Phraseologismen – in der Forschung z.B. als nicht-idiomatisch bzw. transparent bezeichnet – durch ihre Komponentenbedeutungen. Ein Nichtmuttersprachler, der den Phraseologismus nicht kennt, wird die phraseologische Bedeutung häufig nicht richtig konstruieren können.[6] So verbalisiert man die

Bedeutung ‚die Zähne mit einer Zahnbürste reinigen' im Deutschen[7] mit *die Zähne putzen*. Wer die phraseologische Bedeutung von *die Zähne putzen* jedoch nicht kennt, wird ohne Kontext durch die Bedeutungen von *Zahn* und *putzen* (vgl. DWDS[8]) nicht unbedingt unterscheiden können, ob und welche Art von Zahnpflege – die Benutzung von Zahnbürste oder Zahnseide, Zahnsteinentfernung, Beseitigung von Verfärbungen oder etwa professionelle Zahnreinigung – gemeint ist:

1. ‚etw. reibend, wischend blank machen'
2. ‚etw. reinigen, säubern'
3. ‚sich, jmdn. schmücken, festlich kleiden'

Eine Monosemierung und somit die Festlegung der phraseologischen Lesart wird auf der Systemebene mit der Lexikalisierung und im mentalen Lexikon durch den Spracherwerb vollzogen. Die anderen möglichen Bedeutungen der Komponenten bleiben jedoch als Potenzial für kompositionelle Lesarten erhalten, wie im folgenden Beispiel:

– Im ersten Spiel konnten wir unseren Sieg verbuchen. Es ist ein guter Anfang, das [sic!] recht gut verlief. Hasan und Robert konnten je einen Tor schiessen [sic!]. Toll![9]

Für welche Lesart von *Tor* – z.B. ‚einfältiger, törichter Mensch' oder mit der Annahme eines grammatischen Fehlers: ‚zum Hindurchgehen, Hindurchfahren bestimmte große Öffnung' bzw. ‚mit einem Netz umspanntes, vorn offenes Gehäuse, in das der Ball von der Gegenpartei gebracht werden muß' (DWDS[10]) – sich der Sprecher letztendlich entscheidet, hängt vom Kontext, Weltwissen und seiner Sprachkompetenz ab.

Die unterschiedlichen Lesartenmöglichkeiten lassen sich auf die drei Konstituierungsformen von Sprache beziehen (vgl. oben):

1. *Sprachsystem*: Das sprachsystematische Potenzial der einzelnen Komponenten, phraseologische Lesarten sowie evtl. logisch mögliche wörtliche Lesarten.
2. *Sprachverwendung*: Die tatsächlich im Text realisierten Lesarten.
3. *Kognitive Ebene der Sprachkompetenz*: Die in der Sprachverarbeitung konstruierten Lesarten.

Diese Auffassung von Lesarten ist deutlich weiter gefasst und unterscheidet sich somit grundlegend von bisherigen Ansätzen, die die kompositionelle

Lesartenfähigkeit von logisch möglichen Interpretationen einer wörtlichen Lesart auf der Systemebene abhängig machen, d.h. wie z.B. Burger (2010: 62) Lesarten als „die möglichen semantischen Realisation einer bestimmten Wortverbindung" betrachten (vgl. auch Soehn 2006; Soehn und Römer 2007). Unsere Untersuchungen haben gezeigt, dass Phraseologismen mit Ausnahme von Sprachspielen tatsächlich nur selten in einer kompositionellen wörtlichen Lesart vorkommen, d.h. die Konstituierung einer kompositionellen Lesart auf der Ebene der Sprachverwendung ist selten (vgl. Hallsteinsdóttir 2010), denn v.a. bei den frequenteren Phraseologismen ist anzunehmen, dass die phraseologische Bedeutung salient ist und somit eine rein wörtliche Lesart unmöglich macht. Aus diesem Grund sollte möglicherweise eher von einem Lesartenkontinuum ausgegangen werden, das von einer rein wörtlichen bis zu einer rein phraseologischen Lesart reicht:[11]

- Eskortiert von Fangschiffen verließ die „Rainbow Warrior II" im Kielwasser eines Schleppers der Meerespräfektur die Bucht von Marseille in Richtung Spanien.
- Lindemann hatte sich 1956 in ein Faltboot gesetzt und im Kielwasser Bombards über den Atlantik begeben.
- Pünktlich zum Erscheinungstermin des sechsten Bandes kam die etwas angestaubte Korrespondenz jetzt an die Öffentlichkeit – im Kielwasser eines mächtigen PR-Kreuzers, der mit immer neuen Gags die globale Hysterie auf Touren hält.
- Die deutschen Technologiewerte sind am Donnerstag im Kielwasser positiver Vorgaben aus den USA gut behauptet in den Handel gestartet.

Die semiotische Komplexität bedingt eine prinzipielle Modifizierbarkeit von Phraseologismen und sie kommt häufig durch Relationen zu und das Zusammenspiel mit anderen Zeichensystemen zum Vorschein. Die Realisierung von Modifikationen korrespondiert möglicherweise mit den in der Forschung beschriebenen logischen Lesarten, d.h. je logischer die wörtliche Lesart ist, desto einfacher lässt sich ein Phraseologismus modifizieren. Hierzu sind jedoch weitere Untersuchungen erforderlich.

In Modifikationen spielt das in der Forschung als Bildhaftigkeit, Bildlichkeit oder Ikonographie (vgl. Farø 2006) genannte Phänomen eine große Rolle. Die Ikonographie ergibt sich z.B. durch die Bedeutungen der einzelnen Komponenten, kulturelle Symbole und Weltwissen der Sprecher. Die folgenden Beispiele zeigen einige Realisierungsmöglichkeiten der semiotischen Komplexität.

In der Überschrift *Island taget ved hornene* („Island an den Hörnern gepackt") ist die verbale Komponente *tyr* (,Stier') durch *Island* ersetzt worden und

Abbildung 2. *Berlingske Tidende, 21. September 2003*

die Auswahl des visualisierten Tieres (junger Schafsbock) erfolgt in Relation zu dem im Text behandelten Thema: der im Herbst stattfindende Schafabtrieb in Island.

Im zweiten Beispiel (Abbildung 3) kann zunächst eine konkrete Visualisierung der Komponente *Stier* in der Überschrift vermutet werden. Ein Blick auf die untergeordnete Überschrift verrät jedoch, dass der Stier auch die Frankfurter Börse symbolisieren könnte, deren Wahrzeichen bekanntlich Skulpturen von einem Bullen (für steigende Kurse) und einem Bären (für fallende Kurse) sind. Die beiden englischsprachigen Beispiele zeigen verschiedene Stier-Typen. Abbildung 4 zeigt einen gefährlichen, angriffslustigen Stier, mit dem die Firma mit ihren mutigen Rettungsmaßnahmen den Kampf aufnehmen will. Bei der Skulptur handelt es sich beim genaueren Hinsehen um das Symbol der Börse

Abbildung 3. *Gründerelle. Das Magazin für Gründerinnen, Ausgabe 2*
www.wirtschaftsfoerderung-dortmund.de/tiny/oj/ *(30. März 2010)*

Abbildung 4. *Werbung von BanxQuote® R_x. Business Debt Restructuring Solutions*
www.banx.com/images/bull_b&w.jpg *(30. März 2010)*

in Wall Street, wodurch ein direkter Bezug zu den aktuell schweren Zeiten der Finanzwelt herstellbar wird.

Im zweiten Beispiel (Abbildung 5) sehen wir einen durch einen Nasenring domestizierten und unter Kontrolle gehaltenen Zuchtbullen. Die abgeschlossene Zähmung und die Macht über das Zuchttier werden durch das Festhalten der Hörner demonstriert:[12]

Das im Weltwissen der Sprecher verankerte Symbolikwissen, das im deutschsprachigen und dem ersten englischsprachigen Beispiel das Verstehen beeinflusst, kann für den dänischen Phraseologismus nicht eingesetzt werden, denn die

Abbildung 5. *Werbung für Unterwäsche aus dem Jahr 1962*

Komponente *Stier/Bulle* hat keinen vergleichbaren Symbolwert im Dänischen. Im Isländischen gibt es keinen entsprechenden Phraseologismus.

Die semiotische Komplexität und die sich daraus ergebende potenzielle Mehrdeutigkeit und prinzipielle Modifizierbarkeit von Phraseologismen ist, zusammen mit der Unauffälligkeit der Form, eine der Haupterklärungen für Probleme sowohl in der theoretischen Beschreibung als auch der angewandten kontrastiven Phraseologie (vgl. eine ausführliche Argumentation dazu in Farø 2006).

5. Arbitrarität und Motiviertheit

Als zeichentheoretischer Ausgangspunkt dient die bilaterale Saussure'sche Auffassung, dass die Zuordnung von Ausdruck und Bedeutung arbiträr ist und von den Sprechern einer Sprachgemeinschaft ausgehandelt wird. Das Prinzip der

Arbitrarität sprachlicher Zeichen in dem Sinne, dass es keinen zwingenden Zusammenhang zwischen der Ausdrucksseite und der Bedeutung gibt, ist eine wichtige Grundlage aller kontrastiven Analysen (vgl. Farø 2006). Demnach ist weder die Bedeutung noch die Ausdrucksseite eines Zeichens durch das jeweils andere vorhersagbar. Auf die Phraseologie bezogen bedeutet dies, dass die Kombinierbarkeit der einzelnen Komponenten zu einem Phraseologismus nicht durch die phraseologische Bedeutung bestimmt wird und umgekehrt. Die Konsequenz ist, dass nicht von der Ausdrucksseite eines Phraseologismus auf die Ausdrucksseite eines Phraseologismus in einer anderen Sprache und ebenfalls nicht von der Ausdrucksseite auf die Äquivalenz von Phraseologismen und auch nicht auf die Äquivalenz einzelner Komponenten geschlossen werden kann (vgl. Farø 2006; Reder 2006). Der interlinguale Beweis der Arbitrarität sind die falschen Freunde, d.h. Phraseologismen, die „auf der Ebene der lexikalischen Konstituenten und mentalen Bilder, d.h. auf der Ebene der inneren Form" (Dobrovol'skij und Piirainen 2009; 147) Ähnlichkeiten aufweisen, jedoch unterschiedliche Bedeutungen haben.

Eine mit dem Arbitraritätsprinzip eng verbundene Konzeption ist die Motiviertheit bestimmter sprachlicher Zeichen. Die Motiviertheit besagt, dass bei bestimmten Zeichen doch eine Relation zwischen Form und Bedeutung besteht.

Es ist wichtig festzuhalten, dass sich die Motiviertheit und Arbitrarität nicht gegenseitig ausschließen, sondern zwei verschiedene Phänomene sind, die zwei verschiedene Perspektiven auf Sprache erfordern. Die Arbitrarität ist eine auf das Sprach*system* bezogene theoretische Voraussetzung. Die Motiviertheit bezieht sich dagegen auf die Sprach*kompetenz* der Sprecher. Die Motiviertheit teilen wir übergeordnet in drei verschiedene Phänomene auf (vgl. Farø 2006), die auf verschiedenen Strategien basieren können (vgl. Hallsteinsdóttir 2001).

Die *Entstehungsmotiviertheit* bezieht sich auf das Wissen um die Benennungsmotivation/-prinzipien. Sie ist diachron im Sprachsystem verankert und kann i.d.R. nur von Linguisten nachvollzogen werden. Dies gilt beispielsweise für den Ursprung von *jdm einen Bärendienst erweisen* in der Fabel „Der Bär und der Gartenliebhaber" (vgl. DUDEN 11). Diese Motiviertheit ist z.B. für die dänische Variante des Phraseologismus: *gøre ngn en bjørnetjeneste* durch die in den letzten Jahren stattgefundene Bedeutungsentwicklung von ‚ungewollt schlechter Dienst' hin zu ‚guter Dienst' kaum noch vorhersagbar.

Die *retrospektive Motivierbarkeit* basiert auf dem Wissen der Sprecher über die Bedeutung von bekannten Phraseologismen. Durch dieses Wissen kann eine Relation zwischen der Ausdrucksseite und der Bedeutung hergestellt werden. Die folgenden Sätze beinhalten Bedeutungserklärungen[13] mit expliziter retrospektiver Motivierung. Sie stammen von isländischen Sprechern, die alle angeben, den deutschen Phraseologismus selber aktiv zu verwenden:

– *Ihm ein Deutschlehrbuch schenken, hieße Eulen nach Athen tragen. Er ist doch in Deutschland aufgewachsen und spricht Deutsch wie ein Deutscher*: „Überflüssiges tun, unnötiges tun, weil Ähnliches schon vorhanden. [...]. Bedeutungshinweis: Eulen, Vögel der Weisheit, hatten ihren Wohnsitz in Athen" (Hallsteinsdóttir 2001: 243).
– *Aus rein finanziellen Gründen wollen sie die Ost-Firma über die Klinge springen lassen*: „Früher wurden Männer dazu verurteilt, über ein Schwert zu springen und es war Gottes oder der Götter Wille, ob sie es schafften oder nicht. Hier ist gemeint, nicht zu helfen obwohl es gut möglich wäre" (Hallsteinsdóttir 2001: 269).
– *Wir müssen die Beine unter den Arm nehmen*: Sich total beeilen (fast wie eine Kugel rollen, ohne Hindernis: Arme und Beine werden verschlungen miteinander) (Hallsteinsdóttir 2001: 251).

Prospektive Motivierbarkeit bezieht sich auf die Möglichkeit, in der Sprachverwendung eine Bedeutung durch die einzelnen Komponenten bzw. durch Elemente im Text zu konstruieren, d.h. es handelt sich um die Vorhersagbarkeit der Bedeutung unbekannter Phraseologismen im Text in Relation zum Sprecherwissen. So die Bedeutungserklärung eines isländischen Sprechers „Er hat was wirklich Gutes für sie getan. reiner Wein = ist auch ein guter Wein" (Hallsteinsdóttir 2001: 254) zu dem ihm unbekannten deutschen Phraseologismus im Satz: *Er schenkte ihr reinen Wein ein* und die Bedeutungserklärung eines englischsprachigen Sprechers "To be very open. Her heart is on her tounge: she speaks freely about things of the heart, personal, emotional things" (Hallsteinsdóttir 2001: 250) zu dem ihm ebenfalls unbekannten Phraseologismus im Satz: *Sie trägt ihr Herz auf der Zunge.*

6. Äquivalenz

Ein Ziel kontrastiver Arbeiten ist die Ermittlung von *Äquivalenzbeziehungen* (vgl. Korhonen 2007: 586). Unter Äquivalenz versteht man eine Gleichwertigkeit, die sich v.a. auf die Form, die Bedeutung und die Funktion von Sprachzeichen in zwei oder mehr Sprachen bezieht.

Allgemein wird zwischen qualitativer und quantitativer Äquivalenz unterschieden (vgl. Korhonen 2007: 577). Die quantitative Äquivalenz bezieht sich auf die Zahl der Äquivalente, wobei zwischen Monoäquivalenz, Polyäquivalenz und Nulläquivalenz unterschieden wird. Diese Art Äquivalenzbestimmung bezieht sich nur auf das phraseologische System. Andere Äquivalenzmöglichkeiten fallen prinzipiell unter die Kategorie phraseologische Nulläquivalenz (vgl. Abbildung 5). Die qualitative Äquivalenz (vgl. Korhonen 2007: 578–579) umfasst die semantische und strukturelle Beschaffenheit der Äquivalente. Es wird zwischen Volläquivalenz (Form und Bedeutung), Teiläquivalenz (Variation der Form, Bildhaftigkeit, Metaphorik und z.T. Konnotationen und Gebräuchlichkeit) und Ersatzäquivalenz (kein systemhaftes phraseologisches Äquivalent vorhanden) unterschieden. Allein bei der Ersatzäquivalenz werden nicht-phraseologische Äquivalenzmöglichkeiten einbezogen (vgl. Korhonen 2007: 581). Eine freie syntaktische Wortverbindung, also eine Paraphrase, ist prinzipiell immer möglich. Daher sind aus einer linguistischen Perspektive v.a. äquivalente Wortbildungen und Einzellexeme interessant, hierzu gibt es allerdings kaum empirische Untersuchungen.

In vielen kontrastiven Untersuchungen sind die einzelnen phraseologischen Kategorien ein klar bevorzugter Ausgangspunkt (vgl. Malá 2005: 71). Mit einem solchen auf die Form und auf einzelne Kategorien der Phraseologie fokussierten Vergleich geht fast immer eine Kategoriengebundenheit einher in dem Sinne, dass die Einheiten einer bestimmten phraseologischen Kategorie in zwei oder mehr Sprachen verglichen werden. Fleischer (1997: 249) betont jedoch, dass eine sprachspezifische intrasprachliche Kategorie keinesfalls einen kategoriegebundenen Sprachvergleich erfordert, sondern dass sowohl in der kontrastiven Linguistik als auch intralingual die Kategorie an sich nicht für mögliche Forschungsfragen maßgebend sein sollte. Hessky (1997) meint ebenfalls, dass ein interlingualer Vergleich nur dann sinnvoll ist, wenn er von beiden Sprachen ausgeht und nicht nur als intraphraseologische „Einbahnstraße" (Hessky 1997: 258) angesehen wird. Eine mögliche Differenzierung mit Bedeutung als Vergleichsgrundlage wird in Abbildung 6 gezeigt, zu der wir die nicht-phraseologischen Äquivalenzmöglichkeiten auch als mögliche Form in L1 hinzugefügt haben.

Die Vergleichsgrundlage der kontrastiven Phraseologie ist traditionell entweder die Bedeutung oder die Form (vgl. Korhonen 2007: 575; Reder 2006: 91), in neueren Arbeiten auch die Funktion in der Sprachverwendung (vgl. Farø 2006). So ordnen Dobrovol'skij und Piirainen (2009: 145–146) übergeordnet die relevanten zwischensprachlichen Äquivalenzaspekte „den drei bekannten semiotischen Dimensionen – Semantik, Syntaktik (Kombinatorik) und Pragmatik" zu. Korhonen und Wotjak (2001: 228) fordern „(e)in sorgfältig ausgearbeitetes, möglichst auch für die Computerimplementierung geeignetes, mehrdimensionales Kriterienraster als Tertium comparationis", das folgende Äquivalenzparameter beinhalten soll: „Semantik (denotativer Bedeutungskern und Konnotationen; syntagmatisch-semantische Kompatibilität und paradigmatisch-semantische Beziehungen), Lexik, Morphosyntax (praseologismusintern und -extern), Pragmatik, Bildspenderbereich, Gebrauchsüblichkeiten und

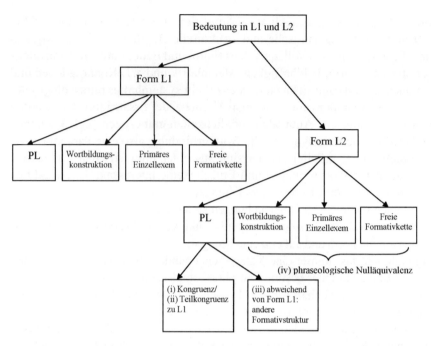

Abbildung 6. *Modifizierte Darstellung der zentralen phraseologischen Äquivalenztypen nach Korhonen und Wotjak (2001: 227)*

-restriktionen, Kollokabilität, Textsortenpräferenzen ..." Und die Liste kann noch lange weitergeführt werden.

Neben der Anzahl ist die *Granularität* der Äquivalenzparameter in der kontrastiven Analyse ein wichtiger Aspekt, denn je feiner die Analyse ist, desto umfangreicher wird die Beschreibung. Die Relevanz einzelner Äquivalenzparameter kann erst nach einer Relevanzanalyse im konkreten Kontext festgelegt werden (vgl. Farø 2006).

Von Farø (2006) übernehmen wir einen funktionalistischen Äquivalenzbegriff, der auf der Grundlage seiner deutsch-dänischen Untersuchung entwickelt wurde und auf den folgenden Prämissen basiert:

– Die Erfassung der Äquivalenz bezieht sich immer auf das gesamte Sprachsystem, d.h. Phraseologismen, Wortbildungen und Simplizia. Eine sprachlich begründete Kategoriegebundenheit im Sinne von L1-Phraseologismus = L2-Phraseologismus gibt es nicht, d.h. es gibt keine den Phraseologismen inhärente Eigenschaft, die eine Äquivalenz in Form eines anderen Phraseologismus vorschreibt (vgl. auch Fleischer 1997: 249).

- Phraseologismen verfügen über ein besonderes semiotisches Potenzial, das sich in bestimmten Situationen entfaltet. Die Ausdrucksseite von Phraseologismen kann demzufolge eine funktionale Rolle spielen, z.B. in Verbindung mit Sprachspielen, häufig tut sie es aber in der Tat nicht. Die Konsequenz ist, dass die Ausdrucksseite für die Lexikologie, Translatologie und Lexikologie relevant sein *kann*, sie *muss* es aber nicht sein.
- Die Äquivalenz von Phraseologismen ist ein unterschiedliches Phänomen in der Lexikologie, Translatologie, Sprachdidaktik bzw. Lexikographie, das jeweils einen theoretisch-methodisch eigenen Untersuchungsgegenstand ausmacht, der aus unterschiedlichen Perspektiven betrachtet werden sollte.

In Farø (2006) werden fünf Grundbedingungen für die Bestimmung von Äquivalenz in der angewandten kontrastiven Phraseologie unterschieden:

1) Zeichentheoretische Grundbedingungen: Arbitrarität und semiotische Komplexität.
2) Disziplinspezifischer Makro- und Mikrokontext:
   a. Kontrastive Lexikologie: Analyseaspekte, Form-Bedeutung, hypothetische Äquivalenzpaare.
   b. Translatologie: Textfunktion, Autorenabsicht, Empfänger, Übersetzungsauftrag, textuelle Funktion des Phraseologismus.
   c. Bi- und multilinguale Lexikographie: Wörterbuchkonzept, lexikographische Funktionen, Benutzervoraussetzungen, finanzielle Aspekte.
   d. Fremdsprachendidaktik: Vorkenntnisse, Muttersprache, Unterrichtskonzept.
3) Granularität der Analyse: grob, mittel, fein.
4) Äquivalenzaspekte: disziplinspezifisch und von der Datengrundlage und Granularität sowie dem Ziel der Untersuchung abhängig.
5) Die lexikologische Beschreibung: die sprachsystematische Wortschatzbeschreibung ist die Voraussetzung der spezifischeren Beschreibung der angewandten Disziplinen.

Äquivalenz ist demnach ein hochkomplexer und in mehrfachem Sinn relationaler Begriff. Fragen nach Äquivalenz – sei es zu einzelnen Phraseologismen, sei es zu ganzen Inventaren – werden im Idealfall immer diese Faktoren berücksichtigen. Das heißt, dass nach der Frage nach Äquivalenz zunächst gewisse Gegenfragen beantwortet werden müssen: Innerhalb welcher linguistischen Disziplin? Wie fein granuliert soll die Beschreibung sein? Welche Äquivalenzaspekte sind relevant? Sind diese Fragen erst beantwortet und der Ausgangspunkt somit spezifiziert, dann erst lässt sie sich gezielt untersuchen.

7. Zu Differenzierungen des Äquivalenzbegriffs mit Blick auf die Praxis

Eine disziplinorientierte Relevanzanalyse erfordert naturgemäß einen Zugang zur Äquivalenz via die einzelnen sprachwissenschaftlichen Disziplinen. Wir beschränken unsere folgenden Ausführungen auf die wortschatzrelevanten angewandten Disziplinen Lexikographie, Translatologie und Fremdsprachendidaktik. Die generelle Voraussetzung für Äquivalenzanalysen ist eine sprachsystematische Grundlage. Dies heißt konkret, dass die Äquivalenz zunächst als reiner lexikogrammatischer und lexiko-pragmatischer Wortschatzvergleich im Rahmen der kontrastiven Lexikologie behandelt wird. Dann erfolgt die Trennung und Spezifikation des Makro- und Mikrokontexts innerhalb des disziplinären Rahmens und nach den theoretisch-methodischen Prämissen der jeweiligen Disziplin.

Es sollte jedoch nicht erwartet werden, dass sämtliche kontrastiv-lexikologischen Daten unbedingt für alle angewandten Disziplinen relevant sind. Auf der einen Seite steht ein deskriptiv-theoretischer Vergleich und auf der anderen Seite die funktional-praktischen Arbeiten in der Lexikographie, Translatologie und Fremdsprachendidaktik mit ihren spezifischen Zielen.

7.1. Kontrastive Lexikologie

Die kontrastive Lexikologie umfasst Wortschatzvergleich auf der Ebene des Sprachsystems mit dem Ziel, den Wortschatz in zwei oder mehr Sprachen zu erfassen, zu beschreiben und zu vergleichen. Ein häufig verfolgtes weiteres Ziel ist es, Daten für angewandte Disziplinen zu liefern. Der Untersuchungsgegenstand sind die sprachsystematischen Eigenschaften von Phraseologismen. Die Lexikologie befasst sich – im Idealfall – mit der Erforschung und Beschreibung des gesamten Wortschatzes, von dem die Phraseologie bekanntlich einen nicht unerheblichen Teil ausmacht.

Traditionelle kontrastive lexikologische Analysen beziehen sich auf das Sprachsystem. Ihr Ausgangspunkt ist meist der Äquivalenzgrad der Bedeutung und der Form auf der Systemebene, wobei Phraseologismen „als *isolierte* sprachliche Einheiten analysiert" (Koller 2007: 606) werden. Kritiker dieser Vorgehensweise haben in den letzten Jahren die Möglichkeiten computerbasierter Analyseverfahren und die Zugänglichkeit von großen Korpora genutzt, um zunächst empirisch fundierte intralinguale lexikologische Beschreibungen auszuarbeiten. Solche Untersuchungen (vgl. z.B. Fellbaum et al. 2006a, 2006b) benutzen Korpusdaten aus der Sprachverwendung, um eine sprachsystematische Beschreibung anzufertigen. Die Validierung der durch die Korpusdaten gewonnenen Informationen geschieht in einem zweiten Arbeitsschritt durch das Hinzuziehen des Sprecher(experten)wissens der einzelnen Forscher, also durch das induktiv-intuitive Einbeziehen der Sprachkompetenz. Diese Beschreibungen sind eine wichtige Grundlage für die kontrastive Lexikologie. Daten zur kognitiven Ebene der Sprachkompetenz der Sprecher sowie Daten zur Sprachverwendung der gesprochenen Sprache sind noch eine Seltenheit, aber im Idealfall müssten diese ergänzend zu Daten zur Sprachverwendung der geschriebenen Sprache und der Intuition der Forscher herangezogen werden.

In der kontrastiven Lexikologie werden hypothetische Äquivalenzpaare (HÄP[14]) auf das Vorhandensein äquivalenzrelevanter Übereinstimmungen und Abweichungen überprüft. Die lexikologische Äquivalenz kann als die vollständige Parallelität einer sehr großen Anzahl von Äquivalenzaspekten beschrieben werden, deren vollständige kontrastive Relationen im Idealfall auf der Grundlage umfassender intralingualer Korpusanalysen und Probandenbefragungen untersucht werden.

In der Phraseologie ist ein interlingualer lexikologischer Symmetriegedanke sehr verbreitet. In den Fällen, in denen bei HÄP offenbar keine Äquivalenz vorliegen konnte, hat man von „phraseologischen falschen Freunden" gesprochen (vgl. Korhonen 2007: 584 – vgl. auch „echte Freunde" in Korhonen und Wotjak 2001: 227).

Wir vermuten, dass eine systematische, umfassende und empirische Untersuchung die angenommene Äquivalenz in vielen Fällen in Frage stellen würde. Dies hat zumindest die Untersuchung von Farø (2006) für äquivalente deutsch-dänische Phraseologismen festgestellt. Die große Vielfalt der Äquivalenzaspekte, deren jeweilige Relevanz sich im lexikologischen Zusammenhang prinzipiell nicht graduieren lässt, macht die lexikologische Totaläquivalenz zu einem eher unwahrscheinlichen Phänomen.

Lexikologische Äquivalenz ist keine funktionsorientierte, sondern eine systembezogene Wortschatzanalyse.[15] Im Sprachsystem kann kaum abstrakt von funktionalen Äquivalenten, sondern nur von potenziell funktionalen Äquivalenzen gesprochen werden. Funktionale Äquivalente können erst in konkreten Situationen, in denen der kommunikative Zweck definiert ist, bestimmt werden.

7.2. Translatologie

Ein Großteil der Untersuchungen, die sich mit Phraseologie und Übersetzung beschäftigen, bezieht sich auf die Klassifikation von eingesetzten Übersetzungsäquivalenten und einer darauf aufbauenden Beschreibung von Äquivalenzproblemen. Das Hauptaugenmerk liegt auf Problemen der Übersetzung (vgl. Koller 2007), aber auch Übersetzungsmöglichkeiten werden beschrieben (vgl. Hallsteinsdóttir 1997). Für die Phraseologie werden bei Koller (2007: 610) drei Analyseperspektiven angegeben, die sich alle auf die Textebene beziehen: die

Übersetzung als Text, der Ausgangstext und der Vergleich von Ausgangstext und Übersetzung.

Beim Übersetzen wird eine durch den Kontext monosemierte Variante der konventionell festgelegten, lexikalisierten Bedeutung eines Phraseologismus im Ausgangstext vom Übersetzer erfasst und im Zieltext wiedergegeben. Übersetzungen als Prozess sind daher laut unserer Dreiteilung an der Schnittstelle zwischen Sprachverwendung und Sprachkompetenz anzusiedeln, während Übersetzungen als Produkt zur Sprachverwendung gehören. Gemeint ist die Sprachkompetenz des jeweiligen Übersetzers sowohl in der Ausgangs- als auch in der Zielsprache, die über sein Verstehen des Ausgangstextes und die Produktion des Zieltextes entscheidet.

Translatorische Äquivalenz umfasst eine adäquate funktionale Beziehung zwischen einem Ausgangstext(teil), der einen Phraseologismus enthält, und einem Zieltext(teil). Der Zieltext vermittelt meist denselben Inhalt wie der Ausgangstext, aber die Funktionen der beiden Texte können abweichend sein. Die translatorische Äquivalenz von Phraseologismen ist als ein Teilaspekt der übergeordneten Textäquivalenz einer Übersetzung zu sehen, und sie legitimiert sich nur durch diese. Die Textäquivalenz beeinflusst somit die Äquivalenz von Phraseologismen. Die phraseologische Äquivalenz in Übersetzungen kann als eine einseitige Relation angesehen werden, die von der Phraseologie des Ausgangstexts und der Sprachkompetenz des Übersetzers gesteuert wird, ohne dass das Resultat unbedingt die gleiche Anzahl an Phraseologismen im Zieltext ist.

Ausgehend von Sprachzeichen stehen viele Möglichkeiten bei der Übersetzung zur Verfügung (vgl. Hallsteinsdóttir 1997, vgl. auch das modifizierte Modell in Abbildung 5):

- Phraseologismus – Phraseologismus
- Phraseologismus – Wort (Wortbildung oder Simplex)
- Phraseologismus – freie Wortverbindung (Paraphrase bzw. Weglassen)
- freie Wortverbindung – Phraseologismus
- Wort – Phraseologismus

Die in Farø (2006) durchgeführte Untersuchung von deutsch-dänischen literarischen Übersetzungen hat ergeben, dass sich Übersetzer bei Phraseologismen einer großen Breite an Übersetzungstypen bedienen. Tendenziell übersetzen sie jedoch kategoriegebunden Phraseologismen mit Phraseologismen. Damit beschränken sich die Übersetzer nicht selten unnötig bezüglich möglicher Lösungen und schaffen unnatürliche oder inadäquate Übersetzungen, denn es gibt keine der Phraseologie immanente Eigenschaft, die eine Übersetzung von einem Phraseologismus mit einem Phraseologismus zwingend macht.

Die Analyse von Übersetzungen modifizierter Phraseologismen ergab eine paradoxe Konklusion: die Modifikation ist eine Realisierungsvariante von Phraseologismen, bei der ihre Form, die Ikonographie und teilweise die phraseologische Kategorie fraglos eine funktionale Rolle spielt. Gerade bei der Modifikation aber scheinen die Möglichkeiten der Übersetzung aufgrund von Ausdruck-Inhalt-Asymmetrien (vgl. Hessky 1992: 111) sehr begrenzt zu sein. Die Übersetzung modifizierter Phraseologismen ist häufig nicht auf der Wortschatz-, sondern nur auf der Text-/Inhaltsebene möglich. Modifikationen – zumindest semantische und formale, denn *metakommunikative* Modifikationen bereiten offenbar weniger Schwierigkeiten – können in diesem Sinn als das wirkliche Problem der Übersetzung von Phraseologismen betrachtet werden.

Eine Analyse der deutschen und der englischen Übersetzung eines Textes aus der offiziellen Touristikbroschüre der Stadt Odense von Januar 2009[16] bestätigt den von Farø (2006) beschriebenen „phraseologischen Dogmatismus", d.h. dass die Form mit den einzelnen Komponenten und die Kategorie eindeutig einen starken Einfluss auf die Übersetzung haben:

1. På pladen har bandet rendyrket genren powerrock, som bandet gennem 3 EP udgivelser og en masse koncerter, **har gjort til deres varemærke** [wörtlich: *zu ihrem Warenzeichen gemacht haben*, Bed. *‚zu seinem Kennzeichen/ Merkmal machen'*].
   - Auf der Platte hat die Band in Reinkultur das Genre Powerrock entwickelt, den sie durch 3 EP-Ausgaben und viele Konzerte **zu ihrem Warenzeichen gemacht hat**.
   - On the album, the band has cultivated the power rock genre, which has become the band's trademark, through their three EP releases and numerous concerts.
2. Begrebet dækker over en unik blanding af guitardrevet rock **med kant** [wörtlich: *mit Kante*, Bed.: *'der besonderen Art'/'mit Biss'.*], melodien i centrum og et udtalt tekstunivers, hvor **der ikke bliver lagt fingre imellem** [wörtlich: **es werden nicht Finger zwischen gelegt*, Bed.: *‚seine Meinung direkt sagen'*].
   - Der Begriff deckt eine einzigartige Mischung aus gitarrenbeheiztem Rock **mit scharfen Kanten**, der Melodie im Zentrum und einem ausgesprochenen Textuniversum, **das keine Wünsche offen lässt**.
   - The concept covers a unique blend of **edgy**, guitar-based rock, with the melody in the centre and a pronounced lyrical universe, and the band **doesn't beat about the bush**!
3. Bandet har i genre tidligere både været forbi det elektroniske grænseland og følsomme ballader, men **er** denne gang **trukket i rocktrøjen** [wörtlich:

hat den Rockpullover angezogen, Modifikation von *trække i arbejdstøjet*, wörtlich: **die Arbeitsbekleidung anziehen*, Bed.: *ein Projekt, eine Aufgabe o.Ä. beginnen*] og **har skruet op for** [wörtlich: **hat herauf geschraubt*, Bed.: *'aufdrehen, lauter/höher stellen'*] guitaren og attituden.
- Die Band hat in diesem Genre früher das elektronische Grenzland erforscht und gefühlvolle Balladen produziert. Diesmal jedoch **hat sie die Rockklamotten angezogen** und die Gitarre und die Attitude **voll aufgedreht**.
- The band has previously dabbled with a more electronic sound and sensitive ballads, but this time they **have pulled on their rock caps** and **cranked up** the guitar and attitude.

Nicht nur die einzelnen Wörter, sondern auch die Phraseologismen im Ausgangstext werden in den Zieltexten so wörtlich wie möglich übersetzt. Im Bsp. 1 werden sogar die Konstituenten der Komponente *varemærke* wörtlich mit *Warenzeichen* übersetzt, statt das lexikalisierte *etw. zu seinem Markenzeichen machen* zu verwenden. Diese Strategie ist ebenfalls bei der wörtlichen Übersetzung des modifizierten dänischen Phraseologismus *trække i rocktøjet* und *skrue op for* im Bsp. 3 zu beobachten. Weiterhin wird im Bsp. 2 *der ikke bliver lagt fingre imellem* im Deutschen und im Englischen kategorientreu mit einem anderen Phraseologismus übersetzt. Bei *rock med kant* handelt es sich vermutlich um eine dänische Version des englischen *with an edge*, die in dänischen Wörterbüchern nicht zu finden ist, jedoch recht häufig in Verbindung mit *Musik* verwendet wird und im Deutschen deutlich seltener als *[Musik(er)] mit scharfen Kanten* vorkommt.

Zusammenfassend kann festgestellt werden: auch wenn kein Phraseologismus mit einer gleichlautenden Ausdrucksseite oder äquivalenten Bedeutung gefunden wird, wird kategorisch phraseologisch übersetzt.

Die Annahme, dass Phraseologismen normale arbiträre Sprachzeichen sind, deren Bedeutung konventionell festgelegt ist, hat für das Übersetzen einen besonderen Reiz. Damit wird erstens die häufig praktizierte Kategoriengebundenheit hinfällig und zweitens kann die Konventionalität auf weitere Ebenen der Kommunikation bezogen werden. Denn eine Übersetzung ist immer in eine zielsprachliche Kommunikation eingebunden, in der die Konventionen der Zielsprache und der Zielkultur sowie das Sprach- und Weltwissen der zielsprachigen Empfänger gelten. Welche Funktion ein Phraseologismus im Text erfüllt und somit auch seine Übersetzung, hängt in erster Linie vom Textinhalt und von den kommunikativen Konventionen des Textes ab, in dem der Phraseologismus verwendet wird – die in der Ausgangssprache und in der Zielsprache nicht unbedingt gleich sind.

7.3. Bilinguale Lexikographie

Die bi- und multilinguale Lexikographie bzw. die Phraseographie (vgl. Hallsteinsdóttir 2006) beschäftigt sich mit der Darstellung der Phraseologie in zwei- oder mehrsprachigen Wörterbüchern. Als Ausgangspunkt gilt, dass zu Phraseologismen in zweisprachigen Wörterbüchern äquivalente Einheiten angegeben und sie eventuell erklärt werden.

Wir beziehen uns hier auf die Funktionslehre der Aarhuser Schule (vgl. z.B. die Übersicht in Tarp 2006 und zur Phraseographie in Hallsteinsdóttir 2009). Sie betrachtet die Frage danach, welche Benutzer welche Wörterbücher in welchen Situationen zu welchem Zweck benutzen, als die grundlegende lexikographische Frage. Das Ziel der Lexikographie ist demnach, durch die Beantwortung dieser Frage dem Wörterbuchbenutzer relevante lexikographische Informationen zu liefern.

Ein funktionaler Ausgangspunkt ist keine Selbstverständlichkeit, denn z.B. von Hanks et al. (2006: 444) wird die Beschreibung des Sprachgebrauchs als die primäre Aufgabe des Lexikographen angesehen: "The task of a lexicographer analysing a corpus is to identify all normal uses of words (not all possible uses), to group them into categories, and to offer an explanation (a „definition") of each word in each of its categories." Eine sorgfältige kontrastive lexikologische Beschreibung ist die *Voraussetzung* phraseographischen Arbeitens, es handelt sich dabei aber um keine lexikographische Aufgabe.

Als kommunikative Benutzungssituationen, die für zweisprachige Wörterbücher relevant sind, gelten die Sprachrezeption und -produktion in der Fremdsprache sowie das Übersetzen in die Fremdsprache oder die Muttersprache (vgl. Tarp 2006). Für die bilinguale Phraseographie bedeutet dies primär, dass Wörterbücher Informationen enthalten sollen, die dem Benutzer einerseits das Verstehen und andererseits das Verwenden von Phraseologismen ermöglichen können. Für das Verstehen reicht meist eine Bedeutungsangabe und eventuell, um das Nachvollziehen der formalen und inhaltlichen Struktur zu ermöglichen, eine komponentenbasierte – „Wort-für-Wort"-Übersetzung (vgl. Ettinger und Nunes 2006: 9). Für das Verwenden gibt Hallsteinsdóttir (2009: 221, vgl. auch Jesenšek 2006: 143, 2007) folgende lexikographische Daten an:

(a) Eine genaue Bedeutungsangabe mit einem metasprachlichen pragmatischen Kommentar zu Gebrauchsregeln und Verwendungsrestriktionen.
(b) Die Angabe der normalen syntaktischen Struktur(en).
(c) Die Angabe der Kontexte, in denen der Phraseologismus normalerweise vorkommt.

Interlinguale lexikographische Äquivalenz betrachten wir als eine Mischung aus einer sprachsystematischen und einer funktionalen Perspektive. Funktional gesehen besteht lexikographische Äquivalenz dann, wenn mit Ausgangspunkt in einem L1-Phraseologismus ein oder mehrere L2-Sprachzeichen oder Paraphrasen dem Benutzer die für seine Benutzungssituation relevanten Informationen liefern. Phraseologische Äquivalente haben aber an sich keinen funktionalen Wert.

Dobrovol'skij und Piirainen (2009: 143) stellen fest, dass in lexikographischen Beschreibungen von einer „prinzipiellen semantischen Äquivalenz" ausgegangen wird. Sie konstatieren, dass sich „in den meisten Fällen zwischensprachliche Äquivalente finden lassen, die aber andererseits so gut wie nie bedenkenlos in allen möglichen Übersetzungssituationen einsetzbar sind." (Dobrovol'skij und Piirainen 2009: 143). Äquivalente können bei einer Totaläquivalenz als Verstehens- und Produktionshilfe fungieren, da aber die Totaläquivalenz eher selten vorkommen dürfte, erfordert die Angabe von äquivalenten Phraseologismen sowie falschen Freunden auch eine Erklärung der Äquivalenzbeziehung.

Lexikographische Äquivalenz ist ein recht komplexer Untersuchungsgegenstand. Die Kombination der lexikologischen Beschreibung, Kotextlosigkeit, Polyfunktionalität und (printlexikographischer) Platzknappheit macht die Etablierung von wirklich anwendbaren Äquivalenzrelationen innerhalb sämtlicher (ex- oder implizit) anvisierter Wörterbuchfunktionen schwierig. Eine Bewusstwerdung über diese Komplexität ist ein notwendiger erster Schritt, der nicht zuletzt durch eigene Erfahrungen mit Vorgaben von Wörterbuchverlagen begründet ist, die durchaus noch auf eine kategoriegebundene Äquivalenz im dem Sinne bestehen, dass ein Phraseologismus mit einem Phraseologismus gleicher Kategorie erklärt werden soll. Auch wenn phraseologische Kategorien für die lexikographische Äquivalenz wenig relevant sind, können sie durchaus für den Lexikographen als ein wichtiges Hilfsmittel fungieren, weil ‚unterschiedliche phraseologische Kategorien unterschiedliche Probleme bei unterschiedlichen Sprach- und Wörterbuchbenutzern verursachen können' (Farø und Lorentzen 2009: 75).

Inzwischen gibt es neben einsprachigen Projekten auch große interlinguale Wörterbuchprojekte, die die Phraseologie von einer Sprache ausgehend kontrastiv beschreiben (vgl. z.B. Ďurčo 2009; Jesenšek 2009). Die Darstellung der kontrastiv-zweisprachig gewonnenen Daten von äquivalenten Wortschatzeinheiten in bidirektionalen Wörterbüchern stellt nach wie vor ein Forschungsdefizit dar (vgl. Hallsteinsdóttir 2009).

7.4. Fremdsprachendidaktik

Die dritte und letzte hier behandelte Schnittstelle angewandter Disziplinen zur interlingualen Phraseologie ist die Fremdsprachendidaktik, in der die Phraseologie auf allen Niveaustufen des Sprachlernens und -lehrens eine immer wichtigere Rolle spielt.[17] Die Phraseodidaktik umfasst die Darstellung von Phraseologie in Lernerwörterbüchern und in Lehrwerken sowie die Entwicklung phraseodidaktischer Materialien und die Erfassung und Beschreibung der Lernervoraussetzungen. Laut Korhonen und Wotjak (2001) sollen in der Phraseodidaktik zusätzlich zu den „phraseodidaktischen Aspekten hinsichtlich der Auswahl und Aufbereitung des Lehr- und Lernstoffs (wie Gebräuchlichkeit, Adressatenbezug und Textsortenspezifik), auch sprachenpaarbezogene Aspekte berücksichtigt werden" (Korhonen und Wotjak 2001: 232).

Sprachdidaktische Arbeiten können übergeordnet aufgeteilt werden in:

(a) die Auswahl und Beschreibung von Phraseologie in der Sprachverwendung als Grundlage für Lehrmaterial und Lernerwörterbücher (vgl. Bergerová 2009b; Durčo 2001; Hallsteinsdóttir et al. 2006; Hessky 1992),
(b) die Methoden der Vermittlung der Phraseologie im Unterricht (vgl. v.a. Bergerová 2009a; Ettinger 1998, 2009; Hessky 1997; Jesenšek 2006; Kühn 1992, 1994) und die Entwicklung von Unterrichtsmaterial[18] sowie
(c) die durch die Sprachkompetenz gegebenen mutter- und fremdsprachlichen Voraussetzungen der Lerner (vgl. Dobrovol'skij 1995; Hallsteinsdóttir 2001; Hessky 1987; Reder 2006, 2008).

Sprachlerner tendieren dazu, die muttersprachliche Phraseologie unreflektiert in die Fremdsprache zu übertragen. Dies geschieht sowohl in der Sprachrezeption als auch in der Sprachproduktion, weil eine durch die Ausdrucksseite der Phraseologismen bedingte Symmetrie, d.h. Äquivalenz, zwischen der Mutter- und der Fremdsprache vorausgesetzt wird. Probleme entstehen z.B. dann, wenn durch die Vorgabe der Phraseologie der Muttersprache in der Fremdsprache fehlerhafte oder nicht existente Phraseologismen produziert werden oder wenn formgleiche oder ähnliche Phraseologismen als Äquivalente interpretiert werden und deshalb die muttersprachliche Bedeutung konstruiert wird. Häufig handelt es sich um falsche Freunde, aber auch andere zwischensprachliche Unterschiede in der Bedeutung können muttersprachlich bedingte Fehler sowohl in der Sprachrezeption als auch in der Sprachproduktion verursachen. Hierzu gehören phraseologische Quasisynonyme, d.h. Phraseologismen mit gleicher oder fast gleicher bildlichen Komponente und ähnlicher Bedeutung und Phraseologismen, die zwischensprachliche asymmetrische Bedeutungsstrukturen aufweisen (vgl. Dobrovol'skij und Piirainen 2009: 146–149; Fabčič 2010).

Eine interlinguale phraseodidaktische Äquivalenz erfordert eine Mischung aus unterschiedlichen Perspektiven. Die Grundlage für Unterrichtsmaterial ist die lexikologische Beschreibung der Phraseologie mit Fokus auf die aktuelle Sprachverwendung – also die Sprache, mit der Sprachlerner in der Tat konfrontiert werden (vgl. Hallsteinsdóttir et al. 2006). Dazu kommen Untersuchungen zur Sprachkompetenz der Lerner, um einerseits durch die Erfassung der muttersprachlichen Voraussetzungen eine gezielte Förderung und Vermeidung von Fehlern und andererseits die Einbeziehung vorhandener Verstehens- und Verarbeitungsstrategien in das Lehren und Lernen zu ermöglichen. Der starke Einfluss der muttersprachlichen Form beim Fremdsprachenlernen macht den Vergleich der Ausdrucksseite der Phraseologie (z.B. Komponentenstruktur, Ikonographie, morpho-syntaktische Eigenschaften, intrasprachlich formbedingte Wortschatzrelationen) zu einem wichtigen Forschungsgegenstand in der Phraseodidaktik.

8. Zusammenfassung

Unsere Unterscheidung zwischen drei Konstituierungsmöglichkeiten von Sprache: dem Sprachsystem, der Sprachverwendung und der Sprachkompetenz, ermöglicht eine differenzierte Erfassung und Beschreibung phraseologischer Eigenschaften. In Relation zu diesen Konstituierungsformen haben wir die Betrachtung von Phraseologismen in den wichtigsten interlingualen Disziplinen diskutiert, die eine Schnittstelle zur Phraseologie aufweisen. Wir haben gezeigt, dass die phraseologische Äquivalenz eine spezifisch lexikologische, translatorische, lexikographische und sprachdidaktische Perspektive hat. Diese Perspektiven sind theoretisch und methodologisch distinkt. Äquivalenz in der Phraseologie ist im Fall der Lexikologie eine sprachsystematisch-beschreibende, in der Lexikographie eine Mischung von Sprachverwendung und des Sprachsystems, in der Translatologie und der Sprachdidaktik aber in erster Linie durch die Funktion eines Phraseologismus in der Sprachverwendung und die Sprachkompetenz der einzelnen Sprecher bedingt. Zwischen der Lexikologie und den angewandten Disziplinen besteht eine einseitige Dependenzbeziehung und insofern müssen kontrastiv-lexikologische Untersuchungen als eine wichtige Grundlage der interlingualen Phraseologie betrachtet werden.

Unsere Hypothese ist, dass sich die hier beschriebenen Eigenschaften semantische Komplexität, potenzielle Mehrdeutigkeit und prinzipielle Modifizierbarkeit nicht nur in der Phraseologie im engeren Sinne, sondern auch generell in der Phraseologie beschreiben lassen. Dieser Beitrag liefert die ersten theoretisch-methodischen Überlegungen für weitere Untersuchungen dazu.

Anmerkungen

Kontaktadressen: erla@language.sdu.dk; kenfaroe@hum.ku.dk

1. Dieser Beitrag basiert auf Ergebnissen aus Projekten, die vom DAAD, The Icelandic Research Council und Carlsbergfondet finanziert wurden. Ihnen sei hiermit für ihre großzügige Unterstützung gedankt. Für wertvolle inhaltliche Hinweise geht ein großer Dank an die beiden anonymen Gutachter.
2. Die sowjetische Forschung lieferte schon eine solide Grundlage für kontrastive Untersuchungen (vgl. Földes 2006: 12, 15). In den etwa 40 Jahren europäischer Phraseologieforschung haben viele Forscher wichtige Beiträge geliefert, z.b. Ďurčo (1994), Gréciano (2000), Hessky (1987), Korhonen (2007), Wotjak (1992) u.v.m. Für einen Überblick über die Forschung zu verschiedenen Sprachenpaaren vgl. Colson 2008 sowie Korhonen (2007) und Korhonen und Wotjak (2001).
3. http://www.widespread-idioms.uni-trier.de/ (30. März 2010).
4. Zur Versprachlichung von Gedanken, in sozialer Interaktion und als ästhetisches Mittel.
5. Dies wurde schon in Hallsteinsdóttir (2001: 58) problematisiert.
6. Dass dies sogar bei unbekannten Phraseologismen durchaus möglich ist, hat Hallsteinsdóttir (2001) gezeigt.
7. Im Englischen, Dänischen und Isländischen mit „(die) Zähne bürsten".
8. www.dwds.de (21. März 2010).
9. Aus einem Bericht über ein Fußballturnier, vgl.
http://www.gsvz.ch/Fussball/fussballturnier_05_lu.htm (21. März 2010).
10. www.dwds.de (21. März 2010).
11. Beispiele aus Deutscher Wortschatz, www.wortschatz.uni-leipzig.de (26. März 2010).
12. Das ist natürlich unsere individuelle Interpretation; im Online-Katalog der Smithsonian Photography Initiative wird die Werbung mit den Schlagwörtern „Bulls", „Women in advertising", „Sex in advertising", „Brassieres" und „Dreams" kategorisiert, vgl. http://photography.si.edu/SearchImage.aspx?t=3&q=dreams&id=4270&index=2 (30. März 2010).
13. Die Beispiele aus Hallsteinsdóttir (2001) sind authentische Bedeutungsangaben aus einer Fragebogenuntersuchung zur Bedeutung den vorangestellten kursiv gedruckten Sätzen.
14. Vgl. die HIP (Hypothetische Idiompaare) von Farø (2006).
15. Der Begriff funktionale Äquivalenz (vgl. Dobrovol'skij und Piirainen 2005) ist in Bezug auf Idiomatik in einem lexikologischen Zusammenhang nicht anwendbar, da „funktional" in einem kontextlosen Zusammenhang ohne einen spezifischen kommunikativen Zweck nicht beschrieben werden kann.
16. Go Odense, Play Life: VisitOdenses Touristikbroschüre Januar 2009, S. 17 in der dänischen, englischen und deutschen Ausgabe.
17. Vgl. über 30 Vorträge zur Phraseodidaktik auf der IDT in Jena/Weimar im Sommer 2009: http://idt2009h6.wordpress.com/ (30. März 2010).

18. Vgl. z.B. *EPHRAS*: www.ephras.org (30. März 2010) und *Multimediales Unterrichtsmaterial zur deutschen Phraseologie*: http://frazeologie.ujepurkyne.com/index2.htm (30. März 2010).

Literatur

Barz, Irmhild. 2006. Wortbildung. In Die Dudenredaktion (Hg.), *Duden 4. Die Grammatik*, 7th edn., 641–772. Mannheim: Dudenverlag.

Barz, Irmhild. 2007. Wortbildung und Phraseologie. In Harald Burger, Dmitrij Dobrovol'skij, Peter Kühn & Neal R. Norrick (Hg.), *Phraseologie: Ein internationales Handbuch der zeitgenössischen Forschung*, 27–36. Berlin & New York: Walter de Gruyter.

Bergerová, Hana. 2009a. Wie viel Phraseologie brauchen künftige Deutschlehrende? In Libuše Spáčilová & Lenka Vaòková (Hg.), *Germanistische Linguistik – die neuen Herausforderungen in Forschung und Lehre*, 71–80. Brno: Academicus.

Bergerová, Hana. 2009b. Nachdenken über ein phraseologisches Lernerwörterbuch. In Peter Ďurčo, Ružena Kozmová & Daniela Drinková (Hg.) *Deutsche Sprache in der Slowakei*, 39–50. Bratislava & Trnava: FF UCM/SUNG.

Burger, Harald. 2010. *Phraseologie: Eine Einführung am Beispiel des Deutschen*. Berlin: Erich Schmidt (4. Aufl.).

Burger, Harald, Annelies Buhofer & Ambros Sialm. 1982. *Handbuch der Phraseologie*. Berlin & New York: Walter de Gruyter.

Burger, Harald, Dmitrij Dobrovol'skij, Peter Kühn & Neal R. Norrick (Hg.). 2007. *Phraseologie: Ein internationales Handbuch der zeitgenössischen Forschung*. Berlin & New York: Walter de Gruyter.

Colson, Jean-Pierre. 2008. Cross-linguistic phraseological studies. An overview. In Sylviane Granger & Fanny Meunier (Hg.), *Phraseology: An interdisciplinary perspective*, 191–206. Amsterdam: John Benjamins.

Colson, Jean-Pierre. 2010. The Contribution of Web-based Corpus Linguistics to a Global Theory of Phraseology. In Stefaniya Ptashnyk, Erla Hallsteinsdóttir & Noah Bubenhofer (Hg.), *Korpora, Web und Datenbanken: Computergestützte Methoden in der modernen Phraseologie und Lexikographie*, 23–35. Baltmannsweiler: Schneider Verlag Hohengehren.

Dobrovol'skij, Dmitrij. 1995. *Kognitive Aspekte der Idiom-Semantik: Studien zum Thesaurus deutscher Idiome*. Tübingen: Narr.

Dobrovol'skij, Dmitrij. 1999. Kontrastive Phraseologie in Theorie und im Wörterbuch. In Rupprecht S. Baur, Christoph Chlosta & Elisabeth Piirainen (Hg.), *Wörter in Bildern – Bilder in Wörtern. Beiträge zur Phraseologie und Sprichwortforschung aus dem Westfälischen Arbeitskreis*, 107–122. Baltmannsweiler: Schneider Verlag Hohengehren.

Dobrovol'skij, Dmitrij & Elisabeth Piirainen. 2005. *Figurative language: Cross-cultural and cross-linguistic perspectives*. Amsterdam: Elsevier.

Dobrovol'skij, Dmitrij & Elisabeth Piirainen. 2009. *Zur Theorie der Phraseologie: Kognitive und kulturelle Aspekte.* Tübingen: Stauffenburg.
Donalies, Elke. 2009. *Basiswissen Deutsche Phraseologie.* Tübingen: Narr Francke Attempto Verlag.
Ďurčo, Peter. 1994. *Probleme der allgemeinen und kontrastiven Phraseologie. Am Beispiel Deutsch-Slowakisch.* Heidelberg: Groos.
Ďurčo, Peter. 2001. Bekanntheit, Häufigkeit und lexikographische Erfassung von Sprichwörtern. Zu Parömiologischen Minima für DaF. In Annelies Häcki Buhofer, Harald Burger & Laurent Gautier (Hg.), *Phraseologiae Amor: Aspekte europäischer Phraseologie*, 99–106. Baltmannsweiler: Schneider Verlag Hohengehren.
Ďurčo, Peter. 2009. Lexikographische Beschreibung der Kollokationen kontrastiv. Vortrag auf der IDT Jena/Weimar, 3.–8. August 2009.
Ettinger, Stefan. 1998. Einige Überlegungen zur Phraseodidaktik. In Wolfgang Eismann (Hg.), *EUROPHRAS 95*, 201–217. Bochum: Brockmeyer.
Ettinger, Stefan & Manuela Nunes. 2006. *Portugiesische Redewendungen.* Hamburg: Buske Helmut Verlag.
Fabčič, Melanija Larisa. 2009. Eine kognitv-semantische Interpretation der phraseologischen Äquivalenz am Beispiel der EPHRAS-Datenbank (Kontrast: Deutsch-Slowenisch). In Csaba Földes (Hg.), *Phraseologie disziplinär und interdisziplinär*, 423–432. Tübingen: Gunter Narr Verlag.
Farø, Ken. 2004. Hvornår går man over åen efter vand? Idiomatiske ækvivalensproblemer i leksikologi og leksikografi [Wann geht man über den Fluss um Wasser zu holen? Idiomatische Äquivalenzprobleme in Lexikologie und Lexikographie]. *LexicoNordica* 11, 85–108.
Farø, Ken. 2006. *Idiomatizität – Ikonizität – Arbitrarität: Beitrag zu einer funktionalistischen Theorie der Idiomäquivalenz.* Kopenhagen: Doktorarbeit an der Universität Kopenhagen.
Farø, Ken & Erla Hallsteinsdóttir. 2006. Neue theoretische und methodische Ansätze in der Phraseologieforschung: Einleitung zum Themenheft, *Linguistik online* 27, 2/06, 3–10. www.linguistik-online.de/27_06/einleitung.pdf(30. März 2010).
Farø, Ken & Henrik Lorentzen. 2009. De oversete og mishandlede ordforbindelser – hvilke, hvor og hvorfor? [Übersehene und mißhandelte Wortverbindungen – welche, wo und warum?], *LexicoNordica* 16, 75–101.
Fellbaum, Christiane, Undine Kramer & Gerald Neumann. 2006. Korpusbasierte lexikografische Erfassung und linguistische Analyse deutscher Idiome. In Annelies Häcki Buhofer & Harald Burger (Hg.), *Phraseology in Motion I: Methoden und Kritik*, 43–56. Baltmannsweiler: Schneider Verlag Hohengehren.
Fellbaum, Christiane, Fabian Koerner & Gerald Neumann. 2006. Corpus-based studies of German idioms and light verbs. *International Journal of Lexicography* 19(4). 349–360.
Fleischer, Wolfgang. 1997. *Phraseologie der deutschen Gegenwartssprache.* Tübingen: Niemeyer (2. Aufl.).
Földes, Csaba. 1997. Konzepte der kontrastiven Phraseologie. *Kontrastiv, Germanistisches Jahrbuch für Nordeuropa* 15. 167–182.

Földes, Csaba. 2006. *Deutsche Phraseologie kontrastiv: Intra- und interlinguale Zugänge*. Heidelberg: Julius Groos Verlag.
Földes, Csaba. 2007. Phraseologismen und Sprichwörter im Kontext von Mehrsprachigkeit und Transkulturalität: eine empirische Studie. *Proverbium* 24. 119–152.
Fuhrhop, Nanna. 2008. Das graphematische Wort (im Deutschen): Eine erste Annäherung. *Zeitschrift für Sprachwissenschaft* 27, 189–228.
Gréciano, Gertrud. 2000. Phraseologie: Spezifische Merkmale, intra- und interlingual. *Revista de Filología Alemana* 8. 233–251.
Gries, Stefan Th. 2008. Phraseology and linguistic theory: A brief survey. In Sylviane Granger & Fanny Meunier (Hg.), *Phraseology: An interdisciplinary perspective*, 3–26. Amsterdam: John Benjamins.
Häcki Buhofer, Annelies. 2006. Vorwort. In Annelies Häcki Buhofer & Harald Burger (Hg.), *Phraseology in Motion I: Methoden und Kritik*, I–XVI. Baltmannsweiler: Schneider Verlag Hohengehren.
Hallsteinsdóttir, Erla. 1997. Aspekte der Übersetzung von Phraseologismen am Beispiel Isländisch – Deutsch. In Eberhard Fleischmann, Wladimir Kutz & Peter A. Schmitt (Hg.), *Translationsdidaktik: Grundfragen der Übersetzungswissenschaft*, 561–569. Tübingen: Gunter Narr.
Hallsteinsdóttir, Erla. 2001. *Das Verstehen idiomatischer Phraseologismen in der Fremdsprache Deutsch*. Hamburg: Verlag Dr. Kovač.
www.verlagdrkovac.de/0435_volltext.htm (30. März 2010).
Hallsteinsdóttir, Erla. 2006. Phraseographie. *Hermes: Journal of Language and Communication Studies* 36. 91–128.
Hallsteinsdóttir, Erla. 2007. Wörtliche, freie und phraseologische Bedeutung. Eine korpusbasierte Untersuchung des Vorkommens von freien und phraseologischen Lesarten bei deutschen Idiomen. In Erika Kržišnik & Wolfgang Eismann (Hg.), *Phraseologie in der Sprachwissenschaft und anderen Disziplinen*, 151–165. Ljubljana: Univerze v Ljubljani.
Hallsteinsdóttir, Erla. 2009. Zweisprachige Lernerlexikografie aus funktionaler Sicht. In Carmen Mellado Blanco (Hg.), *Theorie und Praxis der idiomatischen Wörterbücher*, 209–232. Tübingen: Max Niemeyer Verlag.
Hallsteinsdóttir, Erla. 2009. Wörtliche, freie und phraseologische Bedeutung. Eine korpusbasierte Untersuchung von freien und phraseologischen Lesarten bei deutschen idiomen. In Csaba Földes (Hg.), *Phraseologie disziplinär und interdisziplinär*, 145–154. Tübingen: Gunter Narr Verlag.
Hallsteinsdóttir, Erla, Monika Sajankova & Uwe Quasthoff. 2006. Vorschlag eines phraseologischen Optimums für Deutsch als Fremdsprache auf der Basis von Frequenzuntersuchungen und Geläufigkeitsbestimmungen. *Linguistik-online* 27, 2/06, 119–138. http://www.linguistik-online.de/27_06/hallsteinsdottir_et_al.pdf (30. März 2010).
Hanks, Patrick, Anne Urbschat & Elke Gehweiler. 2006. German light verb constructions in corpora and dictionaries. *International Journal of Lexicography* 19 (4). 439–457.

Hessky, Regina. 1987. *Phraseologie: Linguistische Grundfragen und kontrastives Modell deutsch-ungarisch*. Tübingen: Max Niemeyer.
Hessky, Regina. 1992. Phraseolexeme als harte Nuß für die zweisprachige Lexikographie. In Csaba Földes (Hg.), *Deutsche Phraseologie in Sprachsystem und Sprachverwendung*, 107–124. Wien: Edition Praesens.
Hessky, Regina. 1997. Einige Fragen der Vermittlung von Phraseologie im Unterricht Deutsch als Fremdsprache. In Rainer Wimmer & Franz-Josef Berens (Hg.), *Wortbildung und Phraseologie*, 245–261. Tübingen: Gunter Narr.
Hessky, Regina & Stefan Ettinger. 2009. Deutsche Redewendungen: Ein Wörter- und Übungsbuch für Fortgeschrittene. Stark erweiterte Internetfassung als „phraseologisches Lesebuch". http://www.ettinger-phraseologie.de/(30. März 2010).
Jesenšek, Vida. 2006. Phraseologie und Fremdsprachenlernen: Zur Problematik einer angemessenen phraseodidaktischen Umsetzung. *Linguistik online* 27, 2/06. 137–147.
Jesenšek, Vida. 2007. Zum Problem der Äquivalenz in mehrsprachigen phraseologischen Wörterbüchern. In Annelies Häcki Buhofer & Harald Burger (Hg.), *Phraseology in Motion II: Theorie und Anwendung*, 275–286. Baltmannsweiler: Schneider Verlag Hohengehren.
Jesenšek, Vida. 2009. Phraseologische Wörterbücher auf dem Weg zu Phraseologiedatenbanken. In Carmen Mellado Blanco (Hg.), *Theorie und Praxis der idiomatischen Wörterbücher*, 65–82. Tübingen: Max Niemeyer Verlag.
Juska-Bacher, Britta. 2009. *Empirisch-kontrastive Phraseologie: Am Beispiel der Bekanntheit der Niederländischen Sprichwörter im Niederländischen, Deutschen und Schwedischen*. Baltmannsweilser: Schneider Verlag Hohengehren.
Kilian, Jörg. 2001. Kritische Semantik: Für eine wissenschaftliche Sprachkritik im Spannungsfeld von Sprachtheorie, Sprachnorm, Sprachpraxis. *Zeitschrift für germanistische Linguistik* 29. 293–318.
Koller, Werner. 2007. Probleme der Übersetzung von Phrasemen. In Harald Burger, Dmitrij Dobrovol'skij, Peter Kühn & Neal R. Norrick (Hg.), *Phraseologie: Ein internationales Handbuch der zeitgenössischen Forschung*, 605–613. Berlin, New York: Walter de Gruyter.
Korhonen, Jarmo. 2007. Probleme der kontrastiven Phraseologie. In Harald Burger, Dmitrij Dobrovol'skij, Peter Kühn & Neal R. Norrick (Hg.), *Phraseologie: Ein internationales Handbuch der zeitgenössischen Forschung*, 574–598. Berlin, New York: Walter de Gruyter.
Korhonen, Jarmo & Barbara Wotjak. 2001. Kontrastivität in der Phraseologie. In Gerhard Helbig, Lutz Gotze & Gert Henrici (Hg.), *Deutsch als Fremdsprache: ein internationales Handbuch*, 224–235. Berlin: de Gruyter.
Kühn, Peter. 1992. Phraseodidaktik: Entwicklungen, Probleme und Überlegungen für den Muttersprachenunterricht und den Unterricht Deutsch als Fremdsprache. *Fremdsprachen lehren und lernen* 21. 169–186.
Kühn, Peter. 1994. Pragmatische Phraseologie: Konsequenzen für die Phraseographie und Phraseodidaktik. In Barbara Sandig (Hg.), *EUROPHRAS 92: Tendenzen der Phraseologieforschung*, 411–428. Bochum: Brockmeyer.

Malá, Jiøina. 2005. Phraseologie: Blütezeit einer linguistischen Disziplin (Eine Reise durch die Phraseologielandschaft). *Brünner Beiträge zur Germanistik und Nordistik* 10. 65–77.

Mellado Blanco, Carmen. 2009. Intensivierung durch Vergleich im Deutschen und Spanischen: Intralinguale und kontrastive Analyse der semantischen Beziehungen unter den Vergleichskomponenten. In Csaba Földes (Hg.), *Phraseologie disziplinär und interdisziplinär*, 465–476. Tübingen: Gunter Narr Verlag.

Mieder, Wolfgang. 2009. *International bibliography of paremiology and phraseology*. Berlin & New York: de Gruyter.

Piirainen, Elisabeth. 1999. Falsche Freunde in der Phraseologie des Sprachenpaares Deutsch – Niederländisch. In Annette Sabban (Hg.), *Phraseologie und Übersetzen: Phrasemata II*, 187–204. Bielefeld: Aisthesis.

Piirainen, Elisabeth. 2008. Phraseology in a European framework: A cross-linguistic and cross-cultural research project on widespread idioms. In Sylviane Granger und Fanny Meunier (Hg.), *Phraseology: An interdisciplinary perspective*, 243–258. Amsterdam: John Benjamins.

Reder, Anna. 2006. *Kollokationen in der Wortschatzarbeit*. Wien: Praesens Verlag.

Reder, Anna. 2008. Erkennen DaF-Lernende Kollokationen? In György Scheibl (Hg.), *Tests im DaF-Unterricht – DaF-Unterricht im Test*, 105–115. Szeged: Grimm.

Sabban, Annette. 2007. Culture-boundness and problems of cross-cultural phraseology. In Harald Burger, Dmitrij Dobrovol'skij, Peter Kühn & Neal R. Norrick (Hg.), *Phraseologie: Ein internationales Handbuch der zeitgenössischen Forschung*, 590–605. Berlin, New York: Walter de Gruyter.

Sinclair, John. 1991. *Corpus, concordance, collocation*. Oxford: Oxford University Press.

Sinclair, John. 2008. The phrase, the whole phrase, and nothing but the phrase. In Sylviane Granger & Fanny Meunier (Hg.), *Phraseology: An interdisciplinary perspective*, 407–410. Amsterdam: John Benjamins.

Soehn, Jan-Philipp (2006): *Über Bärendienste und erstaunte Bauklötze: Idiome ohne freie Lesart in der HPSG*. Frankfurt a/M: Peter Lang.

Soehn, Jan-Philipp & Christine Römer. 2007. Wann ist ein Idiom ein Idiom? Eine Analyse von Phraseologismen ohne freie Lesart. In Annelies Häcki Buhofer & Harald Burger (Hg.), *Phraseology in Motion II: Theorie und Anwendung. Akten der Internationalen Tagung zur Phraseologie (Basel, 2004)*, 3–14. Baltmannsweiler: Schneider Verlag Hohengehren,

Tarp, Sven. 2006. *Leksikografien i grænselandet mellem viden og ikke-viden: Generel leksikografisk teori med særlig henblik på lørnerleksikografi* [Die Lexikographie im Grenzland zwischen Wissen und Nicht-Wissen: Eine generelle Theorie der Lexikographie mit Fokus auf Lernerlexikographie]. Aarhus: Handelshøjskolen i Aarhus.

Wotjak, Barbara. 1992. *Verbale Phraseolexeme in System und Text*. Tübingen: Max Niemeyer.

What Inari Saami idioms reveal about the time concept of the indigenous people of Inari

ANNA IDSTRÖM

Abstract

Inari Saami is an indigenous, endangered language spoken in northern Finland. It is demonstrated that the Inari Saami idioms systematically reflect the conceptual metaphor time is nature. The ubiquitous English metaphor time is money, on the other hand, is claimed to be extremely rare in Inari Saami. This finding is explained in the framework of Edward Hall's theory of time concepts by comparing the language with features of the Inari Saami material and social culture. The traditional Inari Saami culture was polychronic; the timing of human action was based on observations in the natural environment and spontaneous reactions to these observations rather than on preset schedules. This time concept results from the prerequisites of human adaptation to the harsh natural conditions of Lapland. The language reflects the culture. It is emphasized that the idioms of endangered, indigenous languages should be urgently and exhaustively documented.

Keywords: Inari Saami; idiom; metaphor; time concept; endangered language.

1. Introduction

The purpose of this paper is to demonstrate, through one case study, why the idioms of endangered languages should be urgently and exhaustively documented to show what kind of insights they can provide about the culture where they have been used. As Piirainen (2004, 2006, 2008), Teliya et al. (1998) and many others have pointed out, it is important to keep in mind that the phraseology of indigenous languages has not been systematically studied. Consequently material is scarce and typologies are not yet possible. Even so, in this paper it is shown that Inari Saami idioms yield some insights into Inari Saami conceptual metaphors and their cultural background. Here I will discuss only one example, namely, metaphors of time.

Conceptual metaphor theory (Lakoff and Johnson 1980, 1999) provides a useful model for analysing the systematic features of the metaphors found in idioms. The proponents of this theory have been criticized for understating the significance of culture as an underlying basis of conceptual metaphors and overstating the contribution of individual cognition to the phenomenon known as "conceptual metaphor" (Dobrovol'skij and Piirainen 2005: 124; Quinn 1991: 65). Thus conceptual metaphor theory alone is not a sufficient basis for understanding the cultural foundations of idioms. It is, however, a worthwhile starting point for such a study and it can be supported by an appropriate anthropological framework. That can involve comparing the results of linguistic analysis with a comparable analysis of literary documents thus involving, as well as a purely linguistic analysis, the material, spiritual and social culture of the people who speak the language.

Dobrovol'skij and Piirainen (2005: 187) and Piirainen (2004: 49) have underlined that an examination of as complete as possible a compilation of an inventory of figurative units within a given domain should be a basic requirement for any reliable study of figurative language. This point cannot be overemphasised. It is necessary to analyse a large number of idioms referring to the same semantic field in order to discover conceptual domains that systematically motivate the figures of speech.

The material researched here consists mainly of phrasal idioms, but, in addition, I have analysed compound words which behave much like phrasal idioms in the sense that informants recognize the mental images – metaphors or metonymies – immediately, and the cultural motivation of the figure of speech seems clear as well. The compound words taken into account in this study belong to the same set of metaphorical mappings as the phrasal idioms and thus provide evidence for the same conceptual metaphor. Furthermore, since the number of available examples is limited, we must analyse what we have.

1.1. *The Inari Saami language*

Inari Saami is an indigenous language traditionally spoken in the area around Lake Inari in northern Finland, in the villages of Kaamanen, Partakko, Nellim, Inari and Ivalo. The language was spoken by Inari Saami families until the 1950s. Thereafter rapid language shift to Finnish took place and Inari Saami ceased to function as a language of communication for decades. It has, since the 1990s, been actively and successfully revitalized, and the revitalization continues today. It is currently spoken by about 350 people, but only around 250 elderly people speak the language as their first language (Morottaja 2007; Marja-Liisa Olthuis, pers. comm.).

This study focuses on the form of Inari Saami language which was spoken before the the language shift to Finnish and the accompanying radical change of the culture, which will be described below. The old Inari Saami still vividly remember the old way of life. The possible changes in the Inari Saami metaphors due to the revitalisation are beyond the scope of this paper, although they would make an interesting research area for further studies. Morottaja (2009) notes that some of the idioms familiar to the old Inari Saami are unknown to the young members of Inari Saami society.

Inari Saami belongs to the Saamic branch of the Uralic language family. The continuum of the Saamic languages stretches from central Scandinavia to the Kola Peninsula in Russia. The most widely spoken Saami language is North Saami with about 20,000 speakers, most of whom live in Norway, in the Kautokeino region. Inari Saami is closely related to North Saami, but these two languages are not mutually intelligible.

Inari Saami culture was traditionally based on fishing, hunting and reindeer-husbandry in the harsh conditions of Lapland (see T. I. Itkonen 1948; T. Lehtola 1998; V-P. Lehtola 2002, 2003 and Morottaja 2005 for details). Since reindeer harnessed to a sledge or skis were the main means of transport in winter and a boat or feet in summer, it was important to know as exactly as possible what the weather and the snow conditions might be. The Inari Saami made every endeavour to predict the weather and timed their actions according to the weather (Idström 2008). The standard of living was modest, occasionally even poor (Koskimies and Itkonen 1917). Human life depended overtly on natural resources, fish and game of the wilderness. Inari Saami culture has been largely neglected by the academic research, but some recent studies on the North Saami reindeer herding culture (Heikkinen 2002: 200–205; Näkkäläjärvi 2000) suggest that the Saami generally consider *freedom* as the positive value of the traditional Saami life. Dependence on nature is seen as the natural way for humans to live, not a limitation to freedom. Since the nineteenth century and increasingly in the twentieth century, however, changes to the environment of the Inari Saami have had significant consequences. Such changes include the damming of fishing rivers used since time immemorial, regulation of lakes in 1940s, motorization and capitalization of the reindeer economy in 1960s, penetration of the road network into the heartlands of Lapland and the consequent influx of Finnish settlers. These have all undermined the foundations of the traditional Inari Saami culture.

Not withstanding these changes and also not unexpectedly given the durability of phrasal lexemes, the old Inari Saami way of life is still reflected in the Inari

Saami metaphors of time. My intention is to describe in detail the relationship between the traditional Inari Saami culture and these idioms.

1.2. Brief theoretical background

To begin the linguistic analysis, I will define the concepts of metaphor and metonymy briefly. *Metaphor* is a linguistic phenomenon which (according to cognitive theory) is based on the cognitive process of mapping between a source domain and a target domain; the target domain is construed and described in terms of the source domain. Metaphoric mapping is based on a sense of some kind of real or imagined similarity or analogy. *Metonymy* is closely related to metaphor, but it links the source domain and the target domain on the basis of contiguity (Allan 2008: 12). For the purposes of this article *idiom* can be defined broadly as a conventional, multiword, metaphoric or metonymic expression. (See Piirainen 2008: 208–213 for more elaborated definition.) The overlapping of the concepts arises from a shift in viewpoint; the same expression can be called a "metaphor" if we want to emphasize mapping, i.e. the cognitive process that causes the noticeable figurative motivation of the expression, or it can be called an "idiom" if we want to emphasize the phraseological aspect, i.e. the fact that the expression is syntactically frozen, shared by the language community as a cultural convention and expresses more than the constituting words alone.

A *conceptual metaphor* is an abstraction for which a "cognitive" status is postulated within the framework of cognitive theory. The systematicity of metaphoric mappings in conventional expressions has become the subject of an expanding discipline since the publication of Lakoff and Johnson's *Metaphors we live by* in 1980. Cognitive metaphor theory rests on the observation that the metaphoric expressions of a language show a tendency to follow a pattern: a target domain is described by several conventional linguistic expressions in terms of a coherent source domain. The domains seem to have a topological, structure-preserving relationship. What causes this phenomenon is not completely clear. Lakoff and Johnson (1980, 1999), Kövecses (2005: 7; 2002: 104; 1995: 140) and many other scholars claim that we *understand* the target domain in terms of the source domain. In the early phase of development of the conceptual metaphor theory, Lakoff and Johnson (1980: 3) wrote: "Our ordinary conceptual system, in terms of which we both think and act, is fundamentally metaphorical in nature." Thirteen years later Lakoff (1993: 208) illustrates this by saying, "What constitutes the LOVE IS A JOURNEY metaphor is not any particular word or expression. It is the ontological mapping across conceptual domains from the source domain of journeys to the target domain of love. The metaphor is not just a matter of language, but of thought and reason. The language is secondary. The mapping is primary..." Lakoff and Turner (1989: 62) underline the point in the following comment about the LIFE IS A JOURNEY conceptual metaphor. "The structure of our understanding of life comes from the structure of our knowledge about journeys." Kövecses (2002: 104) echoes these ideas by saying that, "(s)ource domains are used to understand target domains."

These ideas have attracted criticism (see Murphy 1996, 1997; Vervaeke and Kennedy 1996). The essence of the problem is encapsulated by Sandra (1998: 376), who points out that linguistic research can only speculate about the cognitive processes underlying linguistic expressions. As Itkonen (2005: 45) writes, speculative psychology is not genuine psychology. Keysar and Bly (1995, see also 1999) have empirically demonstrated that metaphorical interpretation may follow from the figure of speech. For example, an archaic English idiom *the goose hangs high* can bring two contrasting interpretations, depending on the context. This result suggests that the language is primary, the metaphorical interpretation (i.e. what happens in cognition) is secondary. On the other hand, recent empirical studies have found evidence of conceptual metaphors existing independently of language (see Casasanto 2009). This of course suggests that the conceptual metaphor indeed is primary, and the systematic features of figurative language follow from this cognitive mapping between two conceptual domains. In conclusion, it seems that there is no consensus about the matter.

An alternative theory attempting to explain "conceptual metaphor" is provided by Quinn (1991, 2003). She claims that metaphor has only a minor role in the *understanding* of the life that we experience. Instead, metaphor is coined and conventionalized on the basis of a cultural schema. A cultural schema exists independently of a language; it emerges slowly from whatever humans experience frequently. A metaphor is apt if it is consistent with the cultural schema. Under these conditions it can become conventionalised. For example, the conceptual metaphor TIME IS MONEY does not exist because we naively believe that time is something like money. Instead, it has been conventionalised, because it describes aptly our culture-specific attitude towards time in appropriate contexts. Strauss and Quinn (2003: 48) stress that the foundation of linguistic meaning is based on cultural schemas. My theoretical position is that the impact of culture should not be ignored as a motivating factor determining the figurative features conceptual metaphor.

Culture does not consist only of its outer manifestations, such as traditional food, music styles or festivals. Katan (2004: 3) condenses the cumbersome and fuzzy concept of culture into a few words. "Culture is ... a system for making sense of experience." This system is transmitted through social interaction as it has been transmitted throughout the whole history of human evolution. It is a myriad of inventions, insights and wisdom of past generations accumulated by the mechanism that Tomasello (1999: 5–6) calls "the ratchet effect." In short, cultural inheritance is the opposite of genetic inheritance. Of course this opposition is a simplification. I refer the reader to Cartwright (2000: 70–71) for a detailed description of the various ways genetic and environmental factors can interact in the process resulting in a given observable feature of an organism. For the purposes of this article we can confine ourselves to the simple, classic definition of culture as a socially transmitted, that is, learned inheritance. Narrower and more detailed alternatives to the definition of culture can be sought in Sabban (2007: 590–591) or in Piirainen (2008: 208–210).

I am supposing that conventional metaphors mirror some aspects of a culture. For example, I will suppose that Inari Saami idioms reflect the time concept of a population of people living in severe natural conditions, and accordingly these idioms will include conceptual metaphors which can be revealed by analysing research data. Of course concepts of time exists independently of language, since days, months and years have natural origins. Concepts of time will also correlate with the way a culture has adapted to its natural environment (see also Steward 1976 [1955]). To show this I will employ Edward Hall's theory of time concepts from the field of cultural anthropology, specifically, since it offers a theoretical framework for understanding the connection between Inari Saami idioms and their cultural background.

1.3. *Edward Hall's theory of time concepts*

Hall (1983) divides the temporal concepts of human cultures into two categories: monochronic and polychronic. This categorisation, even though it is hypothetical and overtly simplified, facilitates an understanding of the Inari Saami conceptual metaphors in a culturally sensitive way. In monochronic societies (such as Anglo-American and northern European cultures) scheduling is used as a classification system that orders life. The pulse of our society is synchronized by preset schedules, clocks and calendars. According to Hall (1983: 48), monochronic time is arbitrary and imposed, that is, learned. People who live in monochronic societies associate schedules with reality. Monochronic cultures are oriented to schedules and procedures (Hall 1983: 48–53). To give an illustration, how often have we experienced some version of the following conversation? "Would you like to go for a cup of coffee with me next week?" – "Yes, that would be nice! Please wait a second, I will just check my diary to see when I have time...." We wake up when the alarm goes off; we hurry to catch the bus which is leaving according to a timetable; we buy whatever we need from the grocery store in accordance with the opening hours; we get our kids from day-care when the clock says so, even if it interrupts their play. This is the nature of post-industrial societies where labour is synchronized with machines that produce goods in factories. Our material welfare is based on this synchrony. (See also Gleick 1999.)

Polychronic societies, instead, are by their nature oriented to people (Hall 1983: 53). The polychronic time concept stresses involvement of people and completion of transactions rather than adherence to preset schedules (Hall 1983: 46). Traditional Inari Saami culture was polychronic; the rhythm of life and the timing of actions did not follow preset schedules. Instead, human life followed the rhythm of nature: the weather and the movements of animals in the wilderness. People made observations about their natural environment and deductions from their observations, against the background of culturally transmitted knowledge concerning the most profitable course of action to take at the moment. This cognitive process determined the dynamic, flexible and usually voluntary timing of actions.

2. Research materials

The data on which this research is based comes from a variety of sources. The most important is the Inari Saami dictionary of idioms (Idström and Morottaja 2006, reviewed by Aikio 2008), which was published by the Saami Parliament in 2006 and has been reprinted twice. A crucial addition is 1,300 pages of the Inari Saami dictionary compiled by Erkki Itkonen (1986–1989). Other written sources used are Koskimies and Itkonen (1978 [1917]) and Erkki Itkonen (1992). Other written documents on Inari Saami are scarce (see http://www.anaraskielaservi.net/language.html for an inclusive list of printed material written in Inari Saami).

It has been claimed that the Inari Saami seem to avoid figurative language (this particular feature of Inari Saami has been suggested by Äimä (1902: 21–22) and a hundred years later by an aged Inari Saami activist, Hans Morottaja, pers. comm.). I take it that this is so, and consequently the number of metaphors analyzed here is not large, but the examples found in the data follow a clear pattern. Further evidence about the validity of the claims argued here can be sought by comparing the linguistic data with the numerous documents on the material, social and spiritual culture of traditional Saami society (e.g. T. I. Itkonen 1948). I shall show that the conceptual metaphor presented below is logical in relation to the Inari Saami way of life.

3. The Inari Saami idioms of time

3.1. Equivalents of TIME IS MONEY in Inari Saami

As an introduction to the analysis of the research material, let us briefly review a familiar conceptual metaphor for time in western, post-industrial cultures, namely, TIME IS MONEY.

(1) You're *wasting* my time.
     This gadget will *save* you hours.
     I don't *have* time to *give* you.
     How do you *spend* your time these days?
     That flat tire *cost* me an hour.
     (Lakoff and Johnson 1980: 7–8)

Finnish equivalents follow the same pattern of mapping.

(2) *Haaska-a-t   kallis-ta   aika-a-ni.*
     waste-PRS-2SG expensive.SG-ACC time-ACC.SG-POSS.1SG
     'You are wasting my precious time.'

    Tämä   tekninen   apuneuvo   säästä-ä
    this   techical.NOM.SG gadget.NOM.SG   save-3SG.PRS
    aika-a-si.
    time-ACC.SG-2SG
    'This gadget will save you time.'

    Anna   häne-lle   aika-a!
    give. IMP   SG3-ALL   time-ACC.SG
    'Give him/her time!'

    Miten   kulut-a-t   aika-a   nykyään?
    how   spend-PRS-2SG time-ACC.SG   nowadays
    'How do you spend your time these days?'

Conversely, it is difficult to find any evidence of this conceptual metaphor in Inari Saami. The research material includes only one clear example of the conceptual metaphor TIME IS MONEY. It is this:

(3) *Ij   mu-st   lah   äigi   vyelgi-ð   kiirko-n.*
     NEG.3SG 1SG-LOC   be. NEG.PRS time.NOM.SG leave-INF church-ILL
     'I don't have time to go to church.'

This can be counted as a metaphor representing time as some kind of property, because it has a possessive construction.

Instead, the material provides a few functional equivalents for the English expression "waste of time", which, as assumed here, represents the conceptual metaphor TIME IS MONEY. These idioms are used in the same situations in which an English speaker might say that something is a "waste of time". For example, if someone proposes a plan, and the others think that this plan is not profitable, they may answer: (4) *Tallet maid kal leibi-lase*. This means: "This plan will not bring us any food." Example (5) means the same.

(4) *Tallet maid kal leibi-lase*
 then supposed EMPH bread.NOM.SG-more.NOM.SG
 'And this is supposed to get us more bread.'

(5) *Tallet maid kal mäli-salgâ.*
 then supposed EMPH soup.NOM.SG-piece_of_meat.NOM.SG
 'And this is supposed to get us a piece of meat in the soup.'

The next idiom has the same function, but it is restricted to the context of hunting:

(6) *Njuoska-n puura-m maid kodá-h!*
 raw-ESS eat-1SG.PRS what kill-2SG.PRS
 'Anything you kill, I will eat raw!'

The idiom (6) is suitable for telling someone that his plan to go hunting is not good; it is a "waste of time" and he is not going to catch anything. The next example (7) is restricted to the context of hunting as well, and the meaning is the same: "You will not catch anything; don't waste your time going hunting."

(7) *Jieh koolgâ sääpi raigâ-ð.*
 NEG.2SG may.NEG.PRS gall bladder.ACC.SG break-INF
 'You will not even break a gall bladder.'

The idiom (7) is based on a schema related to hunting. If a bullet or knife pierces an animal's gall bladder, the gall will spoil the meat. Not all of the meat will be useless, but it must be cleaned and this requires a lot of extra work. So hitting the gall bladder implies bad luck or poor skill, or both. It is probably the next worst thing after not catching anything at all. If someone is told that he will not even get to break the gall bladder, it means that he will not catch anything and the whole trip is a "waste of time".

As these examples demonstrate, the Inari Saami do not use the metaphor "waste of time" in situations where, for example, an English speaker would be likely to use it. They do not mention time at all. Instead, the Inari Saami say something that entails a schema relating to a person performing a task, focusing on the result of the effort, not on the time spent on the task.

3.2. TIME IS NATURE in *Inari Saami*

What is, then, the most salient conceptual metaphor for time in Inari Saami, if it is not TIME IS MONEY? It seems that the concept of time simply was not as important in traditional Inari Saami culture as in urban, post-industrial cultures. Time is the context, not the centre of attention. In the inventory of figurative language investigated in this study the word meaning 'time' is mentioned explicitly in only a couple of cases; yet many of the idioms presuppose the concept of time implicitly. In these cases, the source domain for the metaphor – or metonymy to be exact – is not money but nature. The Inari Saami people frequently refer to certain moments or periods of time by mentioning what happens in nature at that time. This metaphor systematically recurs throughout the research material. I will present some examples.

(8)   *riemnjis*   *kamâs-iið-is*   *koco*
       fox.NOM.SG   leg-ACC.PL-POSS.SG3   hang.SG3.PRS
       'Fox is hanging up his legs.'

It is possible to refer to the beginning of autumn in Inari Saami by saying that a fox is hanging up his legs. First it is important to know that a fox is red. The idiom is based on an image of a fox hanging his legs on the trees like red socks. In the real world the first red leaves are an indexical sign of the summer turning to autumn.

(9)   *illâ-muorâ*   *äigi*
       flaming-coal-tree.GEN.SG   time.NOM.SG
       'the time when the trees have the colour of flaming coals'

Illâ-muorâ äigi means the time in September when the leaves of the trees become yellow and red. It is called 'the time when the trees have the colour of flaming coals'.

(10)   *noro-kyeli*   *äigi*
       gathering-fish.GEN.SG   time.NOM.SG
       'the time when the fish gather together'

October is a good time for catching whitefish, because it is the spawning season when the fish gather. The name for this period of time is *norokyeli äigi*, 'the time when the fish gather together'.

(11) *ponne-suosâ   äigi*
      bottom-sludge.GEN.SG time.NOM.SG
      'time of the ice at the bottom of a lake' (*suosâ* indicates icy sludge)

In autumn when the weather turns to freezing the Inari Saami may say that it is the time of *ponne-suosâ*, ice at the bottom of a lake. In fact, *ponne-suosâ* is a myth; there is no ice at the bottom of a lake.

(12) *taan   muottuu   ääigi*
      this.GEN.SG snow.GEN.SG time.ACC.SG
      'during the time of this snow'

If something is supposed to happen during the ongoing winter, the Inari Saami may say, "during the time of this snow," which means "before this snow has melted." The Inari Saami mention the snow as a metonymical reference to the time when the snow is on the ground.

(13) *Tot   ij   tääiði   kievâ   kuullâ-ð.*
      It.NOM.SG NEG.SG3   may.NEG.PRS   cuckoo.ACC.SG hear-INF
      'He will not hear the cuckoo.'

If someone (a person or a reindeer) looks very sick and is expected to die during the ongoing winter, the Inari Saami may say, *Tot ij tääiði kievâ kuullâð*, 'he will not hear the cuckoo.' The migratory cuckoo birds arrive in Inari at the beginning of June. It is possible to refer to this time by mentioning a penetrating sound ("cuckoo") that begins in the forests when the birds arrive.

The following are a few metonymies relating to spring.

(14) *kiððâ-olmooš*
      spring.NOM.SG-person.NOM.SG
      'spring-person'

Kiððâ-olmooš, 'spring-person', means someone who is making his way through the wilderness at night because of the weather. In April the sun is already warm in the daytime and the snow begins to melt. Hence it is not easy to travel by skis or by reindeer. At night, when the weather is cooler, the snow is solid enough to bear the weight of a person.

(15)   kiđđâ-ergi
         spring.NOM.SG-reindeer_male.NOM.SG
         'spring-reindeer'

In earlier times – until the 1960s – reindeer were used as draught animals in winter. 'Spring-reindeer' means a reindeer who is exhausted in spring after the hard work in winter.

'Spring' is a word referring to a certain period of time. When this word is combined with another word meaning a person or a reindeer, the resulting compound word connects the concepts of time and human or reindeer with nature and what happens in nature in spring; the snow melts. This phenomenon has consequences for people and animals. It is not possible to understand the meaning of the words *spring-person* or *spring-reindeer* and the logical reason why these words are compounded without an encyclopaedic knowledge of the nature of Lapland (which is the Saami country) and the cultural context of the language.

(16)   *Koldâ-keejist   koldâ-kiäčán   páštá   peivi.*
         log-end.LOC.SG   log-end.ILL.SG shine.3SG.PRS sun.NOM.SG
         'The sun shines from one end of a log to the other.'

The idiom above refers to midsummer, when the sun does not set at all, but circles the sky, *Koldâkeejis koldâkiäčán páštá peivi*, 'the sun shines from one end of a log to the other'. If a log is lying on the ground in midsummer, the sun shines on one end of the log in the daytime and on the other end of the log in the night-time. The metonymy describes this situation, which is a fact of life within the polar circle, as a way of referring to the time of midsummer.

(17)   *Kiehâ   lii   čoroh-ân*
         cuckoo.NOM.SG   be.3SG.PRS   unripe-cloudberry-ILL.SG
         puáhčán-âm.
         choke-PTCP
         'Cuckoo is choking on an unripe cloudberry.'

The Inari Saami can refer to the end of June by saying that the cuckoo is choking on an unripe cloudberry. The cuckoo stops calling at the end of June. Thus the Inari Saami imagine that the bird is choking on a cloudberry. The absence of the bird's voice and ripening of the berries are metonymical indexes of time. The causal relation between these indices is a product of a blend, a conceptual integration (see Fauconnier and Turner 2008). What is important with regard to the subject of this article is that, once again, the metonymy for a period of time refers to what happens in nature at that time, imagined or real, or a blend of both.

As these examples show, the Inari Saami have many conventional figurative expressions which involve the concept of time as an essential part of their meaning. In these figurative units the target domain is time, and the source domain is nature. The relation between the source domain and the target domain is metonymical – sometimes illustrated by a blend or an additional metaphor, as in example (8), in which the fox represents, metaphorically, the leaves of the trees. The metonymy is logical. Nature was the index of time in traditional Inari Saami culture, and also other human cultures in the earlier, pre-industrial phases of history; clocks and calendars are later impositions. They are a result of the human attempt to control and systematize our interactions, whereas the flow of time does not depend on these inventions. They are tools which shape our collective understanding of the ongoing reality. The traditional Inari Saami concept of time was different because of their way of life and adaptation to their environment. Thus the most important conceptual metonymy for time in Inari Saami seems to be TIME IS NATURE.

3.3. The Saami calendar

One might think that the time metaphors in Inari Saami reflect a culture where clocks and calendars were unknown or ignored, or merely present due to the colonial influence of the alien, stronger cultures of the south. This, however, would be a misconception. The calendar has always been important to the Inari Saami – the ancient Saami had their own calendar with thirteen months. But the purpose of the calendar was not to synchronize schedules or to make appointments. Instead, its purpose was to predict the weather. Thus the mere existence of the calendar does not indicate preset schedules. On the contrary, the Saami calendar was integral to their way of life, which was based on the polychronic concept of time, and where the conceptual metonymy for time was TIME IS NATURE.

Nowadays the Inari Saami calendar has 12 months according to the standard Western calendar, but even after this mathematical modification, many of the old names of the months have been preserved or reverted to along with the language revitalisation process. A glance at the Inari Saami names for months shows that they follow the same metonymic pattern of mentioning something that happens in nature as the idioms presented above. March is called 'the month of swans' –

the month when the migrant swans come to Lapland, April is called 'the month when the (certain kind of) snow is on the ground', May is 'the month of the reindeer-calf', because the reindeer calves are born in May. August is called 'the month when the reindeer have new, soft hair', November is called 'the dark month.' (See Mattus: *Anarâš kalender*.)

(22) January: *uððâivemáánu*, 'month of new year'
February: *kuovâmáánu* (no recognized metaphor)
March: *njuhčâmáánu*, 'month of swan'
April: *cuáŋuimáánu*, 'month of snow-on-the-ground'
May: *vyesimáánu*, 'month of reindeer-calf'
June: *kesimáánu*, 'month of summer'
July: *syeinimáánu*, 'month of grass'
August: *porgemáánu*, 'month of new hair (of reindeer)'
September: *čohčâmáánu*, 'month of autumn'
October: *roovvâdmáánu*, 'month of oestrus (of reindeer)'
November: *skammâmáánu*, 'month of darkness'
December: *juovlâmáánu*, 'month of Christmas'

A comparison with the English names of months underlines a special characteristic of the Inari Saami conventional figurative expressions. They systematically connect the concept of time with nature even when there would be other possibilities, at least in principle.

(23) January < *Januarius mensis* 'month of Janus'
February < *Februarius mensis*, februa purification feast was held in this month
March < *Martius mensis* 'month of Mars'
April < *Aprilis mensis* 'month of Venus'
May < *Maius mensis*, Maia was a Roman Earth goddess
June < *Junius mensis*, Juno was the goddess of women and marriage
July < Julius Caesar
August < Augustus Caesar
September < seven
October < eight
November < nine
December < ten

The Inari Saami names of months are not motivated by numbers as in many Indo-European languages of European origin: *September, October, November,*

December. Nor are they kings as in *July* or *August.* (Onions et al. 1966; Hawkins 1990.)

3.4. Spatial metaphors of time

The research material includes examples of other conceptual metaphors of time, too. One of them is the metaphor which describes time as a spatial entity.

(18) *ijjâ-kyevdil*
       night.NOM.SG-middle.NOM.SG
       'middle (spatial) of the night'

This expression indicates night-time in April, when travelling by ski in the wilderness is easier at night than in the daytime, when the sun warms the ground making the snow soft and wet.

(19) *peivi-kyevdil*
       day.NOM.SG-middle.NOM.SG
       'middle (spatial) of the day'

This expression means the snow conditions in April in the daytime, when the snow on the ground is too soft to bear the weight of a person on skis. If the weather is cloudy and the wind is in the north, it is also possible to ski in the daytime and it will not be *peivikyevdil.*

(20) *Äigi   mana   huáppu-st.*
       time.NOM.SG go.3SG.PRS fast-LOC.SG
       'Time goes fast.'

It is possible to say in Inari Saami that time *goes* fast, utilizing a metaphor of movement. Also, the Inari Saami case system utilizes oblique (locative) cases in temporal expressions (see Nelson 2007). Further discussion of these spatial metaphors for time are, however, beyond the scope of this paper.

4. Discussion: Reflections of the Inari Saami concept of time in the idioms

All life is regulated by rhythms synchronized with nature. Plants, insects, birds and animals, including humans, follow the rhythmic changes from light to dark and from hot to cold. In Inari Saami culture this was the basic rhythm of life. Rather than relying on preset schedules, the timing of human activities was based on what was observed in the surrounding natural environment and considered important for livelihood. Time was not as strikingly objectified as in modern post-industrial cultures where the TIME IS MONEY conceptual metaphor seems to be prevalent. Traditional Inari Saami time was mainly contextual, not a centre of attention, and definitely not something worth money. Logically, the linguistic Inari Saami metaphors describe time systematically as nature, or as something that happens in nature.

The findings presented above can be explained in the framework of Edward Hall's theory of monochronic and polychronic concepts of time. According to Hall, in monochronic societies time is organized by preset schedules and one thing is done at a time, while in polychronic societies people are involved in several activities at once. The TIME IS MONEY metaphor is appropriate for a monochronic, post-industrial society where the rhythm of daily life is based on paid work. The pulse of society is synchronized by clocks and calendars. The ultimate purpose of this is the effective industrial production and distribution of goods. Consequently, this metaphor is not typical for the Inari Saami.

Instead the TIME-IS-NATURE metonymy is appropriate for the traditional, polychronic Saami society, where daily life followed the rhythm of nature, consisting of reindeer, fishing, hunting and weather. The individual timed his actions by making observations of his natural environment and spontaneously reacting to these observations. For example, fog is an indicator of a good time for fishing whitefish, because the whitefish swim in surface water on a foggy day. There is no preset schedule for determining when to catch whitefish; the fog triggers the action. This schema has even been lexicalised. The expression *riäskápivdemšoŋŋâ*, 'weather for catching whitefish,' means foggy weather.

(21)   *riäská-pivdem-šoŋŋâ*
         whitefish.ACC.SG-fishing.NOM.SG-weather.NOM.SG
         'weather for catching whitefish'

If someone telephones from Inari to Helsinki and says that it is a *riäskápivdem-šoŋŋâ* in Inari, the friend in Helsinki knows that the weather is foggy, even if the fog is not mentioned.

One interesting point emerges clearly from the study. The linguistic material analysed in the framework of the cognitive metaphor theory, with the addition of Hall's theory of time concepts, corroborates the intuition of the Saami about the specific character of their own culture. Their traditional culture is indeed fundamentally different from post-industrial southern cultures with respect to the relationship between humans and nature. Nature was the basis for every aspect of life, including the concept of time. Fortunately, the Saami cultures are relatively well documented, and the vast literature confirms the analysis of Inari Saami metaphors.

On the other hand, linguistic metaphors alone are not a sufficient basis from which to draw reliable conclusions about the culture, at least not in the current state of the art. Linguistic research must be supported by ethnographic documentation of the traditional Saami lifestyle, as well as by general anthropological theories such as Edward Hall's theory of time concepts. The findings of this study raise a question; could the conventional metaphors for time, including the names of the months, be typologized? And if so, would the linguistic isoglosses follow cultural isoglosses, i.e. do the metaphors and metonymies change when the culture changes, for example, from polychronic to monochronic along with the introduction of clocks and industrial systems? It is my hope that this research will be succeeded by other similar studies of indigenous languages to make comparisons and typologizations possible. The language is common to the ethnic group and can be objectively observed. It is a better basis for generalisations about a culture than, for example, a description by an author.

University of Helsinki

Abbreviations

ACC	accusative
ALL	allative
EMPH	emphasis
ESS	essive
GEN	genitive
ILL	illative
IMP	imperative
INF	infinitive
LOC	locative
NEG	negation
NOM	nominative
PL	plural
POSS	possessive
PRS	present
PTCP	participle
SG	singular

Note

Correspondence address: anna.e.idstrom@helsinki.fi

References

Äimä, Frans. 1902. Matkakertomus Inarin Lapista [A travelogue from Inari Lapland]. *Journal de la Société Finno-Ougrienne* 20. 10–25.
Aikio, Samuli. 2008. Inarinsaamen sanontoja [Inari Saami sayings]. *Virittäjä* 3. 474–477.
Allan, Kathryn. 2008. *Metaphor and metonymy: A diachronic approach.* (Publications of the Philological Society 42.) Chichester: Wiley-Blackwell.
Cartwright, John. 2000. *Evolution and human behaviour.* Cambridge, MA: The MIT Press.
Casasanto, Daniel. 2009. When is a linguistic metaphor a conceptual metaphor? In Vyvyan Evans & Stéphanie Pourcel (eds.), *New directions in cognitive linguistics* (Human cognitive processing), 127–145. Amsterdam: John Benjamins.
Dobrovol'skij, Dmitrij & Elisabeth Piirainen. 2005. *Figurative language: Cross-cultural and cross-linguistic perspectives.* (Current Research in the Semantics/Pragmatics Interface 13). Amsterdam: Elsevier.
Fauconnier, Gilles & Mark Turner. 2008. Rethinking metaphor. In Raymond W. Gibbs, Jr. (ed.), *The Cambridge handbook of metaphor and thought,* 53–66. Cambridge: Cambridge University Press.
Gleick, James. 1999. *Faster: The acceleration of just about everything.* New York: Pantheon Books.
Hall, Edward Twitchell. 1983. *The dance of life: The other dimension of time.* Garden City, NY: Anchor Press/Doubleday.
Hawkins, Joyce M. 1990. *Oxford current English dictionary.* Oxford: Oxford University Press.
Heikkinen, Hannu. 2002. *Sopeutumisen mallit: Poronhoidon adaptaatio jälkiteolliseen toimintaympäristöön Suomen läntisellä poronhoitoalueella 1980–2000.* [Models of adaptation. The adaptation of reindeer management to post industrial operational environment in the western reindeer management area of Finland in 1980–2000.] (Suomalaisen Kirjallisuuden Seuran Toimituksia 892.) Helsinki: Finnish Literature Society.
Idström, Anna & Hans Morottaja. 2006. *Inarinsaamen idiomisanakirja* [Inari Saami idiom dictionary]. Inari: Saami Parliament.
Idström, Anna. 2008. Miten talven vaikutus ihmisen arkeen näkyy inarinsaamen kielessä? [How the influence of winter on the daily life is reflected in Inari Saami language?]. *Luonnon Tutkija* 2. 65–67.
Itkonen, Erkki. 1986–1989. *Inarilappisches Wörterbuch.* Vol. I–III. (Lexica Societatis Fenno-Ugricae 20.) Helsinki: Finno-Ugrian Society.
Itkonen, Erkki. 1992. *Inarisaamelaisia kielennäytteitä, aanaarkiela čájttuzeh* [Inari Saami sample texts]. Helsinki: Finno-Ugrian Society.

Itkonen, Esa. 2005. *Analogy as structure and process.* (Human cognitive processing.) Amsterdam: John Benjamins.
Itkonen, T. I. 1948. *Suomen lappalaiset vuoteen 1945* [The Lapps of Finland up to 1945]. Vol I–II. Helsinki: Werner Söderström Osakeyhtiö.
Katan, David. 2004. *Translating cultures: An introduction for translators, interpreters and mediators.* Manchester: St. Jerome Publishing.
Keysar, Boaz & Bridget Bly. 1995. Intuitions of the transparency of idioms: Can one keep a secret by spilling the beans? *Journal of Memory and Language* 34. 89–109.
Keysar, Boaz & Bridget Bly. 1999. Swimming against the current: Do idioms reflect conceptual structure? *Journal of Pragmatics* 31. 1559–1578.
Koskimies, A. V. & T. I. Itkonen. 1978 [1917]. *Inarinlappalaista kansantietoutta* [Inari Saami folk knowledge], 2nd edn. (Mémoires de la Société Finno-Ougrienne 167.) Helsinki: Finno-Ugrian Society.
Kövecses, Zoltán. 1995. Anger: Its language, conceptualization, and physiology in the light of cross-cultural evidence. In John Taylor & Robert MacLaury (eds.), *Language and cognitive construal of the world* (Trends in Linguistics 82), 181–196. Berlin & New York: Mouton de Gruyter.
Kövecses, Zoltán. 2002. *Metaphor: A practical introduction.* Oxford: Oxford University Press.
Kövecses, Zoltán. 2005. *Metaphor in culture: Universality and variation.* Cambridge: Cambridge University Press.
Lakoff, George & Mark Johnson. 1980. *Metaphors we live by.* Chicago: University of Chicago Press.
Lakoff, George & Mark Turner. 1989. *More than cool reason: A field guide to poetic metaphor.* Chicago: University of Chicago Press.
Lakoff, George. 1993. The contemporary theory of metaphor. In Andrew Ortony (ed.), *Metaphor and thought*, 202–251. Cambridge: Cambridge University Press.
Lakoff, George & Mark Johnson. 1999. *Philosophy in the flesh: The embodied mind and its challenge to Western thought.* New York: Basic Books.
Lehtola, Teuvo. 1998. *Kolmen kuninkaan maa: Inarin historia 1500-luvulta jälleenrakennusaikaan* [The land of three kings: The history of Inari from the 1500s to the time of reconstruction]. Inari: Puntsi.
Lehtola, Veli-Pekka. 2002. *The Sámi people: Traditions in transition.* Inari: Puntsi.
Lehtola, Veli-Pekka (ed.). 2003. *Inari – Aanaar: Inarin historia jääkaudesta nykypäivään* [Inari – Aanaar: The history of Inari from the Ice Age to today]. Inari: Inarin kunta.
Mattus, Ilmari (ed.). *Anarâš kalender* [Inari Saami calendar]. Ivalo: Anarâškielâ servi.
Morottaja, Matti. 2005. *Inarinsaamelaiset* [The Inari Saami]. http://www-db.helsinki.fi/saami (assessed 3 February 2010).
Morottaja, Matti. 2007. *Inarinsaamen kielen tilanne sekä kielenhuolto- ja tutkimustarpeet.* [The situation and the need for the research and maintenance of Inari Saami.] http://www.kotus.fi/files/716/inariSelvitys2007.pdf (accessed 3 February 2010).
Morottaja, Petter. 2009. Kirje luhhum: Inarinsaamen idiomisanakirja [Reading a book: The Inari Saami idiom dictionary]. *Kierâš* 12/2009.

Murphy, Gregory L. 1996. On metaphoric representation. *Cognition* 60. 173–204.
Murphy, Gregory L. 1997. Reasons to doubt the present evidence for metaphoric representation. *Cognition* 62. 99–108.
Nelson, Diane. 2007. Events and case in Inari Saami. In Ida Toivonen & Diane Nelson (eds.), *Saami linguistics* (Current Issues in Linguistic Theory 288), 207–226. Amsterdam: John Benjamins.
Näkkäläjärvi, Klemetti. 2000. Porosaamelaisen luonnonympäristö [The natural environment of a reindeer-herding Saami]. Irja Seurujärvi-Kari (ed.), *Beaivvi mánát, saamelaisten juuret ja nykyaika*. [Children of the sun, the roots and the present day of the Saami]. (Tietolipas 164), 143–165. Helsinki: Finnish Literature Society.
Onions, C. T et al. 1966: *The Oxford dictionary of English etymology*. Oxford: Oxford University Press.
Piirainen, Elisabeth. 2004. Cognitive, cultural, and pragmatic aspects of dialectal phraseology – exemplified by Low German Dialect "Westmünsterländisch". *Dialectologia et Geolinguistica* 12. 46–67.
Piirainen, Elisabeth. 2006. Cultural foundation of phraseology: A comparison of standard languages and dialect. In W. Kürschner & R. Rapp (eds.), *Linguistik International. Festschrift für Heinrich Weber*, 321–336. Lengerich: Pabst Science Publishers.
Piirainen, Elisabeth. 2008. Figurative phraseology and culture. In Sylviane Granger & Fanny Meunier (eds.), *Phraseology: An interdisciplinary perspective*. 207–228. Amsterdam & Philadelphia: John Benjamins.
Quinn, Naomi. 1991. The cultural basis of metaphor. In James Fernandez (ed.), *Beyond metaphor: The theory of tropes in anthropology*, 56–93. Stanford: Stanford University Press.
Quinn, Naomi. 2003. Research on shared task solutions. In Claudia Strauss & Naomi Quinn (eds.), *A cognitive theory of cultural meaning*. (Publications of the Society for Psychological Anthropology 9), 137–188. Cambridge: Cambridge University Press.
Sabban, Annette. 2007. Culture-boundness and problems of cross-cultural phraseology. In Harald Burger, Dmitrij Dobrovol'skij, Peter Kühn, Neal R. Norrick (eds.), *Phraseology: An international handbook of contemporary research / Ein internationales Handbuch der zeitgenössischen Forschung*, 590–605. Berlin: Walter de Gruyter.
Strauss, Claudia & Naomi Quinn. 1999. *A cognitive theory of cultural meaning*. Oxford: Oxford University Press.
Sandra, Dominiek. 1998. What linguists can and can't tell you about the human mind: A reply to Croft. *Cognitive Linguistics* 9(4). 362–378.
Steward, Julian H. 1976 [1955]. *Theory of culture change: The methodology of multilinear evolution*, 2nd edn. London: University of Illinois Press.
Teliya, Veronika, Natalya Bragina, Elena Oparina & Irina Sandomirskaya. 1998. Phraseology as a language of culture: Its role in the representation of a collective mentality. In Anthony P. Cowie (ed.), *Phraseology: Theory, analysis and applications*, 55–75. Oxford: Clarendon Press.
Tomasello, Michael. 1999. *The cultural origins of human cognition*. Cambridge: Harvard University Press.
Vervaeke, John & John M. Kennedy. 1996. Metaphors in language and thought: Falsification and multiple meanings. *Metaphor and Symbolic Activity* 11. 273–284.

Comment

Fifteen commandments of a phraseologist

FRANTIŠEK ČERMÁK

Phraseology or, alternatively, idiomatics, is a young discipline still full of misunderstandings due to theories developed for other purposes or, on the surface of it, due to seemingly obvious and clear illustrations of metaphors. There is a long history of generativists fighting the phenomenon of idioms under various labels and with negligible success, some of them wondering why not even the latest Chomskyan or post-Chomskyan theory helps. Cognitivists, on the other hand, being obsessed with metaphor and labouring to identify it everywhere have not made this phenomenon any clearer. On the other hand, being long recognized as a specific domain, idioms are used, often in an oversimplified way, in a number of textbooks for beginners (though with a mixed success) and elsewhere.

Trying to present, in the following, some of the major features and, at the same time, stumbling-blocks in the analysis of idioms, a way is adopted pointing to the gist of problems and fallacies that is almost atheoretical, using plain language, though based on only few examples (however, all of the points mentioned below are discussed in Čermák 2007). Hopefully, a brief comment or dictum, based on the author's lifetime involvement with idioms, both lexicographical and theoretical, which is offered here may provoke some critical thought. Every point given below calls for discussion and lengthy comment, which is hardly possible here (but see the references below).

1. *In idioms, nothing is what it seems to be*: words are not words, they do not have the familiar meaning one knows from dictionaries, while, perhaps, the worst anomaly of theirs is to be found in their specific and unpredictable function, especially a pragmatic one. *You shall be prepared to deal with these fairly and on their own merits*, cf. *kick the bucket* where *kick* does not denote the familiar movement of a foot nor can the *bucket* hold liquid.

2. In your analysis, *you shall not try to decompose the idiom into its constituents*, as this is tempting as well as badly misleading, not being based on any principle and suggests an unwarranted way of analysis. No component is what it seems to be. Should you be tempted to do this, you might end up, having successfully determined *rain* of the idiom *rain cats and dogs* as 'pour', 'fall in drops, etc', facing the remaining *cats and dogs*. Not even the most foolhardy analyst would be able to defend this part of the idiom as meaning 'very hard'.

3. Becoming aware of the kind of special combination underlying the idiom, *you shall not try to generalize this particular feature*, or make it a rule, or, which is worse, an algorithm supposed to produce new idioms. There are no rules, no models to be found here, let alone formalizations enabling their boundless generation. Thus, even the seemingly simple idiom *take a seat* will not allow for a follow-up, such as *take a sofa, take a bench*, etc. signifying a similar habitual movement and often used pragmatically as an invitation.

4. *You shall not try to apply standard methods and criteria while studying idioms.* None of them holds, least of all projections of syntactic theories. Not even the staunchest syntactician, Chomsky, is able to do this. Idioms are always combinations of a kind that have their specific form, meaning and function, cf. the absurd passivization **the bucket was kicked*.

5. *You shall not view the idiom as a nuisance because it does not fit your nice theory*. If the theory cannot accommodate it, it's the theory that is at fault and a nuisance for linguistics. Accordingly, do not try to invent ever-new theories explaining the idioms' substance; there have been too many of them in the past, having all failed. Dwelling on a single counter-example, that generativists are so fond of, may turn out to be a mixture of individual and mutually incompatible interpretations, while, in general, it offers no solution to a large-scale description and interpretation that dictionaries might need.

6. *Idioms defy all sorts of standard language rules* we know from regular use of words. One of the most conspicuous features idioms have, not found elsewhere (next to some scientific terms), is the phenomenon of monocollocable words (word forms, with extremely restricted collocability) that do not exist outside phraseology and, accordingly, do not have an independent existence of their own, cf. *look **askance**, let **bygones** be **bygones**, **kith** and kin*, etc. They represent a constant headache for grammarians as defying any classification and description.

7. In studying idiom, *you shall not limit your scope to the collocation type of idioms only*. Doing so, you shall overlook other types, both smaller and larger.

There are idioms to be found within limits of a single word, but there are also idioms that amount to a sentence or their combination, cf. *breakfast* (≠ break + fast), *nightcap* (≠ night + cap, i.e. in the sense of a drink), *Every cloud has a silver lining*, etc.

8. *You shall not look for nice metaphors and images only* while trying to find idioms in text. Instead, look for irregularities and (paradigmatic and syntagmatic) anomalies in idioms as these are omnipresent in the field while idioms based on metaphors are in minority. Next to metaphors, there are other ways idioms have been formed and these, such as syntagmatic anomalies including many grammar idioms, should not be neglected and left out of description, cf. *as for* (there are no analogous combinations, such as *as in, as from, as on*, etc.), *the ins and outs*, etc.

9. *You shall not handle the idiom as a mere embellishment of one's speech.* Rather, remind yourself of the real reason why the idiom exists, Historically, it is a product of an individual chance formation (not being based on any analogy at all) coming into use because of its useful brevity and vagueness; functionally, it is restricted to a special use, often with an evaluative feature, cf. mostly descriptive *take it in one's head to* not used to give advice (or as an imperative), while *get it into your head* is used in this manner (accompanied by some insistence or impatience).

10. *You shall refrain from being chauvinistic in your interpretation* of idioms viewing them as something that is specific to a language (specifically your language) or society only. It is not. Though some cases may seem to be like this, they are always partial and numerically insignificant in the totality of idioms, cf. specific Spanish *hit the bull's eye*, reminiscent of bull-fight, or Chinese *yan(3) er(3) dao(4) ling(2)* 'cover one's ears to steal a bell', i.e. to cheat oneself (based on an old story).

11. Trying to find and study *the most important and current idioms in a language*, you shall go for those areas and topics that are highly frequent, spoken and laden with evaluative function. Quite a few idioms are primarily spoken, while spoken corpora offering data of this kind are still rather scarce.

12. While comparing idioms in more languages *you shall not enthuse over superficial similarities*. Identical counterparts hardly ever obtain and it is a safe bet that two "identical" idioms are not identical at all. The field is full of false friends, cf. English *out of hand* ('not under control; without thinking'),

French *de la main de* ('master, author') and Czech *z ruky* ('without preparation, improvised'), etc.

13. *You shall keep reminding yourself that idioms are not predictable*, let alone formed on a model found in a neighbouring language. This does not mean, however, that languages do not borrow idioms from each other, though there is no reliable criterion telling you when and what sort of borrowings happen.

14. *If in doubt how to suggest something vaguely while not overcommitting yourself, use an idiom* since idioms are ready-made means for just that, i.e. for avoiding an express and precise formulation, offering, at the same time, an ample scope for conveying pragmatic (evaluative) attitudes.

15. *You shall be careful while using idioms, unless you are a native speaker.* There are always anomalies in their use, too, that have to be observed, cf. a single form (out of more) that is hardly acceptable **he will not be born yesterday*, etc.

Charles University Prague

Note

Correspondence address: frantisek.cermak@lf3.cuni.cz

References

Čermák, František. 2007. *Frazeologie a idiomatika česká a obecná.* [Czech and general phraseology.] Prague: Karolinum.

Čermák, František. Jiří Hronek & Jaroslav Machač (eds.). 2009. *Slovník české frazeologie a idiomatiky. Přirovnání., Výrazy neslovesné., Výrazy slovesné* [Dictionary of Czech phraseology and idiomatics, similes, non-verb expressions, verb expressions, sentence expressions]. Prague: Leda.

Book reviews

Christiane Fellbaum (ed.): *Idioms and collocations: Corpus-based linguistic and lexicographic studies*. London: Continuum, 2007. 224 pp. ISBN 978-0-82-648994-4 (hb), ISBN 978-0-82-644473-8 (pb).

Corpus linguistics has become a much practiced methodology to perform a number of tasks. It is indispensable for lexicographers in providing a much larger range of textual sources than was possible pre-corpora. It is used to create frequency tables to assist language teachers. It can be used to hunt grammatical constructions. This book demonstrates what benefits flow for linguists, lexicographers and phraseologists from a well constructed and sensitively interrogated corpus. The project – some of the outcomes of which are reported in this book – was undertaken as a *Wolfgang-Paul-Preis* project funded by the *Alexander von Humboldt Foundation*. The project was located at the *Berlin Brandenburg Academy of Sciences* (which is also the headquarters of the first dictionary on historical principles, *The German Dictionary*, begun by the Grimm Brothers). The project's aim was to investigate German collocations by means of interrogating the balanced corpus of twentieth century German also constructed at the *Berlin Brandenburg Academy of Sciences*. This corpus demonstrates two elements of successful corpus-based research. As well as having sensitive tools for interrogating a corpus, the corpus itself must be carefully constructed to allow such interrogation.

After a fine introduction by the editor outlining the field, in the first chapter Alexander Geyken describes the characteristics of the corpus. It comprises a core corpus that matches the size of the *British National Corpus* (100 million words), and has an extended corpus of over 900 million tokens. The core corpus is balanced with respect to text types; each decade of the twentieth century is represented by the same number of tokens. The morphologically analyzed and tagged corpus thus constitutes a tool for both credible quantitative and linguistic studies as well as diachronic analysis. Queries can be carried out with a linguistic search engine designed with the needs of linguistics in mind. A statistical module that computes MI scores, t-scores and log-likelihood facilitates the extraction of collocations from the core corpus. Kilgarriff and Tugwell's (2004) WordSketch is a similar tool, applicable cross-linguistically.

In Chapter 2 Alexander Geyken and Alexey Sokirko describe an interactive parsing process by means of which Nominative and Function Verb Groups (NVG/FVG) can be classified. The authors applied a syntactic filter to enable the automatic extraction of candidate structures. The filter is a shallow parser that recognizes phrases where the verb and its argument (NP or PP) are in a head-complement relation. The parser is interactive in that the human lexicographer feeds manually inspected corpus examples back into the parser. A manual inspection of all candidate V-NP and V-PP structures even with a good concordance tool is not feasible because of the high frequency of verbs involved in light verb constructions. In a corpus comprising a billion words, such verbs are presented by hundreds of thousands of tokens. For the task of identifying the NVG *Dienst leisten*, a precision of 99.7% and 97.3% was achieved in two experiments. This is significantly better than the precision one would achieve with a purely Boolean query, which yields only 81% precision. Precision here is crucial, as the lexicographer does not want to inspect pre-classified examples, which would wipe out all savings of time and effort made by employing a machine parser. Similarly, a recall of 93.3% (Exp.1) and 94.8% (Exp. 2) is very high. Identifying a prepositional complement is much harder that an accusative object. Hence it is to be expected that recall and precision of the prior classification will be lower than in the case of direct object in such collocations as *Dienst leisten*.

In Chapter 3 Axel Herold describes the problems associated with extracting all relevant corpus examples of a given idiom. The goal was to investigate the semantic, morphological, lexical, syntactic and diachronic variability of the idioms in unconstructed examples. The queries should be formulated in such a way as to allow for the range of variations not reflected in dictionaries or predicted by intuitions. The corpus query tool Dialing DWDS Concordancer (DDC), used to retrieve the corpus data, allows for the specification of token properties on every level of annotation. Queries can be constructed by giving the exact order of tokens, the maximum and minimum distance between tokens, or no order at all. Tokens can be specified with regard to different linguistic properties. DDC provides support for accessing semantic concepts by exploiting a thesaurus but substitution of lexical material is usually considered on the part-of-speech level, so there is no need to restrict substitution to semantic similarity. It is not possible to construct queries that refer to entities across orthographic sentence boundaries. This makes it difficult to search for anaphoric substitutions for parts of idioms in cases where the antecedent is part of an adjacent sentence. However, the lexicographers can manually examine the wider context of each sentence that corresponds to the query. In many cases, they will detect anaphoric use of some idioms, but in many cases, it is almost impossible to explore anaphora.

Having shown how the corpus was collected and parsed, in Chapter 4 Gerald Neumann, Fabian Koerner and Christiane Fellbaum show how it can be used for lexicographic purposes. The chapter describes the custom-built lexicographic workbench for the collection, analysis and representation of the corpus data. After the collocations are extracted from the corpus (Herold), an example corpus is created that illustrates the item's usage. Each example is labelled according to its bibliographical origin and date; labels are also assigned referring to morphological, syntactic and lexical variations. Manual inspection distinguishes examples with literal and idiomatic uses; sometimes both readings are intended by the writer. The linguistic and lexicographic analysis is performed manually by means of a template in the form of a specialist electronic dictionary entry where a wide range of properties of the citation form and all variations found in the corpus are recorded along with the appropriate corpus examples. Such manual inspection is not possible without a good query system to collect the data in the first place.

From this point on, the book turns to the use of the previously outlined tools for linguistic analysis. Here the efficacy of the massive effort in constructing the tools is demonstrated in the high quality analyses which it provides.

In Chapter 5 Katerina Stathi performs a fine-grained analysis of adjectival modification in German idioms. According to Nunberg et al. (1994) and Dobrovol'skij (1999), adjective modification can serve as a diagnostic of semantic analysability. Idioms are roughly divided into un-analysable ones, as *kick the bucket* and analysable ones like *spill the beans*, which can be modified along the lines of *spill the political beans*. Stathi challenges this classification as being too simplistic since it ignores the whole range of possible and casually occurring adjective modifiers within idioms. Analysis of corpus examples allows Stathi to identy five types of adjectival modification, which can be correlated with different types of idioms arranged in a hierarchy.

In Chapter 6 Elke Gehweiler, Iris Hoese and Undine Kramer explore diachronic changes of the semantics in German idioms. Like other aspects of the language, phraseology is a dynamic phenomenon. Corpus-based analyses of German VN idioms show that a number of idioms changed during the twentieth century. Some idioms have more than one idiomatic meaning in addition to a literal meaning. *Schlagseite haben* has five idiomatic meanings. Those idioms that have two or more related idiomatic meanings are considered as polysemous. Homonymous idioms have at least two semantically unrelated non-compositional meanings (Palm 1994). Homonymous idioms are only very rarely attested. For each idiom, the authors give citation forms, number of occurrences, the periods of usage and the meaning paraphrase for each variant. Then they compare the citation forms from the corpus with those given in four dictionaries. Third, they attempt to account for the 'surprises' found. It is only with the help of their large DWDS corpus that they could discover and document the manifold variations of the citation forms. Types of idiom changes are as follows: re-motivation (old idiom develops a new meaning), transition from technical to common language. The authors found that the dictionaries do not necessarily list all the meanings of a phrasal lexeme. For polysemous meanings, their frequency and diachronic development can be commented on with markers such as "seldom" and "becoming obsolete", "low frequency". Access to a corpus helps to establish frequencies and periods of usage for phrasal lexemes. Users can search this database for the phenomena they are interested in, they can search for idioms that have modifiers, those that are resistant to syntactic transformation like passivization or conversion, or examples showing wordplay.

In Chapter 7 Christiane Huemmer highlights the importance of context and discourse for the investigation of idioms. She examines a structurally diverse range of multi-word units, including verb phrases, noun phrases and adjectival phrases. She shows how the underspecified meanings of idioms, and in particular their metaphorical core components, can be made context-specific via modification and how the idioms' meaning potentials can be activated by the larger context. Just as with simple lexemes, the behavioural profile of an idiomatic set phrase is intimately related to its meaning. Huemmer follows Dobrovol'skij (2000, 2004) in arguing that idioms are both motivated and arbitrary: motivated in that the many features of contextual embedding are rooted in formal, lexical and semantic properties; arbitrary in that they are used in a conventionalized way that represents one of many possible motivated links between meaning and contextual embedding. Each idiom has three levels of meaning – literal, metaphoric, and idiomatic. The author takes three idioms and shows by means of a case study that formal properties (such as phrase structure) and three levels of meaning determine idiosyncratic behaviour of the idiom.

In Chapter 8 Anna Firenze focuses on the variation of the determiner. Many idioms show grammatical deviance in their determiners, namely a frozen definite determiner in their canonical form although none of the rules for its use in the literal language seem to apply. Fellbaum (1993) argues that variation of the frozen determiner indicates that the noun is interpreted referentially. In contrast to the theories based on the linguist's intuition as data and their and consequent subjectivity (such as 'dis-agglutination inevitably leads to the loss of the idiomatic reading' [Eisenberg 1998]), the corpus data show that the behaviour of the contracted preposition in idioms is identical to the behaviour of the same expressions with literal meanings and hence, they are not as frozen as is often assumed. In this case, it does not differ from the dis-agglutination of contracted prepositions in free usage. Zero article, possessives, demonstratives and quantifiers were also considered. 800 VN idioms were analysed.

Angelika Storrer investigates German support verb constructions (SVC) in Chapter 9. SVCs form a class of multi-word units that differs both from typical idioms and from typical regular VP constructions with respect to three properties: semantic compositionality, component substitution and morphosyntactic flexibility. The chapter argues that morphosyntactic flexibility is determined not only by the referentiality of the predicate noun, but also by the type of construction the predicate noun occurs in. SVCs that realize their predicate noun in the direct object slot (DO-SVCs) seem to be generally more flexible than SVCs where the predicate noun occurs within a prepositional phrase (PP-SVCs). The author finds that adjective modification is frequent even in constructions that are quite restricted with respect to determiner variation. Thus, flexibility depends on two factors: the referentiality of the predicate noun and the type of construction containing the predicate noun. PP-SVCs are generally much more constrained in number and determiner variation than DO-SVCs. Both constructions can be modified by adjectives. Idiomatic SVCs are restricted to both flexibility and modification no matter if the nouns occur in a direct object slot or within a prepositional phrase. When grouping SVCs according to their typical constraints, a cross-classification along these two independent factors seems to be more adequate than a simple partition in referential and non-referential constructions. The choice between support verb constructions and their corresponding base verbs is not as arbitrary as has been assumed in the literature. The chapter shows that for further analysis, it is important to have a specialized workbench where the corpus occurrences are linguistically annotated (presence or absence of modifiers and determiners), sorted into different files – for different base verb of SVC or for different types of substitution difficulty.

In Chapter 10 Christiane Fellbaum investigates the class of grammatically marked idioms. The chapter examines three types of German VP idioms. In each case, the argument structure of the verb is part of the lexical entry and is required for its idiomatic reading. The syntactic construction is an integral part of the idiom's meaning as much as its lexical make-up. The association of a particular syntactic construction and a specific meaning has been discussed by Fillmore et al. (1988), who examine English idiomatic constructions like (1) and (2):

(1) *the X-er and the Y-er (the more the merrier, the more guests the merrier the party, the smaller a laptop is, the easier it is to carry in a bag)*

(2) *XY? My son a professor? Mary work in a soup kitchen? Freddy out of money?*

The open slots in these frames admit a wide range of lexical items from several syntactic categories. As Fillmore et al. (1988) show, the constructions carry very complex and subtle meanings that cannot be captured by the dictionary definitions for their constituent lexemes. Unlike the constructions considered by Fillmore et al. (1988), Fellbaum focuses on idioms with specific lexical content. In the case of the idioms with *stehen* and *geben*, their marked syntax sets them apart from their use in freely constructed language. The high number of idioms involving a Beneficiary that are semantically opaque suggests that the double-object frame here carries the shared core message (semantic prosody) 'do something nasty to somebody'. The patterns carry much of the idioms' meanings, compensating for the lack of semantic transparency.

In summary, what does this excellent book have to offer to phraseologists? First and by no means of least importance, it demonstrates how careful one needs to be in setting up a corpus so as to ensure that what is wanted from the corpus is able to be gained from it. Like any data collection process, the quality of the data finally determines the quality of the generalizations that can be made on its basis. Size certainly matters. Just as the equipment at CERN (*Conseil Européen pour la Recherche Nucléaire*, or *European Council for Nuclear Research*) has expanded as new particle accelerators have been needed, so corpora have expanded. That large corpora are needed is indicated by Geyken et al. (2004) who suggest that until corpora reach a critical mass, they cannot provide reliable information about phrasal lexemes. Exactly what that size turns out to be is still, to some extent, an open question. The quality of the material in a corpus also matters. While newspapers offer easy electronic data, newspapers are only one family of text types. If one views corpora as providing data on the phraseology of a language, then some attempt must be made to create a representative corpus. While much has been written on this, what constitutes 'representative' is still a contested matter. A corpus is a sample of parole, not langue. There is no way to sample langue directly so all one has is parole of various kinds. But that does not mean the distinction can be laid aside. It is clear that the authors are well aware of this through the sensitive handling of the data they have used. They are interested in langue as well as parole. Second, the book shows that there is no substitute for sensitive human intervention. After extracting data from a corpus, human analysis is still needed. This always makes use of native speaker intuitions. Even the judgement that two different forms constitute one lexeme in two different forms is not something a computer can always be relied on to provide. Third, the book shows clearly what a great data set can do for testing hypotheses. The chapters of linguistic analysis are quite revolutionary in the proposals they provide for a better understanding of the linguistic properties of phrasal lexemes. These proposals would not have been as carefully supported if it had not been for the careful way in which the data was assembled.

ELENA DNESTROVSKAYA
Correspondence address: elena.dnestrovskaya@canterbury.ac.nz

References

Dobrovol'skij, Dmitrij. 1999. Haben transformationelle Defekte der Idiomstruktur semantische Ursachen? In Nicole Fernandes Bravo, Irmtraud Behr & Claire Rozier (eds.), *Phraseme und typisierende Rede*, 25–37. Tübingen: Stauffenburg.
Dobrovol'skij, Dmitrij. 2000. Ist die Semantik von Idiomen nichtkompositionell? In Suzanne Beckmann, Peter-Paul Koenig & Georg Wolf (eds.), *Sprachspiel und Bedeutung: Festschrift für Franz Hundsnurscher zum 65. Geburtstag*, 113–124. Tübingen: Niemeyer.
Dobrovol'skij, Dmitrij. 2004. Idiome aus kognitiver Sicht. In Katrin Steyer (ed.), *Wortverbindungen: Mehr oder weniger fest*, 117–143. Berlin & New York: Mouton de Gruyter.
Fellbaum, Christiane. 1993. The determiner in English idioms. In Cristina Cacciari & Patrizia Tabossi (eds.), *Idioms: Processing, structure, and interpretation*, 271–295. Hillsdale: Erlbaum.
Fellbaum, Christiane (ed.). 2007. *Idioms and collocation: Corpus-based linguistic and lexicographic studies*. London: Continuum.
Fillmore, Charles J., Paul Kay & Mary C. O'Connor. 1988. Regularity and idiomaticity in grammatical constructions: The case of *let alone*. *Language* 64. 501–538.
Geyken, Alexander, Alexej Sokirko, Ines Rehbein & Christiane Fellbaum. 2004. What is the optimal corpus size for the study of idioms? Paper presented at the annual meeting of the Deutsche Gesellschaft für Sprache, Mainz.
Kilgariff, Adam & David Tugwell. 2004. Sketching words. Paper presented at the 11th EURALEX International Congress Université de Bretagne-Sud, Lorient.
Nunberg, Geoffrey, Ivan A. Sag & Thomas Wasow. 1994. Idioms. *Language* 70. 491–538.
Eisenberg, Peter. 1998. *Grundriss der deutschen Grammatik: Das Wort*. Stuttgart: Metzler.
Palm, Christine. 1994. Habent sua fata idiomata: Beobachtungen zur Polysemie von Phraseologismen. In Barbara Sandig (ed.), *Europhras 92: Tendenzen der Phraseologieforschung*, 431–460. Bochum: Brockmeyer.

Wolfgang Mieder: *"Yes we can": Barack Obama's proverbial rhetoric*. New York: Peter Lang, 2009. 352 pp. ISBN 978-1-4331-0667-5 (pb).

Wolfgang Mieder, Professor of German and Folklore at the University of Vermont, the founding editor of *Proverbium: Yearbook of International Proverb Scholarship*, is an outstanding and internationally recognized paremiologist and phraseologist. Among the more than one hundred and fifty books that he has published on proverb studies, there is a large number of publications on language and politics, e.g. *The politics of proverbs: From traditional wisdom to proverbial stereotypes* (1997), *The proverbial Abraham Lincoln* (2000), *"No struggle, No progress": Frederick Douglass and his proverbial rhetoric for Civil Rights* (2001), *"Call a spade a spade": From classical phrase to racial slur* (2002), *"Proverbs are the best policy": Folk wisdom and American politics* (2005). It is little wonder, therefore, that Barack Obama – well-known for his impressive rhetoric and metaphorical language – has attracted the author's special attention. Nevertheless, this new book differs from those mentioned above in that it examines the rhetoric of a contemporary politician. Without any doubt Obama is the most eminent political leader of the present: his speeches and books have been followed and read by millions of people all over the world and are accessible through the modern media even today. This aspect alone makes the book outstanding and significant for a readership interested in language and politics in contemporary history, in "a new politics for a new time" (Obama).

The book is structured as a collection of four comprehensive articles. More specifically, Mieder's phraseological analysis includes Obama's books *The audacity of hope* (2006) (Chapter 1, pp. 1–31) and *Dreams from my father* (1995) (Chapter 2, pp. 33–62) as well as 229 speeches, news conferences, interviews and addresses dating from 2002 to his inaugural address on 20 January 2009. The speeches are examined in Chapter 3 "The proverbial speeches and media events" (pp. 63–106) and Chapter 4 "The proverbial rhetoric to the presidency" (pp. 107–146), the latter presenting in-depth studies of Obama's seven most significant addresses on his way to presidency. While this structure entails that some aspects are repeated several times, it has the great advantage that the individual chapters can be used separately, for example, for educational purposes. The 184-page index of 1714 proverbs and proverbial phrases found within Obama's works (from *to clean up one's act* to *to be in the golden years*) with an exact contextualization of writings and events is an additional asset of the book.

The mere fact that Mieder locates 195 phraseological units in Obama's 365-page book *The audacity of hope* proves that idioms, set phrases and proverbs are an integral part of Obama's impressive style. Mieder shows that he uses them to add colour and emotion as well as communality and common sense to his writing and to show himself to be part of the general population. On the one hand, he thus follows in the footsteps of Abraham Lincoln, Theodore Roosevelt, Benjamin Franklin, Martin Luther King and other figureheads of American political history, who also made extensive use of the folk speech patterns of their constituents. On the other hand, as Mieder shows, the percentage of actual proverbs in his speech is rather low. In comparison to his predecessors Obama is less didactic (*Look before you leap*) and does not rely on clichés; his pre-formulated language is rich in modern expressions and texts such as *winner-take-all (economy), golden parachute, been there done that, make (no) waves, cookie-cutter formula, break the glass ceiling* and *to listen to one's guts*. For example, when using biblical quotations, he adapts them to the modern age overcoming the gender bias (*I'm my brother's keeper and my sister's keeper*).

Chapter 2, dealing with Obama's book *Dreams from my father: A story of race and inheritance*, has the title "'Black as pitch' and 'White as milk'. Barack Obama's proverbial autobiography". What is true for Mieder's book as a whole becomes particularly obvious here. We learn about Obama's proverbial rhetoric and, at the same time, we get to know Obama himself. The many contextualized idioms and phrases taken from his books reveal their fascinating contents and encourage one to read them in their entirety. Mieder rightly characterizes Obama's description of his experiences at his private school in Hawaii as "a linguistic and phraseological masterpiece, indicating that he has command over the entire register of the English language, from slang and lingo of the youth culture to the intellectual vocabulary of a highly educated person" (p. 42). With reference to a rich variety of examples Mieder illustrates to what extent idioms, proverbs and phrases add to the authenticity of Obama's book. His keen interest in African proverbs and traditional folk speech reveals itself when Obama describes how he searches for and discovers his African roots on a journey to Kenya.

A topic discussed in several chapters of the book is ghostwriting. To what extent can we be sure that the speeches and writings whose style is admired by so many people are authentic 'Obama'? Of course, politicians, who sometimes have to deliver a speech every day, rely on a team of competent wordsmiths who draft them. Several books have shed light on American presidents and their speechwriters and the topic has recently been focused on in relation to Barack Obama in the US press as well as in blogs on the internet. On the one hand, he said in an interview, as Mieder quotes (p. 38): "I would feel uncomfortable putting my name to something that was written by somebody else or co-written or dictated. If my name is on it, it belongs to me." On the other hand, Obama thanks his editors in the introductions to his books and mentions Jon Favreau as his director of speechwriting in his White House staff announcement. For Mieder phraseology can be used as ample proof of authenticity. Having scrutinized Obama's books as well as his more spontaneous contributions in interviews and news conferences from 2002 until the beginning of 2009, he comes to the conclusion that his style is absolutely consistent. "The important point here is that Obama communicates today very much in the same way as he did when he was a little-known politician in Illinois" (p. 65). The consistently high percentage of proverbial language that permeates the entire communicative corpus with parallel expressions in written und oral texts specifically supports Mieder's "gut reaction" (p. 76) that these stem from Obama personally.

In Chapter 3 Mieder classifies the phraseological units that he has isolated. The over one thousand expressions used in Obama's speeches and media events are arranged in groups such as "classical proverbs and phrases" (pp. 96–98), "somatic phrases" (i.e. referring to parts of the human body) (pp. 98–100), "binary or twin formulas" (pp. 100–101), "sport expressions" (pp. 101–102). Mieder's frequency analysis reveals to what extent language (and above all phraseology) mirrors ideas. He describes so-called proverbial leitmotifs that are comprised of recurrent idioms and phrases. One of those key concepts is "change", with the following phrases underscoring Obama's message: *turn the page* (used 64 times in the corpus!), *the buck stops here, all hands on deck, now is the time, put one's shoulder to the wheel, let this be the day* and, of course, his campaign slogan *Yes we can*, which he might have picked up from the popular song *Yes We Can Can* (1973) by the Pointer Sisters, as Mieder explains.

In addition, Chapter 3 shows that Obama not only makes use of prefabricated language but also coins phrases and slogan-like structures that have the potential to become proverbial in due time. *You invest in America, America will invest in you, What's good/bad for Main Street, is good/bad for Wall Street, You can't change direction with a new driver who follows the same old map, No ifs, ands, or buts* can be found among those "pseudo-proverbs" (pp. 73–77). In addition, there are meta-communicative formulae that are associated with him: *but make no mistake* and *let me be perfectly clear*. Time will tell whether they last beyond Obama's use and have a chance of entering quotation dictionaries.

In Chapter 4 Mieder deals with Obama's seven most important speeches in his campaign for the presidency. They demonstrate that Obama is an excellent orator who controls the power of words (p. 108): "He uses a political language that finds a balance between the popular and the intellectual, coming from the heart and reaching across all divides in an attempt to reunite a nation for the common purpose of leaving an economic crisis, an unjustified war, and many social problems behind." This chapter is also a personal statement.

The author is not only one of the best paremiologists in the world, an accurate linguist who counts proverbial phrases, and occasionally even commas in these (see p. 74) in a huge corpus of writings and speeches, and who does not take for granted what is claimed on the Internet about the origin of an African proverb, but traces it himself in Chinua Achebe's novels (pp. 59–60). Mieder openly states that he read parts of Obama's books with tears in his eyes and that he, as a recent naturalized citizen of the United States, was deeply moved by Obama's inaugural speech. The three great Americans that the President admires, Abraham Lincoln, Frederick Douglass, and Martin Luther King, are his heroes as well. The chapter is concluded with the author's personal letter to Barack Obama.

Phraseologists – and this reviewer confesses to belonging to this species herself – occasionally have a problem: They tend to be a bit overenthusiastic about their field of research. Where 'ordinary' people just listen to a pop-song, they detect an idiom in the lyrics; when the other family members sit in front of the TV and enjoy watching a film, they notice that in a certain scene a proverb has been inadequately translated in the dubbed version. Although I am similarly thrilled by Obama's use of phraseological units in his speeches and writings and, among other things, encourage my students to deal with the topic in term papers and theses, I could not help smiling from time to time when faced with Wolfgang Mieder's fascination. For instance, he wishes that Obama had included Frederick Douglass's proverbial quotation *If there is no struggle, there is no progress* (p. 116), he bemoans the fact that Obama prefers terms such as "aphorism", "saying" and "truth", but does not use "proverb" a single time in his writings (p. 43), or he recommends the President to use an anti-proverb occasionally (p. 83). It is a pleasure to read a highly scholarly book that is written with so much warmth, energy, and enthusiasm.

The language of politicians has often been criticized. One popular view is that it is "empty and full of hollow phrases". Phraseological units are mainly referred to pejoratively as "clichés" or "platitudes" in this context. An assessment that is not supported by empirical evidence and that neglects their pragmatic and stylistic functions. Barack Obama's becoming the 44th President of the United States undoubtedly has a lot to do with his linguistic prowess and his truly powerful rhetoric. As Wolfgang Mieder shows convincingly, effective and sincere political communication needs proverbs, sayings and other elements of so-called folk speech. The book, with its impressive contextualized phraseological index and an extensive bibliography dealing with politics and proverbs as well as with Obama's rhetoric, is a treasure trove for paremiologists and linguists. However, it can also be recommended to non-specialists who simply want to learn more about the linguistic side of the first African American President of the United

States. My paperback edition comes in an up-to-date jacket with fresh colours and a modern style, high-resolution photograph of Obama. The attractive design reflects its contents appealingly. In this case, you *can* judge the book by its cover.

SABINE FIEDLER
Correspondence address: sfiedler@rz.uni-leipzig.de

References

Mieder, Wolfgang. 1997. *The politics of proverbs: From traditional wisdom to proverbial stereotypes*. Wisconsin: University of Wisconsin Press.
Mieder, Wolfgang. 2000. *The proverbial Abraham Lincoln: An index to proverbs in the works of Abraham Lincoln*. New York: Peter Lang.
Mieder, Wolfgang. 2001. *"No struggle, no progress": Frederick Douglass and his proverbial rhetoric for Civil Rights*.
Mieder, Wolfgang. 2002. *"Call a spade a spade": From classical phrase to racial slur*. New York: Peter Lang.
Mieder, Wolfgang. 2005. *"Proverbs are the best policy": Folk wisdom and American politics*. Utah: Utah State University Press.
Obama, Barack. 1995. *Dreams from my father: A story of race and inheritance*. New York: Three Rivers Press.
Obama, Barack. 2006. *The audacity of hope: Thoughts on reclaiming the American Dream*. New York: Crown.

Thomas Kotschi, Ulrich Detges and Colette Cortès. 2009. *Wörterbuch französischer Nominalprädikate*: *Funktionsverbgefüge und feste Syntagmen der Form <être + Präposition + Nomen>*. Tübingen: Gunter Narr, xxiv + 926 pp. ISBN 978-3-82-336481-8.

The *Wörterbuch französischer Nominalprädikate* ('Dictionary of French Nominal Predicates') is most welcome as it fills a gap in the lexical reference works available for the French language. It contains an inventory of so-called light verb constructions, corresponding to what are generally called *constructions à verbe support* in Romance linguistics, or *Funktionsverbgefüge* in German linguistics. The constructions included in the dictionary are identified on the basis of corpora of modern French and are provided with their German translations. This makes the dictionary extremely valuable for advanced learners of French (and their teachers) in schools and in higher education, as well as for professional translators. In addition, it provides the Romance linguist with a wealth of descriptions of the grammatical and semantic features of the constructions concerned, along with authentic illustrative examples for each linguistic pattern. It is thus a precious resource for further research in this area of linguistic phenomena where syntax and phraseology overlap and which is characterized by a high number of idiosyncrasies on the level of language use. These irregularities cannot be predicted by the systematic rules of language and therefore need to be described minutely and case by case. This is done in this book.

As indicated in the subtitle, the dictionary focuses on a particular subgroup of light verb constructions. Their base form consists of the verb 'to be' followed by a preposition and a noun: *être* + Prep + N, as in *être en délire*. In a sentence they typically constitute the predicate. The verb may vary to form a series of related constructions for referring, for example, to different phases of the process (different types of *Aktionsart*), as in *être en délire* → *entrer en délire, tomber dans le délire*, or for changing the number and kind of arguments, as in *être en fureur (contre N)* → *mettre quelqu'un en fureur (contre N)*. The constructions also vary as to their degree of fixedness and semantic transparency. At one end of the scale, they may merge with fully idiomatic phrases sharing the same structural pattern. Such phrases – although not belonging to the class of light verb constructions proper – are also included in the dictionary. For example, it contains *être en boîte* (the base form) and the corresponding members of the series *mettre quelque chose en boîte, mettre un film en boîte* as well as the fully idiomatic phrase *mettre quelqu'un en boîte*.

The reference work in question is an example of a valency dictionary. It differs from existing dictionaries based on a similar theoretical background (see Busse and Dubost (1977) for French and Herbst et al. (2004) for English) in that the entries are not single lexemes but multi-word constructions, which, as a whole, determine the number and nature of their arguments.

The dictionary derives its raison d'être from a whole range of considerations. For instance, one must take into account the general importance of the patterns in the language. In French, *être* + Prep + N and related phrases are among the most frequent and versatile constructions, along with V-N-constructions involving the verbs *avoir* or *faire*, for example. In addition, one must consider the textual functions of the constructions due to the fact that they often constitute structural, semantic, or stylistic alternatives to single verbs. It is these functions which – although somewhat neglected in recent linguistic research in favour of an investigation of their grammatical properties – make them particularly interesting for areas of application such as second language acquisition, and especially for the teaching and acquisition of advanced level written competence, as well as for translation and text production generally. Then there is the notoriously large number of peculiarities with regard to the form, meaning and distribution of the constructions. These constitute a particular difficulty for L2 speakers. But the native speaker, too, will want to check his or her intuition in one case or the other, in particular when it comes to specialized contexts. More specifically, such idiosyncrasies may involve:

- the form, structural variation, and syntax of the constructions. A first difficulty concerns the question of whether or not the noun is preceded by its article, or which of the two variants is the preferred variant in actual usage (e.g. *être à (la) disposition de quelqu'un*). Another example of unpredictability concerns the choice of the verb in the series based on a particular noun. One verb may be habitually preferred to a semantically similar one, without any obvious reason. Moreover, this phenomenon may differ from series to series. The choice of the verb may also be linked to the syntax and the cotext/context of the construction (*placé sous l'autorité de quelqu'un* vs. **mis sous l'autorité de quelqu'un*). In addition, the range of syntactic options, such as the attributive or adverbial use of Prep + N without the verb *(en perspective; au nom de)*, seems to be largely a matter of usage, too, and cannot be predicted either.
- the semantics of the constructions. These are typically said to be transparent, but mostly this is true only in retrospect. The exact meaning of the word combination cannot necessarily be derived from its component parts when one encounters the expression in a text. The meaning may perhaps be inferred more or less precisely (e.g. *cachette* 'hiding place' – *en cachette*: 'secretly, in secret'; *perte* – 'loss'; *en perte* 'characterized by *financial* losses'), but quite often remains no more than a good guess. This may be particularly true for the non-native reader. In such cases, the dictionary makes it possible to compare the text in question with the explanation and example provided, allowing the hypothesis to be confirmed or rejected.
- the distribution of the construction. Many constructions are stylistically marked, being typically encountered in more formal or in technical contexts, where they may have a rather specialized meaning (e.g. *viande sur pied; (cellules etc.) en culture*). Yet another need for a dictionary of this kind arises from the fact that the constructions cannot be accounted for either adequately or exhaustively by general dictionaries. This is precisely due to their complexity. One can envisage electronic dictionaries that include the range of constructions and their meanings under the nominal key term, along with relevant corpus examples, but the entries would be intimidating in their length. Therefore, focusing on syntagmatic structures and the juxtaposition of similar structures provides a good basis for immediate grasp and comparison. Moreover, it is of instructive value in its own right.

The dictionary is structured as follows. First, the detailed introduction explains the 'macro-structure' and the 'micro-structure' of the dictionary as well as its mode of description. The main body of the dictionary comprises nearly 800 pages (pp. 1–798), each of which is subdivided into two columns for clarity of presentation. The left-hand column contains a grand total of 950 nouns (in alphabetical order) and the constructions of which they form part. The constructions listed for a particular noun may be grouped according to semantic criteria, such as different meanings in the case of a polysemous noun (e.g. *charge* 'costs'; 'load, burden'; figuratively: 'burden'). Each construction on the left is provided with a valency description, comprising statements about the complementation patterns and systematic information on the semantic properties and collocational range of the complements. The description is not technical at all, but makes use of familiar abbreviations which are immediately comprehensible (e.g. *équipe: Nqn – se mettre en ~ avec Nqn*, as in *Simon s'est mis en équipe avec Thomas et Étienne pour le concours.*) Syntactic information is included, such as the attributive use of *en boîte* – when referring to food – as in *les tomates en boîte* ('canned tomatoes'). Registers and domains of usage are indicated, such as 'sport' *(être/ se trouver en garde* as used in boxing and fencing) or 'politics' *(être en cohabitation (avec quelqu'un)*). The right hand column contains the German translations of both the noun and of each construction listed on the left (*boîte* '(a) can'; for a film: *être en boîte* 'be in the case'). The translations are very well done, including cases in which contiguous concepts and their constructions need to be differentiated. This, for example, is true for the constructions involving the historically related *confiance* and *confidence*, which may both be rendered by German *Vertrauen* in many contexts although the meanings of the respective constructions are clearly different and do not overlap. Each translation is followed by an example taken from the corpus. More than one example is provided if the construction has more than one reading and requires a different translation in German (as in *partir en fume* for *in Rauch aufgehen*; figuratively '*sich in Rauch auflösen*'). The layout is optimal, with the structural patterns on the left directly facing their translation and a relevant corpus example on the right.

The dictionary further contains an index of nearly 100 pages (pp. 801–896), which consists of the German terms used in the translations. This makes it possible to look up a construction starting from German. Typically, more than one French entry is listed for a particular German word, for what in German can be expressed with a single concept may correspond to different constructions in French with different key terms (and vice versa). The dictionary therefore also lends itself to interesting contrastive observations and studies.

Another 30 pages (pp. 897–926) are devoted to the sources of the examples. These include dictionaries, electronic corpora, e.g. Frantext, works of literature and non-fiction, a number of journals and magazines as well as internet sources. Works of literature are strongly represented in the corpus, all the more so because Frantext itself draws heavily on literature. This is justified since, as pointed out above, many of the constructions belong to the more formal registers and are more likely to occur in written texts and literature. Since some of the sources derive from 19th century literature, it may not always be clear to what extent a construction is still in use today. Assessments are made of the present-day currency or otherwise, based largely on the authors' own judgment. It seems clear that intensive research to confirm this would have been beyond the scope of this publication.

The authors and their team are to be congratulated on a comprehensive and innovative documentation of language use, with systematic analyses and an abundance of examples. We should be grateful to the publisher for supporting a dictionary that is both attractive in appearance and enjoyable to use. The reader will stand in awe of the intricacies of language use documented here, intricacies which the native speaker often seems to master with ease but which can confront the L2 learner with serious difficulties.

ANNETTE SABBAN
Correspondence address: sabban@rz.uni-hildesheim.de

References

Busse, Winfried & Jean-Pierre Dubost. 1997. *Französisches Verblexikon: die Konstruktion der Verben im Französischen*. Stuttgart: Klett-Cotta.
Herbst, Thomas, David Heath, Ian F. Roe & Dieter Götz. 2004. *A valency dictionary of English: A corpus-based analysis of the complementation patterns of English verbs, nouns and adjectives*. Berlin & New York: Mouton de Gruyter.

Stefaniya Ptashnyk. 2009. *Phraseologische Modifikationen und ihre Funktionen im Text: Eine Studie am Beispiel der deutschsprachigen Presse* (Phraseologie und Parömiologie 249). Hohengehren: Schneider. xi + 264 pp. ISBN 978-3-83-400624-0.

This monograph is a revised and extended German translation of the author's Ukrainian doctoral dissertation (Ivan Franko University, Lviv). It investigates German phraseological modifications, i.e. modifications of common or usual phraseological units (*Phraseologismen* or *phraseologische Einheiten*) in present-day German print media. Ptashnyk uses an impressive body of texts as her database: complete editions of each issue of the newspapers *Die Woche* (for

1998), *Die Zeit* (1996–1999), *Süddeutsche Zeitung* (1998, 1999, and 2001), and *die Tageszeitung* (1999) as well as the magazines *Focus* (1999) and *Der Spiegel* (1997 and 1999). These were manually searched for modifications of phraseological units, producing a database of 512 examples of phraseological modification. A second body of approximately 2500 examples of phraseological modification was compiled by searching the years 1987–2001 of the written corpora of the *Institut für Deutsche Sprache* in Mannheim, which consist of German, Austrian and Swiss newspapers and magazines. The phenomenon is, however, considerably more frequent than Ptashnyk's two corpora of examples suggest. A manual search of a single issue of *die Zeit* (9 April 2010) yielded some 50 examples. So it is highly unlikely that several years' of newspapers and magazines would only produce 3000 examples.

The book consists of seven chapters plus introduction and conclusion. The introduction (pp. 1–6) describes the aims of the study, the database and the structure of the book. Chapter 1 (pp. 7–43) provides an overview of previous research on phraseological units and the defining criteria and typologies used in the German and Russian tradition of phraseological studies. Chapter 2 (pp. 44–76) introduces the topic of investigation, occasional modification (*okkasionelle Modifikationen*), defining it in contrast to common or usual phraseological units (*usuelle Phraseologismen*) and phraseological variants, i.e. common variants of phraseological units that have the same meaning. Chapters 3–6 comprise the core of the book. Chapter 3 (pp. 77–132) is the author's classification of structural modification – in her definition subsuming both lexical and grammatical changes to a phraseological unit – and contextual modification, which is her term for semantic changes without structural changes which are based on the interplay between literal and phraseological meaning in the context of the text. Chapter 4 (pp. 133–158) focuses on semantic processes in phraseological modifications, while Chapter 5 (pp. 159–175) discusses the relationship between phraseological units and derivations from these leading to new phraseological units. It further analyses the process of standardisation of phraseological modifications, a process through which modifications change from occasional (*okkasionelle Phraseologismen*) to common phraseological units (*usuelle Phraseologismen*) and become lexicalized. Chapter 6 (pp. 176–237) discusses the textual functions of phraseological modifications. It is followed by a summary of the preceding chapters and suggestions for future research (pp. 238–245). While the detailed table of contents makes up for the absence of an index, an inclusion of a list of figures and tables would certainly have been desirable.

The book addresses a difficult and complex topic and the reader is grateful for the chapter summaries, as it is easy to lose sight of the wood for the trees, as it were. This is partly due to the subject, as phraseological units in the wider sense are structurally diverse and the author investigates occasional modifications, i.e. individual changes to these. But to some extent, as will be shown below, Ptashnyk herself is responsible for the reader's difficulty in keeping track of the detailed system of categories. In her definition of phraseological units the author follows Burger et al. (1982) and Burger (2003). The resulting set of phraseological constructions include fully idiomatic, partly idiomatic, and non-idiomatic phraseological units consisting of verb phrases, nominal phrases and adverbial phrases. More specifically, the set of phrases comprises *Zwillingsformeln* (phraseological pairs and, in the author's definition, also including triplets), *Modellbildungen* (constructions with a fixed pattern such as *Zug um Zug*, where different but identical nouns can replace *Zug*), comparisons (e.g. *frieren wie ein Schneider*), and independent clauses, including elliptical clauses. The category 'independent clauses' includes proverbs, commonplaces, so-called *feste Phrasen* (idiomatic set phrases or sentences which are closely related to the context), routine formulae such as greetings or expressions of surprise, and literary and non-literary quotations that have become general knowledge and are used as fixed expressions. Ptashnyk thus uses a wide definition of phraseological units, but one that is distinct from formulae in the sense of Wray (2002) by only including units consisting of more than one word and by restricting the concept of phraseological units to those that are common knowledge within the language community, i.e. the population of German speakers. The database of phraseological units that is taken to be shared by the community of German speakers and against which potential modifications are checked are the phraseological units occurring in the following dictionaries: *Zitate und Aussprüche: Herkunft und aktueller Gebrauch (Duden 12)*, *Redewendungen und sprichwörtliche Redewendungen (Duden 11)*, *Duden Deutsches Universalwörterbuch*, and Müller's *Lexikon der Redensarten*. Unfortunately, none of these is listed in the bibliography, so that it is unclear which edition has been used.

In her categorization of modifications Ptashnyk distinguishes between semantic modification, structural modification and contextual-semantic modification (p. 49), but the diagram which, according to the text, serves to illustrate this threefold division shows something different, an overlap between semantic and structural modification. In other words, the figure points to semantic modification without structural modification, structural modification without semantic modification, and structural modification with semantic modification. Thus, it appears that Ptashnyk has not fully succeeded in solving the problem of categorization. In Chapter 3 (*'Strukturelle und semantische Besonderheiten phraseologischer Modifikationen'*) the division into three categories (structural, semantic and contextual modification) is replaced by a division into structural modification and contextual modification (p. 81 and p. 131). Despite the chapter heading, this chapter is predominantly a structural categorization of phraseological modification. It includes the following types: substitution of one or more lexemes, expansion, reduction, coordination, contamination, morphological and syntactic modification. Some of these definitions are problematic. Thus coordination also includes the addition of a second constituent in a relative clause (example 3.57), which makes it difficult to distinguish from expansion. In contrast to structural modification which may but need not involve semantic modification, contextual modification does not involve structural change. It is a cover term for wordplay that is based on the realization of the literal subsequently or concurrently with the phraseological meaning, or exclusively with only an allusion to the phraseological meaning.

Chapter 4 (*'Semantische Prozesse bei strukturellen Modifikationen'*) is a semantic analysis of the structural types described in the previous chapter. The author distinguishes three major types: retention of the core meaning of the phraseological base, partial retention of the core meaning of the phraseological base and deactivation of the core meaning of the phraseological base. The term "deactivation" is used by Ptashnyk for cases in which the structure of a phrasal unit is used as a model for a new phrasal unit. The process involves the substitution of two (or more) essential elements, as in *neues Gift in alten Eiern*, which uses *neuer Wein in alten Schläuchen* as its phraseological base, but in which the use of this pattern is merely a stylistic device.

Chapter 5 (*'Phraseologische Modifikationen und die Dynamik in der Phraseologie'*), despite being comparatively short, is the one that will be of interest to a much wider readership than the previous chapters, as it shows common patterns of lexicalization of phraseological units. First deactivation is shown to be a productive way of deriving new phrases from existing patterns. Ptashnyk illustrates this for the phraseological unit *Von der Sowjetunion lernen heißt siegen lernen*, which functions as the phraseological base for numerous modifications. These can be described as follows: *Von* NP *lernen heißt* VERB-INFINITIVE *lernen* (examples 5.2–5.15), the English equivalent of which would be *learning from* NP *means learning to* VERB-INFINTIVE. This pattern is a phraseological unit in its own right of the type *Modellbildung* (p. 35), i.e. a semi-fixed construction. A second route to the lexicalization of a phraseological unit is derivation based on the metaphor used in a phraseological unit, and which is described as an extension of the phraseological image (*Ausbau des phraseologischen Bildes*). Ptashnyk illustrates this with the phraseological units *jemanden ins/in das Boot nehmen/holen* ('to take someone on board (of a boat)', and *jemanden mit im Boot haben* ('to have someone on board (of a boat)') and *mit im Boot sein* ('to be on board (of a boat)') (pp. 163–166), all of which she derives from the phraseological unit *in einem Boot sitzen* (literally 'to sit in one boat', the equivalent of the English phraseological unit *to be in the same boat*). A similar claim is made for *ein/kein/das Rad (der Geschichte, der Zeit u.a.) dreht sich* (literally 'a/no/the wheel ((of history) turns') and *das (große)Rad/ein (großes) Rad drehen* (literally 'to turn the (big) wheel/a (big) wheel'), both of which Ptashnyk derives from the phraseological unit *das Rad der Geschichte zurückdrehen* ('to turn the wheel (of history) back'). This derivation is, however, doubtful in the case of *das (große) Rad/ein (großes) Rad drehen*, as it implies that someone has the power to decide political or economic processes (p. 168). The phrase clearly implies a powerful agent, while the wheel of history is something that is not determined by a human agent, but rather by blind fate, which is at the origin of the image of the wheel of history. It appears much more likely to derive from the English phrase *(to be) at the wheel*, which implies that someone directs the course of events. The origin of this phraseological unit therefore needs further investigation. Moreover, this case shows that influence from English needs to be considered, in particular in the area of economy and politics, in which lexical borrowing from English is particularly frequent. English may also have played a role in the development of the phraseological units relating to the image of the boat; such as *to have someone on board* and *to be in the same boat*. A diachronic analysis may show whether English has played a role in the development of the new phraseological units containing the *Boot*. A third type of modification which frequently becomes productive is the replacement of a lexeme by a near-synonym. This is demonstrated by Ptashnyk in the case of *den Teufel an die Wand malen* (literally 'to paint the devil on the wall', which means 'to portray the worst-case scenario'), in which *Teufel* ('devil') is frequently replaced by *Gespenst* ('ghost'). In all of Ptashnyk's examples *Gespenst* is postmodified by a genitive phrase. This suggests that the change is motivated by the possibility of postmodification, which is first documented in the well-known phrase *das Gespenst des Kommunismus* in the opening sentence of Marx' and Engels' *Communist Manifesto*, a fact which seems to have escaped Ptashnyk. A fourth derivational process is the reduction of a phrasal unit consisting of a verb phrase to a nominal one, as in *schmutzige Wäsche* ('dirty linen'), which is derived from *schmutzige Wäsche (vor anderen Leuten) waschen* ('to wash dirty linen in public').

Chapter 6 ('*Textuelle Funktionen phraseologischer Modifikationen*') relates the frequency and the position of phraseological modification to their textual functions. Phraseological modifications are most frequent in headings, followed by leads and the beginning of texts (p. 181). The textual functions are categorized as structural devices, stylistic devices and pragmatic devices (with various subcategories) that serve to influence and entertain the reader. Ptashnyk emphasises that the textual functions often co-occur (p. 234) and readily admits that her analysis is speculative, as it is not based on statements by the respective journalists, but on her own interpretation; on the basis of this interpretive method alone, it is impossible to assess to what extent a journalist's audience designs work.

While it is regrettable that Ptashnyk has not managed to solve her classification problem and despite several instances of over- and misinterpretation, this book provides new insights into phraseological units. It is of major interest to scholars working in the areas of discourse structure, audience design, and lexicalization.

MARTINA HÄCKER
Correspondence address: martina.haecker@uni-paderborn.de

References

Burger, Harald. 2003. *Phraseologie: Eine Einführung am Beispiel des Deutschen*. Berlin: Schmidt.
Burger, Harald., Annelies Häcki Buhofer & Ambros Sialm. 1982. *Handbuch der Phraseologie*. Berlin & New York: Mouton de Gruyter.
Wray, Alison 2002. *Formulaic language and the lexicon*. Cambridge: Cambridge University Press.

Alison Wray: *Formulaic language: Pushing the boundaries*. Oxford & New York: Oxford University Press, 2008. 305 pp. ISBN 978-0-19-442245-1.

Wray's *Formulaic language: Pushing the boundaries* is, as the similarity of titles suggests, a sequel to her monograph *Formulaic language and the lexicon* published in 2002. Since then, she has assessed another host of empirical data which lead her to an informed discussion of follow-up questions such as: "Do we use formulaic language by default? What determines the level of formulaicity in language? How central is formulaic language in natural language learning by humans? How central should formulaic language be when modelling such learning for computers?" and "Does formulaic language constrain what we say and what we think?" (p. 5).

Wray considers boundaries to be "the real test cases" for hypotheses (p. 4); in order to locate them, trespassing is necessary. Therefore Wray goes far beyond unambiguous formulas but takes into account anything that appears to be a complex unit stored in the mind, including deliberately memorised sequences, oral narratives, performance scripts and even signalling systems such as racing car flags and military bugle calls (see p. 4). What is more, her metaphorical account of "pushing the boundaries" does not stop at revisiting our understanding of the form and function of complex linguistic units, but applies just as well to methodological and theoretical issues. While she liberates linguistic theory from the remnants of underlying, but questionable logical assumptions (e.g. that complex units are necessarily built of smaller ones), no new theoretical boundaries are set up. Instead, the reader is repeatedly reminded of the (often ignored) interdependence between research question, theory and applied method. Thus, Wray avoids the fallacy of comparing apples with oranges when she discusses linguistic approaches from fields as different as generative theory, functional grammars, corpus-driven models, or most prominently cognitive approaches (e.g., Jackendoff 2002; Hunston and Francis 2000; Goldberg 2003, 2006). Quite to the contrary, being well familiar with different theoretical stances, she explores formulaicity with fearless freshness from any possible angle. By assuming that formulaic language is a default, and analytical segmentation and recombination only secondary, plausible alternative explanations are offered to account for a number of linguistic phenomena, such as creativity within formulaicity.

The book is structured into four parts. The first three parts provide the theoretical and empirical basis for the final discussion in part four. Wray starts out with a summary of her publication from 2002 making the reader familiar with the concept of Morpheme Equivalent Unit (MEU), amongst others. A MEU is defined as "a word or word string, whether incomplete or including gaps for inserted variable items, that is processed like a morpheme, that is, without recourse to any form-meaning matching of any sub-parts it may have" (p. 12). In other words, basic linguistic units are not characterized by an abstract formal criterion, but by function and storage principles. This entails firstly, that the lexicon is heteromorphic, i.e. larger units and their analysable subparts are stored side-by-side; secondly, that analysis of subparts only takes place if need be (Needs-Only-Analysis NOA); and thirdly, that MEUs enable the speaker to manipulate the hearer – formulas are rich in overtones and can thus direct the hearer's way of thinking. Wray admits that her account of mental storage and NOA is still speculative; she presents her hypothesis as a possible alternative worth considering and implicitly invites the reader to explore it further, as she often does throughout the book.

The second part examines the state of the art and discusses the contributions of different linguistic approaches. She refrains from lengthy general and evaluative summaries, but focuses her far-reaching account on those aspects which are effectively linked to her specific research. More than once, divergence is attributed to different research questions. The theoretical overview is complemented by a discussion of how to identify MEUs. Wray suggests a diagnostic approach which operationalizes the researcher's intuition. Criteria for identification known from former phraseological research – such as grammatical, semantic and stylistic oddities, certain phonological patterns, usage preferences, association with specific situations or registers, inappropriate usage etc. – are not used for ontological and static identification, but as a checklist that serves to make the basis on which the researcher grounds her intuition more transparent. After all, if the agenda is "pushing the boundaries," it is better to attribute an MEU falsely and subjectively than to miss a single real one. A first application of this diagnostic approach is added (Namba 2008), affirming the reader's overall impression that Wray always tends to immediately check her methodological suggestions for feasibility and her theoretical hypotheses against empirical evidence.

Part three contains six case studies from fields as different as computer-aided communication, language learning, meaning construction strategies and memorizing techniques. Formulaic language is examined in terms of its various (potential) functions in and effects on communication. The study on a machine-translation program for oral interactions, TESSA, suggests that formulas help the program to be less susceptible to errors: if several synonymous formulas are stored, the computer is able to disregard non-salient differences. TALK, on the other hand, is a computer program for assisting speech-disabled people. The study is illuminating in two regards. Firstly, frequent types and loci of formulas in conversations are identified (e.g., perspective, topic/function, and interjections). Secondly, the study suggests that fluency is more important for conversing parties than accuracy. The two studies about beginning and advanced L2 learners suggest that memorized, functionally well-chosen formulas have obviously positive effects on retention, motivation and confidence. Observed errors of the beginners seem to indicate that adults can obviously not "bypass linguistic analysis" (p. 151). The study with the advanced L2 learners reveals that learner errors are not necessarily due to lack of competence; the propensity of risk-taking in expressing one's self grows with the degree of linguistic proficiency, i.e. questions of cultural identity can intervene (see also Pawley 1986). This observation ties in perfectly with the results of Wray's study on comedians, where again risk taking by using spontaneously assembled speech instead of memorized phrases is a feature of high professionalism, but also of naturalness. Effects of NOA, i.e. constituent blindness towards known formulas vs. constituent analysis to derive meaning from unknown formulas, are at the bottom of another study in part three: the "coonass court case" of linguistic abuse. Part three is both thrilling and entertaining thanks to the variety of the studies, their sometimes exotic (or even absurd) settings and the wealth of aspects to formulaicity depicted. Wray's capacity of making out the deeper implications of observed phenomena and establishing interconnections while strictly keeping her focus is impressive.

Part four then continues in a similar way, tying in even more empirical data into the profound discussion of her five main questions. Firstly, "do we use formulaic language by default?" Apart from some traditional arguments for default holistic processing, such as failing intuition in view of word frequencies, fossilized archaisms, etc., Wray approaches the question from an evolutionary angle; what if formulas were the phylogenetic starting point of language? (Her approach is, however, different from Croft's (2000) seminal publication on the topic). Studies in closed language communities, be it Maori or the jargon amongst aviation maintenance staff, seem to suggest that in a setting where almost all contexts are shared by all members, phonological units tend to refer to highly complex concepts. In other words, the cognitive view that words are mere pointers to concepts is taken to an extreme (see also Sperber and Wilson 1995; Croft and Cruse 2004). Using Thurston's (1988) terminological distinction between "esoteric" and "exoteric communication" (insider vs. outsider communication), Wray assumes that human language may have been fully holistic at first, as our ancestors presumably formed esoteric communities, i.e. communities of insiders. However, as soon as communication with outsiders became necessary, language needed to become more autonomous and NOA set to work. The outsider "look[ed] for patterns which [were] not there," whereas insiders may have become aware of where potential problems lie and regularized idiosyncratic complex forms (p. 211). Consequently, segmentation and analysis may be only a secondary feature of language, rather than constituting its central building blocks. If one puts this idea to its logical conclusion, grammar is possibly nothing but a chimera, i.e. a heuristics to flexibly construct and convey meaning independent of context. Wray sees her hypothesis as an alternative account to explain the puzzling discrepancy between the complexity of potential grammatical constructions and our limited processing capacity. Moreover, Wray points out that the formulaic default also offers a viable explanation of why formulas are a prime means of identity construction: insiders use their 'jargon' all along (and outsiders are free to "refuse" it).

The second question scrutinized in part four is, "What determines the level of formulaicity in language?" Arguing that it is mainly the speaker's assumptions about her interlocutor and her own communicative motives that influence the degree of formulaicity, Wray implicitly applies Sperber and Wilson's (1995) notions of "mutual cognitive environment" and the "principle of relevance" to her specific linguistic feature. A speaker apparently opts for a certain degree of formulaicity according to her judgements about the interlocutor's group membership and her assumed familiarity with the holistic expression. On the other hand, Wray cites numerous examples of people with language impairment and of L2 learners who sacrifice creative flexibility for the sake of fluency. Thus the formulaic restrictions of native-speaker-like competence (Pawley and Syder 1983) could also be explained by fluency constraints. Wray concludes that "[i]n all situations, formulaicity and creativity were set in a specific, appropriate balance, and the challenge for the speaker was to maintain the optimal relationship between them" (p. 258).

The third question in part four is, "How central is formulaic language in natural language learning by humans?" and the fourth asks, "How central should formulaic language be when modelling such learning for computers?" According to Wray, a simplified notion of one right balance between analytic and holistic L2 learning is precluded. Therefore the focus has to be put on the situation, circumstances and purposes (as Wray keeps reminding the reader persistently). If the motivation is to be prepared for many different situations, and if learning cannot go hand in hand with learning new situations, teaching freely combining words and functional items may be the more effective strategy than inflexible, context-bound formulas. In view of computer programs, formulas obviously help cope with vagueness and restrict over-generation. If patterns are drawn from usage data, like in TESSA, a vast corpus tagged for propositions and a trainer might be an alternative to theory-led programs.

Finally, "Does formulaic language constrain what we say and what we think?" As might be expected, Wray starts her discussion with Orwell's famous vision. However, she also draws on more realistic settings, e.g. events in China during the Cultural Revolution. Although formulas may manipulate the hearer to think in a certain direction, they also always require "continuing access to novel thought" in their application (p. 261). It is therefore not so much thought, but the linguistic expression of thoughts that can be restricted by full reliance on formulas. Computer-aided communication and non-linguistic signalling systems demonstrate that unforeseen situations are difficult to deal with. However, new specific situations entail communicative creativity in the long run: there are such things as dialects in racing flag communication. Consequently, creativity can never be precluded completely.

"Perhaps one of the most striking consequences of the approach taken in this book is the extent to which even quite evident boundaries between phenomena have often dissolved in the course of discussion" (p. 277). Despite this seemingly blatant conclusion, Wray avoids the trap of leading the reader to the mere truism that everything is interconnected, (too) complex, fuzzy and vague anyway. Instead, the reader can enjoy a number of "light-bulb moments", such as the possible culture-boundedness of the concept "word" and its consequences, or insights into why learning idiomatic expressions poses problems to L2-learners. The loss of clear boundaries is interpreted as a natural consequence of viewing formulaic language as a "linguistic solution to a non-linguistic problem", i.e. "the speaker's promotion of self" (p. 101).

Alison Wray's *Formulaic language: Pushing the boundaries* is a prime example of modelling a wide range of very different observable phenomena into a coherent, comprehensive and plausible picture. When a "grand picture" is drawn, details may not always be as carefully painted as the reader might wish. Some of her ideas are only sketched, some are slightly reductionist, e.g. the relation between proficiency and free combination, and some might not be free from circularity such as her scenario of language evolution, which presupposes that the first units were phonetically complex. However, on the one hand, she seems to be very well aware of this sort of shortcomings: her book concludes with a long list of topics for further research. On the other hand, Wray is always inspiring. She offers an intelligent and fresh approach to linguistic theory, which is put in a clear writing style and is very accessible thanks to the vast amount of well integrated examples and empirical studies. Moreover, thrilled by the wealth of angles from which her subject can be approached, she also grants the proper dues to those scholars who inspired her and refrains from fruitless dissociations. All this makes reading *Formulaic language: Pushing the boundaries* enthralling from beginning to end.

SIXTA QUASSDORF
Correspondence address: sixta.quassdorf@unibas.ch

References

Croft, William. 2000. *Explaining language change: An evolutionary approach*. Harlow: Longman.
Croft, William. & D. Allan Cruse. 2004. *Cognitive linguistics*. Cambridge: Cambridge University Press.
Goldberg, Adele. 2003. Constructions: A new theoretical approach to language. *Trends in Cognitive Sciences* 7(5). 219–224.
Goldberg, Adele. 2006. *Constructions at work*. Oxford: Oxford University Press.
Hunston, Susan & Gill Francis. 2000. *Pattern grammar*. Amsterdam & Philadelphia: John Benjamins.
Jackendoff, Ray S. 2002. *Foundations of language*. Oxford: Oxford University Press.
Namba, Kazuhiko. 2008. *Formulaic language in bilingual children's code-switching*. Cardiff: Cardiff University (Centre for Language and Communication Research) dissertation.
Pawley, Andrew. 1986. On speech formulas and linguistic competence. *Kansas Working Papers in Linguistics* 11. 57–87.

Pawley, Andrew & Frances. H. Syder. 1983. Two puzzles for linguistic theory: Nativelike selection and nativelike fluency. In Jack. C. Richards & Richard.W. Schmidt (eds.), *Language and communication*, 191–226. New York: Longman.
Sperber, Daniel & Deirdre Wilson. 1995. *Relevance: Communication and cognition.* Oxford: Blackwell.
Thurston. William R. 1988. How exoteric languages build a lexicon: Esoterogeny in west New Britain. In Ray Harlow & Robyn Hooper (eds.), *VICAL 1: Oceanic languages. Papers from the fifth international conference on Austronesian linguistics, Auckland,* 555–579. Auckland: Linguistic Society of New Zealand.
Wray, Alison. 2002. *Formulaic language and the lexicon*. Cambridge: Cambridge University Press.